Hunter Valley

WINEGUIDE

Nick Bulleid

series editor
Max Allen

photography
Adrian Lander

PIZZEY *WIF*

First Published 2000
By Pizzey WIF Pty Ltd
ACN 089 540 465
ABN 95 089 540 465

Pizzey WIF Pty Ltd 37 Callantina Road, Hawthorn, Victoria, 3122 Australia

Nick Bulleid 1947–
        Hunter Valley Wineguide

        ISBN 0 9578355 0 7

        1. Wineries - NSW - Hunter Valley Region - Guidebooks
        I. Title

Series Editor: Max Allen
Editor: White Kite Productions Pty Ltd
Design: Andrew Rankine Design Associates Pty Ltd
Photography: Adrian Lander
Printed by: Brown Prior Anderson

Con *tents*

Thanks *to* ...

No one grows to know and love a region like the Hunter without the help of others. Luckily for me, in the Hunter there are many people who have been generous with their time, hospitality and good bottles. The Tyrrell family, Len Evans, Gerry Sissingh, the Brokenwood partners and Iain Riggs have all given me help and companionship along the way. It's been a lot of fun.

It's hard to tread anywhere in the world of Australian wine without finding that James Halliday has been there first. James and I have shared many bottles of Hunter wine, and his book (with Ray Jarratt) *The Wines and History of the Hunter Valley* was an excellent reference work for me. Max Lake also provided great inspiration – through his chapters 'It'll only take half an hour' and 'A morning with Audrey Wilkinson' in *Hunter Winemakers*. These really whetted my appetite for Hunter history.

Thanks also to Hugh Thomson and Freya Hohnen for wielding corkscrews; to Dr Henry John for the glasses and the Pokolbin community for the hall; to Roger Paterson, who became de facto store manager for my wine samples (and for being Roger Paterson); to Gus Marr and his staff at the Cessnock City Tourist Board; to Max Allen for suggesting to Boyce Pizzey that he give the job to someone he'd never met and for editing my words (although I'm writing this before I've seen what he's done).My family deserves special thanks. Susan was extraordinarily patient when I kept on deferring chores in favour of *the book*. Thanks, too, to Hugo and Theo who almost understood why Dad was hogging the 'puter yet didn't seem to be having fun.

And lastly, to all those countless people with whom I have shared good bottles and great conversation: many thanks.

Fore *word*

I first met Nick in the early 1970s. John Parkinson was working for me and he said, 'I've met a bloke who hasn't been a big wine lover and he seems very interested. He appears to have a naturally good palate.'

It didn't take Nick long to develop this natural gift. Through the Junior Wine & Food Society of that day and the Rothbury Society, he quickly established himself as a leading tasting contender, winning the coveted Purple Ribbon Best Taster of the Year no less than three times. He started appearing at various wine shows, serving a long apprenticeship as an Associate Judge in Sydney. Indeed, when eventually he was made a Judge he sent me a simple fax: 'I can't believe it. WHO DIED?'

Since then he has served all sorts of shows with distinction and great application. Indeed, his passion for wine led him to leave his job as a marine biologist and to take up a wine career completely. Our gain was a considerable loss to the study of water movement on plankton and nutrients. This is his first book.

There hasn't been a good book about the Hunter around for a long time. When I started visiting the Hunter there were only six working wineries. At the Hunter Valley Wine Show in 1999 over 120 wineries competed and there were still 20 or 30 who didn't show.

The best chapter I've read on the Hunter was written by Max Lake, about Audrey Wilkinson, in Max's *Hunter Wine and Hunter Winemakers*. In his book Nick appears to share Max's view, gives further information about him, and writes of the revival of the vineyards and what's going on there today. In short, this book is up to date, though packed with history and opinion. I recommend it to anyone who loves wine and wants to learn more about it. I recommend it especially to anyone who has not yet appreciated just what the Hunter can do. At its best the Hunter is one of the great wine regions of the world.

Len Evans AO OBE

Intro*duction*

In 1969, while at University in England, I had a letter from my father, who had recently arrived in New South Wales from our previous home in the Bahamas. He told me that he was shortly going to visit a place called the Hunter Valley, where they made wine. Wine had been one of my father's interests for many years, although scarcely a passion. But, in spite of frequent exposure at home, I still thought that wine was dreadful sour stuff you could barely drink. My preference, like a good West Indian, was dark rum, and in that I had more in common with New South Wales' early settlers than I did with my father. Nevertheless, for some reason the name 'Hunter Valley' stayed with me. Little did I know what was in store.

My first visit to the Hunter was in 1971. This trip was to taste the Tyrrell's red wines in wood, which, we were to find, had been described by Murray Tyrrell as 'the worst vintage in living memory' – hardly a good omen. We left Sydney's southern suburbs after breakfast and fought our way through the remains of rush-hour traffic as far as a row of traffic jams through Hornsby and Berowra. We wound our way round the old Pacific Highway, across the Hawkesbury River and through Peate's Ridge, Ourimbah and Kangy Angy and were then held up by traffic at the railway crossing at Wyong.

Having stopped at the roadside near Dora Creek for a hurried snack lunch, we arrived at Tyrrell's in the early afternoon, five and a half hours after we had left home. Once we had tasted the Tyrrell's reds, we had barely enough time to visit the newly built Rothbury Estate winery before setting off back to Sydney to arrive home too late for dinner.

The last time I drove to the Hunter, I joined the expressway at Pearce's Corner, Wahroonga, and sat on cruise control until I left It at Freeman's Waterholes, about thirty minutes from Pokolbin. The trip took two hours from the Harbour Bridge. The Hunter's a lot closer to Sydney nowadays.

And a lot of other people have noticed that. In the early 1960s there were seven wineries in the Hunter: Elliotts, Lindemans, McWilliam's, Penfolds, Tyrrell's and two Draytons.

When I started researching this book, I counted 130 wineries, if you include vineyards with their own label. Numerous people had discovered the lure of owning a vineyard and winery only two hours from home – and I was one of them, initially picking grapes at Brokenwood during the 1975 vintage and then becoming a partner in 1978.

For many years, and before the opening of the expressway, I couldn't bring myself to repeat that first journey. And so, each weekend, I braved the rigours of the Wollombi Road which, in those years, included 30 kilometres of indescribably bad, corrugated and pot-holed dirt. These trips virtually shook my MG B to pieces and filled every belonging and orifice with fine dust. Almost every Brokenwood partner and friend had some tale to tell about accidents on that road. The trips back with cases of wine did nothing to improve the car's suspension. In 1976 I took two weeks' leave to work as a cellar rat at Rothbury with Gerry Sissingh ('How much are you paying us for this winemaking course, Bulleid?' asked Len Evans), interspersed with chats at Tyrrell's with Ralph Fowler and visits to Brokenwood to analyse grape samples. Over the next few years, different facets – provided by the Rothbury Estate Ribbon Dinners, the cycle of the seasons at Brokenwood and eventually judging at the Hunter Valley Wine Show – were added to this gem I had discovered. I still feel a thrill of excitement as I turn right off Mount View Road on to Oakey Creek Road and towards the vineyards.

The Hunter Valley had got to me.

Hunter *History*

The first sighting of the Hunter River by European settlers was in 1797, when one Lieutenant John Shortland chanced on it while searching for escaped convicts. Its initial value to the new communities to the south was as a source of timber and coal for the steamships that provided much of the transport for Sydney and its surroundings. The first overland route to the Hunter was discovered in 1820 by John Howe and a road-way was constructed largely along his path from Windsor to Singleton in 1823. This is now the Putty Road, familiar as a picturesque, if rather winding, shortcut for travellers from western Sydney to the Hunter. Howes Valley, towards the northern end, commemorates the route's pioneer.

The first road between Sydney and Newcastle was cut in 1826. After leaving the Sydney basin past St Albans and reaching the top of the ranges, this road continued north towards Cessnock. Today its course is largely followed by the Wollombi Road and you can still see many of the original convict-built features along the way. (More about those in the chapter 'Travelling'...)

Road transport quickly opened up the Hunter Valley to new settlers, who found that the sandy loams of the river flats were suitable for many types of agriculture.

No record exists of who planted the first vines. These early land grants were developed as mixed farms and, although several were planted with grapes, winemaking was far from the principal activity. William Kelman is one of the main contenders. Kelman had married Catherine, the sister of James Busby, who had taken up a land grant of 2000 acres on the Hunter River between Singleton and Branxton in 1824, which he called Kirkton. Busby is widely regarded as the founder of the Australian wine industry, although lately he has been seen to have played a role as a thinker and author who enthusiastically encouraged others rather than as a practitioner. Busby had imported vines from France, Spain, Luxembourg and the United Kingdom, and cuttings from these were taken to Kirkton. There is no record, however, of when these were planted; and they are more likely to have been planted and managed by Kelman than by Busby. In any case they thrived, as the vineyard grew to 10 acres by 1834 and 15 by 1843. Busby left for New Zealand in 1833 where he played a longer and more important role in a fledgling national wine industry than he had in Australia.

George Wyndham, who planted vines at Dalwood, near Branxton, in 1830, could also have been the first. Wyndham bought the property at a bankruptcy sale and became a successful farmer, later buying land as far afield as Inverell. His first vines failed, but he persevered and made his first vintage in 1835. His vineyard was eventually bought, in 1904, by Penfolds, who made Dalwood into a national brand. The name is still used in international markets. The property became Wyndham Estate after Penfolds sold up and moved to the Upper Hunter in 1963.

Another early settler was James King, who took up a land grant of 1920 acres on the Williams River near Raymond Terrace, which he called Irrawang. He planted vines in 1832 and made his first wine in 1835, the same year as Wyndham.

King was also instrumental in founding, in 1847, the Hunter River Vineyard Association (HRVA) – an extremely influential body in the early development of wine in the Hunter. In 1833 there had been a mere 20 acres of vines in the Hunter, but by 1843 the area had grown to 262 acres and by 1850 to 500 acres, owned by 32 growers, marking the beginning of the Hunter's first boom.

King's vineyard also spread rapidly. By 1854, the vineyard had grown to 15 acres and King reported his most successful variety as semillon. One of King's wines won a medal at the Paris Exhibition in 1855 and the wine was placed on the table of the Emperor Napoleon III during the closing ceremony. History doesn't record whether the Emperor tasted the wine or what his opinion was but one could say that, with that small gesture, the invasion of Europe by Hunter wine had begun.

If one ignores the replanted vineyard of Wyndham Estate, none of these early vineyards and names survives to this day.

However, in 1843, Dr Henry Lindeman planted vines on land he had bought near Raymond Terrace, which he named Cawarra. Although this vineyard, too, no longer exists, Lindeman's influence was to go much further, as he gradually acquired several vineyards through the Lower Hunter and even Kelman's Kirkton. In time, Lindemans was to become an international brand.

In 1860, Hunter production was in excess of 60,000 gallons, or 270,000 litres – the equivalent of 30,000 cases. For a new industry in a young colony, started largely by settlers from a non-wine producing country, this was a very impressive start. However, to put this volume into some kind of perspective, it is somewhat less than today's annual production of Tamburlaine and about ten per cent of The Rothbury Estate. This quantity is the most likely reason that no wine from this era appears to survive – although I hope from the bottom of my heart that somewhere there might be a forgotten cellar ...

Most of this production was drunk locally by country people and comparatively little found its way to the cities, even to Sydney. As James Halliday points out in *The Wines and History of the Hunter Valley*, 'it is easy to forget how difficult transport was. There was no rail link between Sydney and the Hunter until the 1880s, when the first rail bridge was built across the Hawkesbury River. Some of the smaller vignerons made the arduous journey to Sydney by bullock dray with their produce, but the roads were totally unsuited to this.' Until rail took over, shipping was the most important transport for supplies to Newcastle and the Hunter – and, therefore, of wine to Sydney. At that time, the Hunter River was navigable past Singleton.

Halliday quotes the *Sydney Morning Herald* of 1861: 'Messrs Wyndham and Lindeman have united in establishing an agency in Sydney for the sale of their wines, which is conducted by Mr J D

Lankester. Although, Messrs Wyndham and Lindeman have this year produced about 40,000 gallons, the greater proportion which will, in course of time, be forwarded to Sydney for their disposal.' A similar joint venture nowadays between Orlando Wyndham and Southcorp would seem unlikely.

In the previous year, 1860, an edition of the *Herald* reported that 'Frequent shipments have previously been made to Melbourne ... already more than 3,000 dozen of the Irrawang and Kaludah wines have been sold ...' There are many Hunter companies today who would welcome sales of this size to Melbourne.

All of these early vineyards were established to the north of the Hunter River, in the area between Raymond Terrace and Singleton. But it wasn't long before vineyards spread to the south, away from the river and on to the slopes below the Brokenback Range. It's not known what prompted this shift, although it's tempting to think that vignerons simply found they could make better wine there. Whatever the reason, their counterparts today would find it very difficult to manage vineyards in that wetter climate nearer the coast, as downy mildew arrived in the Hunter in 1917 and changed the lives of vignerons forever.

Vineyard establishment spread to the area around Lochinvar and Allandale. In the 1860s, Joseph Holmes planted The Wilderness and Caerphilly, either side of the Branxton Road near the intersection with The Wilderness Road. At about the same time, George Campbell established Daisy Hill.

Planting in the Pokolbin area seemed to start with a rush. In 1866, the Wilkinson family took up several parcels of land along the foothills of the Brokenback Range between what is now Mount Pleasant and Tyrrell's. Frederick Wilkinson planted Oakdale and selected Côte d'Or for his father, Lieutenant Alfred Wilkinson. Frederick's brothers Charles, William and

John planted Mangerton, Maluna and Coolalta shortly after. Coolalta, along the south side of De Beyers Road and opposite JYT, was later bought by Lindemans, who recently renamed it Cawarra to perpetuate the name of Dr Lindeman's first vineyard, now defunct. John McDonald planted vineyards and built the Ben Ean winery in 1870. The Stephens family planted Ivanhoe shortly after.

Martin Bouffier, a German settler, is credited with planting the first vineyard in the immediate Cessnock area, in 1866, but none of the vineyards that followed survived the leaner years or the urban sprawl that accompanied the development of coal mining.

The next few years were very prosperous. Actual figures for wine production or vineyard area are sketchy. Max Lake suggests a total of 5480 acres of Hunter vineyard in 1866 (the current total is just under 10,000 acres), but others have thought his figure too high. The production figure of 168,123 gallons in 1866 suggests a vineyard area of between 500 and 1000 acres; there were 2126 acres in the whole of New South Wales at the time. Nevertheless, vineyard establishment was certainly rapid.

With the improvement in transport to Sydney, sales flourished. For a while, Lindemans and Penfolds shared cellars in Sydney's Queen Victoria Building – a great irony, considering their merger nearly a century later. These, in the early 1900s, claimed to be 'the largest city cellars in the world underground'. The stock carried was over 500,000 gallons, or 250,000 cases, an astonishing amount, implying that much of it was sold as fully mature, bottle-aged wine.

The bank crash and recession in the 1890s had caused difficulties for many vineyards, but this was nothing compared with what was to come.

After Federation in 1901, customs barriers were removed and South Australian wines entered New South Wales unimpeded.

These wines were cheaper than the Hunter's, thanks to subsidies and probably higher yields. The Hunter simply could not compete and a period of decline followed. To add to the economic woes, the vine disease downy mildew arrived in the Hunter in 1917. The disease remains a threat to this day, but management strategies have been developed for reducing its impact. These would not have been available in the years immediately following downy's arrival, and the damage caused was considerable. Max Lake records that, in 1925, three quarters of the crop was lost to the disease.

Many pioneering families sold out and famous names disappeared. During the 1914–18 war the remaining wine (and the brand name) of Carmichael's Porphyry vineyard was sold to Lindemans and the vineyard abandoned. This was one of the last remaining vineyards in the Raymond Terrace area. Lindemans also bought the Kirkton Vineyard, which had been founded by Busby and Kelman, in 1914. Through a sad twist of fate, the last wine produced from Kirkton before the vineyard was abandoned was in 1924, that vintage being served at Kirkton's centenary celebrations in 1930. Lindemans also bought Catawba and Warrawee but, by 1923, they had gone into receivership. By 1922, the Hunter's vineyard area had fallen to 2700 acres. Not all the vineyard sales resulted in decline, however. Some provided opportunities for established wine companies from other regions to gain a toehold in the Hunter and, later, to grow substantial businesses. In 1904, part of John Wyndham's original property Dalwood was bought by Penfolds, which was to become one of the major players in the Hunter for the next seventy years. Then, in 1921, a vineyard on the slopes of Mount Bright, planted by Charles King in 1880, was bought by an Irish father and French mother for their son, who studied in France before taking over as winemaker. That winemaker was Maurice O'Shea. O'Shea rapidly built a considerable reputation which lives to this

day, but his audience was small and even he struggled to survive. He sold part of his business to McWilliam's in 1932 and the balance in 1941.

Industrial strife in 1929 saw a lockout of miners for sixteen months, which decreased the money in local circulation and hit the vineyards hard. The Great Depression followed. Fortified wines were gradually gaining a greater foothold in the market and, although most Hunter wineries still produced these, the wines from interstate would have been cheaper and more widely distributed. Vineyard area declined throughout the inter-war period – from 2556 acres in 1925 to 1380 in 1936.

In those bleak years, many small producers survived by selling their wine in bulk, to be bottled by other wine producers or wine merchants. Maurice O'Shea was a noted buyer and later Hardys in South Australia and Mildara in Victoria joined him. More significant were the sales to wine merchants, for in them lay the beginnings of the Hunter's revival.

One of these merchants was Leo Buring. Buring had been an important winemaker, working at the Minchinbury Cellars in Rooty Hill, now in Western Sydney, between 1902 and 1919 and after that as a consultant. He bought premises in George Street, Sydney, and started a restaurant and wine merchant's business, which he called Ye Olde Crusty Cellars. Through a curious twist of fate, Buring was the first manager appointed to Lindemans in its receivership. After leaving the company in 1930, he bought much of the stock for his business from Lindemans' new receiver. (In 1962, in turn, Lindemans would buy Leo Buring's company, following his death in 1961.)

This was one of the few wine businesses of the time and in its early years many wines were bought in bulk from other producers. These were stored and bottled at cellars in

Redfern, now occupied by wine auctioneers Langtons. Even after Buring bought the Orange Grove winery in the Barossa Valley (in 1945) he continued to bottle wine from Hunter makers under his own label, which by then had national distribution. Semillon from Jack Phillips' Glandore Winery, now Brokenback, was bottled as one of the first national branded wines, Leo Buring Rinegolde. It's hard to believe now that, in its early years, such a large and important wine as Rinegolde was a Hunter semillon. Wines from Draytons and Elliotts were also sold under the Buring label.

Another important merchant, Johnnie Walker, started the Angas Steak Cave in Pitt Street, Sydney, shortly after which he started selling wine under the Rhinecastle label. Tulloch was a frequent supplier and this prompted Walker to take groups of his customers to the Hunter to visit Tulloch's and other wineries. Other wine merchants – such as Douglas Lamb, with his St Patrice label, Henri Renault in Kent Street and Kassel – also bottled Hunters and poured many people their first glass of wine. Seabrooks and Crittendens were doing the same in Melbourne. Australians were beginning to develop a love for wine.

These first glimmers of change were either not recognised or came too late for some producers and, by 1956, the area under vine in the Hunter had fallen to 1153 acres (467 hectares). Jack Phillips pulled up Glandore in 1960. There can have been little interest in Oakdale when Frederick Wilkinson's son Audrey died in 1962. Phillips' vineyard lay bare of vines for the first time since it had been planted and it failed to make its centenary by just four years. The Hunter reached its low point in 1963, when Max Lake started the first new winery in living memory.

I tell the story under the Lake's Folly entry, but it's worth pre-empting here, that Lake's quest was to re-create an historic wine that he had tasted: the 1934 Dalwood Cabernet Verdot from the Penfolds vineyard at Branxton. Was this folly? None of us has tasted that wine, so we cannot say. But, folly or not, Lake's undertaking was a turning point. Jim Roberts planted Belbourie in 1964 and built a new winery from stone used in George Wyndham's original Dalwood. David Hordern added a vineyard to his Upper Hunter property Brogheda in 1966 and Dr Lance Allen established Tamburlaine the following year. It can hardly have gone unnoticed that Penfolds had planted what was, for the time, the massive area of 600 acres in the Upper Hunter. In the late 1960s, wine took off in the Hunter. The second Hunter boom was underway.

A new company, Hungerford Hill Vineyards, bought a cattle property from Allan Hungerford opposite Tallawanta in 1967 and, in 1968, planted about 80 hectares of vineyard. By 1970, the area had grown to 240 hectares. Most of this lay on either side of Broke Road and to the west of McDonalds Road. On the southern side it encircled Tallawanta and the block that was shortly to become Brokenwood. It also included the land across McDonalds Road from Brokenwood, Leavers Block, which had produced good red wine in the early 1900s. (I remember some lovely Hungerford Hill shiraz from these vines, but they were pulled out barely ten years after they had been planted and the block has been vacant ever since.)

The Rothbury Estate syndicate also planted its first vines in 1968 and, by 1972, had 320 hectares across its four main vineyards: Rothbury, Brokenback, Homestead Hill and Herlstone. Rothbury had the novel idea of marketing its wine entirely to a mailing list of members of its Society. This was a groundbreaking scheme, as direct marketing had barely made an impact in any type of Australian commerce, let alone the conservative wine industry. The Society was never able to handle Rothbury's entire production, but it later became a model that many other wine companies would use successfully.

Saxonvale was the only one of these large new companies to establish vineyards in the Broke Fordwich area. It, too, gained a foothold in Pokolbin when it merged with a smaller syndicate that had bought the Happy Valley winery from Barrie Drayton. It also bought the Pokolbin Estates vineyard next to Tamburlaine, bringing its vineyards to over 160 hectares. However, it had the misfortune to be bought by the Gollin empire the year Gollin collapsed and was, after that, never able to market its wines in the way their quality deserved.

In 1971, the McGuigan family and other investors re-established the Dalwood vineyards that Penfolds had vacated in their move to the Upper Hunter, naming their company Wyndham Estate. This venture was originally one of the smallest of the boom-time babies, but eventually it outgrew all of them. The largest was yet to come. At its peak, the Arrowfield vineyard totalled over 480 hectares, a size that has rarely been exceeded since. Other vineyards in the Upper Hunter included Chateau Douglas, Mount Dangar, Denman Estate, Hollydeen, Mindaribba, Richmond Grove and Rosemount. The scope of the Hunter had reached over 4000 hectares of vineyard by 1976.

The unfortunate thing about almost all of these developments was that they had been planned at the time of the red wine boom and, naturally, largely involved the planting of red grapes. And just as those vineyards came into full bearing, the Australian public decided it wanted white. You can discover what happened to many of these companies from the entries under the individual wineries. Suffice to say that all except Rosemount have changed hands, in some cases several times, and virtually none remains in its original form.

There were also many smaller wineries and these tended to follow the Lake's Folly example, rather than that of corporate development. For this reason alone, they were generally more successful; in most

cases they had owners or shareholders with a day job, who could support the ventures during their growing pains. Among them were Allandale, Brokenwood, Peterson's, Quentin Vineyard (which became Marsh Estate), The Squire (Robson) Vineyard and Terrace Vale. Other new starters – De Beyers, Bimbadgen, Honeytree, Lochleven and Weinkeller – were vineyards only, selling their grapes to other winemakers.

The 1980s were a period of consolidation. While some vineyards were being uprooted, others were being established. But the greatest changes were occurring in tourist and related facilities. For the first time, Cessnock seemed to acknowledge the successful industry it had on its doorstep, instead of ignoring it or treating it as an embarrassment.

When I first started visiting the Lower Hunter, there was little choice about where to stay: two rather ordinary motels in Cessnock offered accommodation, as did several pubs, where one could be lulled to sleep by the sounds from the public bar. There was not a single bed in the vineyard area; only one restaurant, at Saxonvale's Happy Valley (now Golden Grape Estate); and not one place where you could buy a restorative tea or coffee. Since then there has been an explosion of facilities for the visitor; at a conservative estimate, these facilities include 180 places to stay, 70 restaurants, numerous shops and tea rooms and several golf courses. Less than two hours' drive from the Harbour Bridge, the Hunter has become Sydney's playground.

This tourist boom brought many new visitors and, with the memory of the over-planting in the 1970s fading, some bought land and planted vineyards. (Which of them know that the vines on Leaver's Block lasted barely ten years?) The third vineyard boom had started. A major difference between these settlers and their forebears in the 70s is that most have planted as grape growers and have not put in wineries. They have also started with a diversified base, building accommodation for rent, planting olive trees and establishing art galleries in their cellar doors. Rather than make wine, which means a winery and big capital expenditure, they have their wine made by a contract winemaker, taking it back as labelled stock.

Previously, contract winemaking could be very inconsistent, but there are now several very professional companies who specialise in this and standards are high. There is also a new professionalism in the way vineyards have been originated. Most new entrants to the industry recognise that a thousand dollars of a viticultural consultant's time can save a hundred thousand in mistakes. Nevertheless, many are finding that marketing their wine is the most difficult part of all.

Through the 1990s, the centre of gravity of new vineyards moved to the Broke Fordwich area. Two major factors were the availability of smaller blocks of land and the availability of water to assist vineyard establishment and maintenance. In spite of the fact that some grape growers are beginning to have difficulty selling their fruit, the planting seems to continue unabated. There are new vineyards all over the Pokolbin and Broke Fordwich areas. A huge new development off the Great North Road is offering self-contained blocks with home and vineyard.

How long will the current Hunter boom last? It's difficult to say, but history shows not long. Frequent repetition doesn't diminish George Santayana's words: 'Those who cannot remember the past are condemned to repeat it.'

And that past crops up in many unexpected ways. In the early days of The Rothbury Estate, workmen clearing out the tractor shed on the Brokenback Vineyard unearthed – quite literally; they were buried under soil – several unusually shaped, flat bottles of white wine. They were the original Rinegolde – semillon from the Phillips Glandore Vineyard, believed to be from the 1940s and bottled, in the Mateus Rosé-like bottle, by Leo Buring. I was lucky to taste that wine

on two occasions and both times it was rich, soft and toasty – a wonderful Hunter semillon.

In about 1975, I bought an unlikely lot at auction – two half bottles, one a 1969 Penfolds Bin 389 and the other a 1926 Lindemans St Cora Burgundy. St Cora was, in the 1970s, the Burgundy equivalent of Cawarra Claret: a cheap, non-vintage red for drinking the day you bought it. I suspected this was different and a reply from Lindemans confirmed that the wine would have been a Hunter. The wine was simply brilliant, with very ripe, sweet fruit, full body and wonderful earthy complexity. Served masked to some friends in the industry, it was picked as Hunter shiraz from perhaps the 1950s.

Then, in 1980, I was talking to grape-pickers in the Richebourg vineyard, near the village of Vosne Romanée in Burgundy, when one of them asked me back to the cellars. I was met by his mother, Mme Mugneret, who was wildly waving a leather-bound copy of *The Vineyards of New South Wales* by Sir Henry Parkes. Her great, great-grandfather had been Philobert Terrier, the winemaker and manager of St Helena Vineyard at Lochinvar in the mid-1800s. 'That vineyard,' I found myself saying 'was about 20 kilometres from where mine is.'

That history is still tantalisingly close. The current owners of the land where Kelman and Busby's Kirkton once stood still turn vine stumps out of the ground. Take the road up towards the Pokolbin lookout and, after you pass Maluna, look to the right across the valley and you'll see the terraces of the Orizaba vineyard. This belonged to the Kelman family and was pulled up in the 1940s. Hidden behind the pepper trees on the corner of McDonalds and Oakey Creek Roads you'll find the ruins of the old Ivanhoe winery, with water tank and fermenters still intact. Gaze at Neil Stevens' shiraz vines on the slopes of Mount Bright, planted in the 1860s. Are they the oldest in Australia? I can think of few older.

We cannot know why or how or how many of today's vineyards will disappear, but history dictates that some certainly will. Hopefully they will reappear, and those new, enthusiastic vignerons may look to our experience to guide them. Maybe they will even taste our wines. Meanwhile, you can taste them today, and enjoy them.

Hunter *Terroir*

The Hunter Valley is the basin formed by the Hunter River and its tributaries, which ultimately flow to the east, reaching the Tasman Sea at Newcastle. The valley is bounded to the north by the Liverpool Ranges and the Barrington Tops, which reach a surprisingly high 1555 metres and where the Hunter River itself rises; to the west by the wild Wollemi National Park; and to the south by the Brokenback Range and the Wattagans. All these areas are covered by eucalyptus forest, so the valley provides a pastoral contrast to the craggy, tree-lined hills. The important tributaries are the Wollombi Brook to the south and the Paterson and Williams rivers to the north-east. It was near the Williams River that many early Hunter vineyards were planted but, since the arrival of downy mildew, viticulture there has become too difficult.

There's a popular misconception that all vineyards are set in beautiful landscapes. Sure, the sense of grandeur as you face Chateau Palmer is indescribable, but it doesn't alter the fact that the Médoc is a flat strip of gravel along a murky, grey river whose monotony is broken principally by an oil refinery. The name *Coonawarra* is magical, but the vineyards are dead flat and featureless.

Yet, if ever there was a region to *support* the misconception, it's the Hunter Valley. Here, there is a different view with every corner turned – a group of gum tress, a shirt-front of vineyard, a dramatic sandstone bluff. Everywhere you look there is contrast. The Hunter is the brooding mass of the Brokenback Range that lies like an evil skeleton's backbone above the tumbling slopes of red Pokolbin earth. The Hunter is that graceful sweep below the precipitous Sentry Rock down to the meandering Wollombi Brook. The Hunter is those wandering rows of casuarinas that stitch their way across the quilt of vineyards on the creek flats. The drama of the hills, the slopes, the flats translates into the grapes that grow there ... and every bottle tells the story.

The French word *terroir* has no obvious equivalent in English, other than the rather non-specific 'environment' or the technical 'bioclime'. Basically, it encompasses all aspects of the vine's surroundings, including climate, soil, slope and direction faced. Since, the French argue, no two areas can be the same in all respects, it is inevitable that the vine's *terroir* is also different. This will be expressed in the wine's character to the extent that, in the finest detail, no two wines will be the same. Although the concept of *terroir* has been rejected by some, particularly in the United States, as French mumbo-jumbo, the idea that a vine's fruit should be a reflection of where it's grown ought cause no surprise. The fact that the French tend to use the term to describe the fine detail of local differences, whereas the New World (including Australia) thinks on a broader scale, doesn't diminish the concept.

Climate

In many respects the Hunter is not a great place to grow grapes. Most soil types allow only low vigour and yields, which is fine if you're a winemaker selling at a premium price but not if you're a grower in the business of just selling grapes. Rainfall is at a seasonal low in late winter and spring, exactly when you most want it. Cyclones or upper air disturbances can bring moist tropical air to dump three months' rainfall in a weekend over the harvest. Humidity is a two-edged sword: it can reduce moisture stress, but it also encourages powdery and downy mildew. Coastal southerlies, preceded by thunderstorms and hail, can sweep north and drench vineyards each week throughout summer. (To be fair, the Upper Hunter is less affected by this last scourge.) If you're a grape grower looking for purely financial return, you'd do better in a more consistent area like McLaren Vale.

But start making wine and the story is different. From two grape varieties – semillon and shiraz – the Hunter makes two of the most distinctive and superb wine styles in Australia (in the case of semillon, I could say the world). Let's find out how.

The Hunter is warm, even hot. When the Yarra Valley was being rediscovered and the cooler parts of Western Australia had burst on to the scene back in the 1980s, it was fashionable to say that you couldn't make high-quality wine in a hot climate. (Try telling that to a winemaker in the Rhône Valley!) That prejudice has largely gone, but I would banish it even further and say that temperature, within broad limits, has nothing to do with quality, affecting only style. Hot climates make styles of wine that cold climates can't make, and vice versa. And the Hunter makes its styles of wine brilliantly.

The Hunter has a maritime climate. So, in addition to warm days, it has warm nights, when the physiological processes that ripen fruit can continue. Much of the warmth the Hunter gets is early in the season, which gives the vines a quick start. Being maritime, it also has quite high humidity, which allows the leaves to keep their pores open longer during hot weather and reduces heat stress. This allows photosynthesis and growth to continue, when in drier air it would not.

As a result, Hunter vines grow with high efficiency for such a warm area. Budburst can start later in the Hunter than it does in McLaren Vale, Margaret River and parts of the Riverland, yet its fruit ripens two to four weeks earlier.

Most of the southern part of the Australian continent has a winter rainfall pattern and this is most obvious in Western Australia and South Australia. This feature is also found in southern Europe around the Mediterranean and in California. However, the east coast of Australia is affected by a band of summer rainfall, assisted by the East Australian Current that sweeps down from the Coral Sea to Bass Strait. This rainfall pattern wraps around Victoria as far as Melbourne, including the Yarra Valley, bringing summer rains in a manner similar to that experienced in northern Europe, particularly France. Dr Andrew Pirie of Piper's Brook, who studied seasonal influences on wine style as part of his doctoral thesis, believes that this moist summer climate is responsible for the more delicate structure and finer tannins in the wines of eastern Australia.

In such a warm climate, it should be no surprise that it is the varieties that thrive in the warmer parts of Europe – shiraz, semillon and verdelho – that do well.

Soil

Read the cellar door brochures and you'll hear a lot about 'red basalt' 'volcanic' soils and 'limestone' in the Hunter – volcanic perhaps to conjure up images of primal excitement, limestone because of its supposed superiority for growing grapevines. In fact, most of the soils in the Hunter are sedimentary and derived from Permian sandstone. The Brokenback Range and the hills that form the western boundaries of the Pokolbin, Broke/Fordwich and Upper Hunter areas are largely Hawkesbury sandstone, with small patches of shales, conglomerates and tuffs. The soils are formed from the erosion of these. In the Mount Bright area above Pokolbin, there is a small patch of volcanic rock and soil. Limestone is also found in the Mount Bright/Mount View area and eroded patches may be found in many parts of the Hunter.

More important for vines than the actual origin of the soil is how well it drains. If drainage is poor, the vine roots will become waterlogged; if it is too rapid, vines will lack the moisture they require for growth and respiration.

Very broadly, there are three main soil types in the Hunter. The first is the red clay loam that appears on the hilltops and slopes. You'll see this most clearly in the Lower Hunter on Chick's Hill, where the Lake's Folly and Rosehill vineyards are planted; on the slopes around Mount Pleasant near the Tyrrell's winery; and on the upper slopes either side of the Wollombi Brook near Broke, particularly above the Hope Estate Winery. In the Upper Hunter,

they again lie on the slopes, most famously on the Roxburgh Vineyard. Red soils are well drained and provide a good medium for vines. In the Hunter, the red soils are red wine country, where the best shiraz is also grown.

Also on the slopes you'll find chocolate brown podsols – the second Hunter soil type – which tend to be used for red grapes, too.

You'll find the third major soil type on the flats along the creek beds where grey sandy loams overlie white or yellow clays. Some of these soils are a little richer and allow greater vine vigour, except for those that are almost bare sand and where vigour is low. Look at Tyrrell's' HVD vineyard, Mount Pleasant's Lovedale and the vineyards close to the Wollombi Brook. This is where whites grow best, so you'll find mostly semillon and chardonnay.

Slope and aspect

The direction a vineyard faces is not as critical in a warm area like the Hunter as, for instance, in the marginal climates of Germany. Nevertheless, slopes provide cool air drainage at night, raising night temperatures and allowing flavour and colour development to continue better than on the flats, where the cold air collects. This is probably another reason why the slopes of red soil are the best sites for red grapes.

Geographical Indications

Winemakers and vignerons in the Hunter have been redefining the region as part of the new Geographical Indications (GIs) programme. These GIs will give our wines protection in international markets but, until you can describe the boundaries of a region (and the characteristics of the area within), you can't legally protect it. The regional definition is therefore important.

The Hunter Valley GI boundary largely follows the catchment of the Hunter River, although only a small area of the land enclosed is actually used for wine production.

Broke Fordwich was the first part of the Hunter to become a defined sub-region, based on the sandy river flats and red clay slopes alongside the Wollombi Brook, and on its distinctive climate. This climate is a little warmer and drier than the Pokolbin area and avoids some of the summer rainfall that plagues the rest of the Lower Hunter. Broke Fordwich and the Pokolbin together make up the Lower Hunter. The Upper Hunter is warmer and drier still, making it the most reliable area for grape growing. However, semillon and shiraz from the Upper Hunter rarely scale the heights of those from the Lower Hunter.

Winemaking and *Grape Varieties*

In most respects, the principals of winemaking have changed very little in the Hunter over the years. Winemaking is about protecting the inherent quality of the grapes; it's about good housekeeping. The changes mostly concern the materials now used. Stainless steel is easier to keep clean than concrete or old oak casks. Refrigeration and inert gas cover help the winemaker protect flavours from oxidation. But other equipment is, in principle, very similar to what was used before.

The one major change is the use of small new oak but, in the Hunter, it is only with chardonnay that new oak has become more or less universal.

White varieties

Semillon

There's not the slightest shadow of doubt in my mind that semillon is the greatest white variety for the Hunter and I'm prepared to justify a non-populist view. Chardonnay, it's true, will often make a wine that is more immediately appealing, particularly when the wines are young. But often that chardonnay will not be a distinctively Hunter white, especially if it comes from a rain-affected vintage. Semillon almost invariably *tastes* like a Hunter, whether the harvest weather has been wet or dry. What's more, it is the most distinctively regional semillon there is in Australia (*pace* Margaret River) and probably the world.

Semillon is a warm area variety. Its 'home' – Bordeaux – is at the cool end of its optimum range. Go any cooler and you get wines with strong vegetative flavours and a really lean, unbalanced palate. Yet the paradox is that, in the Hunter Valley, when it is picked to make a wine of 10 to 11 per cent alcohol (most table wines in Australia approach or exceed 13 per cent), you get a balanced wine without under-ripe flavours. The wine is light, crisp and, to the chardonnay lover, lacking fullness, but what it does have is delicacy and intensity. It can even show aromatic characters, probably the reason that for many years it was known as Hunter River riesling. But leave the wine in bottle for at least four years and it transforms into a soft, richly flavoured wine, unrecognisable from its demure beginning.

Some winemakers have tried to overcome that lack of fullness in the young wine by maturing it in new oak. However, semillon is a much more delicate and less resilient wine than chardonnay and most of these wines have ended up as lean oak drinks. Semillon needs alcohol and body to withstand oak maturation and it doesn't often have this in the Lower Hunter. The Upper Hunter, which escapes some of the wet summer weather that hits Pokolbin, usually manages to get semillon riper, so oak-matured semillons are more successful there. All the same, they're now relatively rare.

Semillon skates on thin ice. It has a large, soft, fleshy berry with a delicate skin. If the weather holds, the ice stays firm and the winemaker gets the ripeness he or she wants. If the rain comes, the ice melts, bunch rot breaks through those fragile skins and the harvest becomes a frantic life-saving effort to salvage what fruit you can.

The general procedures used for making semillon in the Hunter have changed little since the 1960s. The grapes are generally harvested in about the second week of February when between 18° and 21° brix. This sugar concentration yields about 10 to 11.5 per cent alcohol, unusually low compared with the other premium varieties and with semillon in other regions.

The juice is generally given as little skin contact as possible and sometimes whole-bunch pressing of uncrushed bunches is used. (Occasionally, a winemaker may try to build a fuller palate by allowing up to twenty-four hours' contact between juice and skins to make the wine more attractive for early drinking.) After crushing and pressing, the juice is clarified using a range of procedures that include cold settling, filtration and centrifugation. The aim is to get a delicate juice free of other flavour influences. Up to two grams per litre of tartaric acid may be added to adjust the acidity when this is needed.

The must ferments to dryness in stainless steel tanks at around 13° Celsius, which takes about ten days. This is, admittedly, much cooler than during the years before refrigeration was commonplace. Occasionally semillon is still made using 'chardonnay methods' – that is, fermentation with some grape solids in oak barrels at ambient temperature – but these wines are now few.

After the fermentation has finished and the wine is dry, it is clarified by a combination of settling, filtration or centrifugation, as with the juice. Then it is fined, which prevents deposits forming in the bottle, and is bottled early, typically in the May to August period following vintage.

Most companies release their semillons when they are only a few months old, although a few keep some wines for bottle maturation before release. The young wines are crisp and lively, often with a light body and fresh, lemony and grassy fruit. If cellared, they go into a flat spot at around two years of age, when they are no longer fresh but not yet developed. (Riesling does the same thing.) Then, after four or five years, semillon transforms itself, deepening in colour, softening and becoming rounder in the mouth, and developing the most brilliantly complex flavours of vanilla and buttered toast. (If you want a one-glass lesson in aged semillon, buy a bottle of Mount Pleasant Elizabeth or Tyrrell's Vat 1. You'll be convinced.) I have many Hunter semillons in my cellar over ten years old, a few over twenty, and the ones I've tasted are simply wonderful.

The great news is that there are more good semillons in the Hunter now than I have ever seen before. Some have been made to be more immediately attractive when young – they will still age quite well – while many are still made in the leaner, tighter style which will develop over many years. Although interest in semillon is growing, this wine still hasn't captured as much attention as it deserves. Consequently, several companies offer older semillons at the cellar door and these are often great bargains.

Chardonnay

Chardonnay had been grown for many years in Penfolds' HVD vineyard, yet its potential had been unrecognised. It had merely been a component of Penfolds' popular Bin 365 Pinot Riesling, a chardonnay–semillon blend, meaning pinot chardonnay and Hunter River riesling. It's also well known that the vines in HVD came from the Kurtz vineyard in Mudgee, although it had not been recognised there for what it was. Philip Norrie has shown, in his book *Vineyards of Sydney*, that the chardonnay cuttings for Alf Kurtz came from the Roth brothers' Craigmoor vineyard and that these, in turn, had come to Bill Roth from a Sydney vineyard, Kaluna. One manager of Kaluna – his family eventually bought the vineyard in 1918 – had been Ambrose Laraghy, who had worked at Kirkton, where duplicates of the vines in the Busby collection had been planted. The paper trail is complete. It seems the Hunter had an even bigger role in chardonnay's success in Australia than had been thought.

But it was Murray Tyrrell who really started the ball rolling. He planted chardonnay in an attempt to see what this grape, which made the great white burgundies of France, would do in the Hunter. His wines excited, then incited, the whole industry and were for years the benchmark by which other chardonnays were measured.

The irony is that in the Hunter, more particularly the Lower Hunter, chardonnay is quite inconsistent, thanks to the vagaries of the weather. (Chardonnay is more consistent in the Upper Hunter.) In the tastings I have done for this book, I have found three totally different styles, not all of them planned by the winemaker, but all of them out there for sale. Firstly there's the richly flavoured wine made from ripe grapes, the familiar full-bodied, peachy Australian chardonnay that's delicious almost as soon as it's bottled. Second, there's the leaner, crisper, lighter bodied wine that's made when the grapes have had to be picked early, as a result of rain. This wine can be almost a semillon look-alike and often ages for years in bottle. Lastly, there's the wine that didn't escape the rain and the botrytis, which starts off with intriguing fruit-salad flavours, but which turns deep gold and blows out, becoming old and tired within three years.

It is the first type of Hunter chardonnay that winemakers strive for and these are wonderfully rich, complex wines. Sometimes, they develop quite quickly at first but can then plateau and remain almost unchanged for years. The early Tyrrell's chardonnays did this, and also some from Rosemount.

Unlike the techniques for making semillon, those for chardonnay have been evolving rapidly over the last twenty years and vary somewhat from winery to winery. The description below covers the most common methods.

For premium chardonnay, barrel fermentation is used. The grapes are picked at $23°$ to $24°$ brix, if possible, to give about 13 per cent alcohol, but in wet vintages winemakers often have to settle for less. The grapes are either de-stemmed and crushed, or placed directly into the press and pressed as whole bunches. The juice is partly clarified, leaving it slightly milky in appearance, and then pumped to new or previously used small oak barrels, usually 225 litre barriques or 300 litre hogsheads. French oak is best. The barrels are either held at the ambient temperature of the winery or slightly cooled in a cold store. The must ferments with cultured or natural yeast and, after it is dry, stays in the barrel, during which it undergoes malolactic fermentation. This softens and broadens the palate of the wine and gives greater complexity, often with overtones of butterscotch and smoky bacon. It also increases the length of flavour in the mouth. Some winemakers allow malolactic in only some barrels, while a few, for instance Lake's Folly, prevent malo altogether. The wine matures in barrel, in contact with the yeast lees, which gives further complexity while retaining freshness. It is then fined, filtered (usually) and bottled anywhere from six to twelve months after vintage.

Oak barrels are expensive and require a lot of labour to manipulate, so winemakers usually ferment the less expensive chardonnays in stainless steel tanks with either planks of new oak or oak chips. These are both perfectly legitimate and effective for cheaper wines if handled well. Wines made this way are often combined with barrel-fermented wine to produce the right complexity at the right price.

Many drinkers reacted against the over-oaked chardonnays of the past and some winemakers responded with unoaked chardonnay. This style has not been particularly successful, as winemakers have usually reserved their best, and ripest, grapes for barrel fermentation and kept the lesser grapes for unoaked chardonnay; and under-ripe chardonnay is pretty boring. Another factor is that chardonnay, unlike most other whites, develops a lot of its flavour during fermentation from flavourless precursors, and fermentation in oak seems to maximise that conversion. Careful use of oak, respecting the depth of flavour in the fruit, is the best course.

Verdelho

Verdelho is almost entirely restricted to Portugal and the islands of Madeira, where it is largely used for fortified wines. Even in Australia, it has been quite limited in distribution, planted mainly in Western Australia and the Hunter. It ripens early in the season, so there's usually little difficulty in getting very ripe flavours and a full body from high alcohol, even in a tricky area like the Hunter. Verdelho handles wet weather well, aided by a tough skin, but those same skins

are a two-edged sword: they can also make the wine rather firm and tannic, which some winemakers disguise by leaving a small amount of residual sweetness in the wine. It's like putting more sugar in a strong cup of tea.

Verdelho is made using the same methods used for semillon. It goes into bottle early and is usually at its best in the year it's made or the one following. A good verdelho should have a full body, with a rich, almost oily texture similar to that of chardonnay. The flavours are ripe and tropical, usually with suggestions of pineapple and rock-melon. Be prepared to find a hint of sweetness, but this shouldn't cloy and the wine should finish dry. Occasionally you may come across a verdelho that has aged brilliantly in bottle, becoming rather like a full-bodied semillon, but the grapes for it were probably picked earlier, resulting in wine that is less alcoholic than is common now.

Verdelho performs well in Hunter vine-yards and has great immediate appeal, so you'll see a lot more of verdelho in the future.

Other white varieties

Gewürztraminer, currently unfashionable and usually thought of as a cold area variety, often does surprisingly well in the Hunter. More than any other, it was the grape that first brought success to Rosemount. In the Hunter, it is made either quite lean and crisp with lightly aromatic fruit, or big and full-bodied with pungent flavour. (I wish more winemakers had the courage to make the second style.) All traminers should show varietal characters of lychee, rose water and lavender. Traminer is the perfect match with Thai food, and a trip round the cellar doors will give you the chance to find the style you like best.

Riesling rarely makes great wine in the Hunter and I know of only two vineyards that still have the variety planted.

You'll occasionally find chenin blanc, which makes a soft, slightly broad style of white without particularly intense fruit. There are some pleasant examples about but, frankly, anything chenin can do in the Hunter I think semillon can do better.

Sauvignon blanc provides some flavour variation in this region but doesn't show distinctive varietal character. If you like the variety, you'd do better to look elsewhere.

The occasional Hunter viognier that has come my way has shown some promise, so watch this space.

These last few varieties are usually made in the same way as semillon and bottled early, without maturation in oak, so that the varietal character can speak.

Red varieties

The ways in which reds are made in the Hunter usually depend more on the winemaker's preference than on the grape variety. I'll use shiraz to describe the range of methods used and then enlarge on those for other varieties.

Shiraz

It comes as a surprise to most people that shiraz is a rather insignificant variety on the world scene. It is certainly present in several countries in the New World (only France in the Old World), but its importance falls far short of the other mainstream red varieties – cabernet sauvignon, merlot, grenache and even pinot noir. Only in Australia, in the Rhône Valley and, increasingly, in the south of France, is shiraz an important grape. There's no obvious reason why this should be so, other than history and fashion. Apart from a warm climate, shiraz has no special requirements. What's more, it has the natural fullness and tannin balance to drink well when young, while also aging well.

In the Hunter, the grapes are typically picked in the last two weeks of February and into early March. Most winemakers aim for wines of 13 per cent alcohol, sometimes more, but often bad weather forces them to accept 12 to 12.5 per cent. The fruit is crushed and de-stemmed and transferred to either stainless steel or open concrete fermenters. Sometimes a cold soak is used, where contact between the juice and skins before fermentation helps to extract colour, flavour and tannins. The must ferments at between 20 and 30° Celsius; cooler temperatures give a fruitier, softer but less complex wine; warmer temperature give more extract and complexity but less obvious varietal character. Either cultured or natural yeast is used. During fermentation the skins, which have floated to the surface, are mixed into the must by being pushed under the surface with hand plungers, by having the wine pumped over them or by a process of emptying the fermenter into another tank and then refilling it. They may also be held under the surface by means of header boards. Some winemakers use rotofermenters (like giant concrete mixers), which rotate to keep skins and must mixed.

When the fermentation is nearly complete, the wine is pumped off, either into another tank or into barrels, where the fermentation finishes. The skins are transferred to the press, where the remaining wine is squeezed out. Shortly after this, the wine goes through malolactic fermentation. If the wine has been in a tank, it is now transferred to barrels. Sometimes, winemakers leave the wine in contact with the skins for up to eight weeks after the fermentation has finished, which changes the tannin structure and produces wine with a different texture.

The traditional style of Hunter shiraz was made without new oak. The wines matured in large casks, typically ovals of 1000 to 2000 litres, which allowed the tannins to soften, but without imparting any vanilla-like new oak flavour, and the wines to develop complexity. This style is still widely made, usually by the larger companies like McWilliam's and Tyrrell's. Lindemans use new oak for their Stephen Vineyard Shiraz but not for the standard Hunter River Shiraz.

New oak barrels were first used for Hunter reds in the 1970s and time has shown that they need to be handled carefully, as new oak, particularly American oak, can easily dominate Hunter fruit. Both American oak and French oak are now common for shiraz, and the amount of new oak flavour is matched to the strength of the wine by using a combination of new and older barrels. The impact of oak is much stronger when it's new.

Hunter shiraz usually lacks the power of its counterpart in, say, McLaren Vale or the Barossa. As a result it often suffers in comparison during masked tastings and in wine shows, particularly when those other wines carry a lot of new oak. The typical young Hunter shiraz is a medium-bodied wine showing red berries, spicy fruit and plenty of soft, mild tannin. It can age for a considerable time, more than its constitution often suggests. With bottle age, it becomes much more complex, with earthy, leathery overtones and a beautiful perfume. It also acquires a silkiness and grace, becoming a smooth, wonderfully complex and richly flavoured wine.

Cabernet sauvignon

Cabernet sauvignon is an enigma in the Hunter. Common wisdom, particularly amongst winemakers, has it that the variety doesn't succeed in the region; that the wine shows harsh astringency, lacks natural balance and is often dominated by gum-leaf type characters rather than sweet blackcurrant and blackberry fruit. The more successful Lake's Folly Cabernets and the early examples from Brokenwood and Saxonvale are thought of as aberrations that do nothing to change that belief. And yet James Halliday (*The Wines and History of the Hunter Valley*) quotes several sources to show that cabernet had a good reputation in the Hunter last century and was widely planted.

It's hard to reconcile this picture with current attitudes. However, judgement on the quality of cabernet would have been made by an insular New South Wales industry before Federation and without the comparison with cabernet from Coonawarra, Margaret River or, probably, the Yarra Valley.

I have a feeling that cabernet tends to do better in the Broke/Fordwich area than it does in Pokolbin, though why that should be I don't know. Broke is slightly warmer, less humid and slightly less affected by wet weather during vintage than Pokolbin, but none of these seems to account for the difference in performance. The Upper Hunter can grow good cabernet if yields of vigorous vines are kept under control.

Cabernet sauvignon ripens later in the season than shiraz and is often picked slightly less ripe, to give a wine of about 12.5 per cent alcohol. It has small berries with tough skins, so survives the wet vintages much better than does shiraz.

The winemaking differs little from shiraz, except for a few points. French oak tends to be used in preference to American and the wine is often blended with small amounts of other varieties like merlot and cabernet franc to improve its complexity and balance.

Hunter cabernet ages well in bottle, but needs to start with a good tannin balance. Highly astringent cabernets simply stay hard and don't soften; if anything, the tannins appear more bitter and the wine more hollow with age. Good examples develop the beautiful cigar-box like bouquet typical of cabernet, with the additional earthy complexity typical of the region.

Merlot

This is the most important variety in the Bordeaux region of France, at least in terms of area, but it's relatively new to Australia and the Hunter. Merlot's flavour is not unlike cabernet sauvignon's, but the familiar blackcurrant character has additional overtones of plums and leafiness and occasionally some earthiness. The structure is quite different, though, with a much plumper, rounder middle palate and softer tannins than cabernet. Its colour, when young, is also less intensely purple and it develops more quickly in bottle.

In the Hunter, merlot ripens a little earlier than shiraz and is usually made using the same methods. It's still early days for merlot, but some characteristics are already appearing. Merlot's supple, soft nature is compatible with that of the Hunter red style. Its early ripening is useful in beating the rain in wet vintages. However, merlot has thinner skins than cabernet sauvignon and can be damaged by bunch rot in those wetter years.

It's hard to see merlot ever making large inroads on the popularity of shiraz in the Hunter Valley, but it does offer the red drinker further choice.

Pinot noir

Pinot noir is chardonnay's great red companion in the Burgundy region of France and in Champagne, but there the similarity ends. Where chardonnay is adaptable in the vineyard and easy to handle in the winery, pinot is a minx. Pinot generally performs best in a cooler climate than that of the Hunter – which is ironic, as it was Murray Tyrrell who put pinot noir on the map in Australia. (Even Murray, though, has been heard to say that he can make great semillon and shiraz every year, while with pinot noir it's only three years out of ten.) True, pinot has its supporters; Tyrrell is one, Ian Scarborough and Evans Family are others. True, with age pinot can develop a lovely, mellow Hunter Valley softness and earthiness, but so can shiraz – only better.

In the Hunter calendar, pinot noir is the first red variety to ripen and is usually picked even before semillon. The winemaking methods involve all the usual pinot variations – a cold soak before fermentation, some whole berries and uncrushed bunches, fairly hot fermenting, and *pigeage* (foot

stamping) to mix the skins and stalks into the must. New oak must be restrained with pinot noir and the oak is almost invariably French; American oak and pinot simply don't work together.

Hunter pinot won't be as obviously varietal as examples from, say, southern Victoria, but it should have a pleasant softness and sweet fruit. It will develop earthy Hunter characters quite quickly with bottle age. Either drink it straight away or cellar it to become complex and mellow.

Chambourcin

In many respects, I think of chambourcin as the red counterpart of verdelho in the Hunter. It's a hybrid of the familiar grape vine we know well, *Vitis vinifera*, and an American species. The American genes make it resistant to the downy mildew that plagues vines and distresses vineyard managers in wet weather. It carries quite heavy crops, yet doesn't seem to have much difficulty getting them ripe. One distinguishing feature is that it makes intensely purple wines, more so than any other familiar grape. Chambourcin is a soft, fleshy wine with an attractive berry flavour, which gives it great immediate appeal.

For all the above reasons, Chambourcin is rapidly becoming more widespread in the Hunter and you'll see a lot more of it. Drink it while it's young.

Other red varieties

There is a little cabernet franc grown in the Hunter; and while Italian varieties like sangiovese, barbera and nebbiolo are beginning to put in an appearance, these will be hard to find for a few years yet. It looks as if sangiovese, for one, may be suited to the Hunter.

viti*culture*

A year in the vineyard. What you can expect to see, and when.

June

In many respects, the vineyard year starts in June. The vines have been bitten by cold nights, perhaps even frosts. They have now lost their leaves and are dormant sticks that can be pruned. In most parts of Australia, pruning's a rather cold and sometimes solitary task. In the Hunter, the mornings may start cold, even frosty, with a crunch under foot, but by midday you can be pruning in a T-shirt, and sunshine and clear blue skies warm the spirit. Come four o'clock, you are looking forward to that fireside glass of muscat.

July

This is the peak month for pruning, when seemingly random growth is cut back to an elegant architecture, ready for the year to come. Most Lower Hunter vineyards use cane pruning, which reduces the vine to a simple 'T'. More vigorous vineyards in Broke or the Upper Hunter often use spur pruning, which leaves the vine's arms with a spiky appearance. Damaged trellis is repaired. You may see spreaders carpeting the soil with lime or gypsum, to make that red Hunter clay more welcoming for the vine's roots.

August

The purple coral pea, *Hardenbergia*, blankets the embankments and the sunnier edges of bushland. The last vineyards are being pruned. The severed canes are dragged out of the vineyard and burned, blue wisps of smoke rising against the background of the gum-tree lined hills. The cover crops that were planted in May are ploughed in. Vineyard managers who maintain a clean, tilled vine row will be 'hilling up' the soil under the vines to give the roots greater scope. At the end of the month, buds on the earliest varieties – gewürztraminer, pinot noir and chardonnay – are beginning to shoot. If the soils are dry, vineyards with irrigation will get their first drink.

September

The days are now warm and sunny. By mid-month, all varieties will be shooting. Green will begin to return to the vineyards, bringing hope for the coming season. The creamy-white flowers of the spotted gums powder the bush.

October

Vine growth is well underway and, hopefully, there has been rain. The weeds love the rain, too. Tractors now thread their way between the vine rows, either tilling the soil or slashing the weeds and grass low. Vineyard managers will be applying preventative sprays for downy and powdery mildew.

November

Most varieties flower during this month. You can smell the delicate scent of the flower bunches as you walk through the vineyards. Flowering is a critical time and good weather is crucial; for every flower that's not pollinated, you lose a grape. It is rare in the Hunter for rain to affect flowering badly, but drought or scorching westerlies can be worse. A spray applied to the flower bunches now will prevent botrytis spores from growing and causing bunch rot later in summer.

December

Vine growth is at its greatest. Some vineyard managers train the canes by tucking them in to the trellis, the traditional Hunter way. Some hold them upright and at attention by lifting foliage wires. Others trim them into loose hedges. Scattered rain now is very useful, because the young grapes are swelling; but too much, and you can get trouble. Each afternoon, you'll see vineyard managers looking to the west, as that's where the thunderstorms come from, and the hail. Clouds with hail have a green tinge to them. Murray Tyrrell used to let off rockets to disperse the hail clouds, but you don't see those used now. Some managers will apply a precautionary spray against bunch rot.

January

This is the last chance for a winemaker's holiday. The grapes are going through veraison – the reds changing colour, the whites becoming translucent. Rain may now become a problem, bringing bunch rot. If you hear guns, don't run for cover – the locals are really quite friendly. The bangs are from gas guns, used to frighten birds away from the ripening fruit. Some vineyards under the bush on Mount Bright or above Milbrodale Road will use bird netting. Vintage for pinot noir and gewürztraminer may start towards the end of the month.

February

Semillon and chardonnay both start to come in during the first week. Most of the grapes are now mechanically harvested, but you'll still see the picking teams out there each morning. If you know a vineyard owner or winemaker, you can sometimes join in. If it's muddy, don't wear gum boots; you'll leave them behind. Picking can be a riot. It's hard work, but you hear all the local gossip, the new jokes, what happened on *Friends* last night – that sort of thing.

If the weather is fine, vintage may be relaxed; if it's wet, all hell breaks loose. By the third week, most of the whites are picked and shiraz starts. Cabernet sauvignon follows about a week later.

March

The last of the reds come in before the middle of the month. (Those wineries taking fruit from other districts like Cowra or Mudgee are still flat out, though, as grapes ripen later there.) If there has been rain, the vines start to put out fresh, new growth, freed from that burden of grapes. Piles of grape skins appear in the vineyard, waiting to be spread as mulch.

April

The vines are now laying down reserves for the following spring. The leaves are starting to turn yellow. It's a quiet time in the vineyards, giving the staff a chance for congratulation or to reflect on what might have been. The semillons are being 'cleaned up' and can be assessed for the first time. Chardonnays and reds may still be going through malolactic – the worst time to taste them.

May

The leaves have turned into a glorious palette of gold, amber and red. With cold nights, they will start to fall. Some vineyard managers will plant cover crops to provide a green manure that can be ploughed in later. A few will make an early start to pruning. The year closes.

Vint*ages*

2000

The great news is that the Hunter farewelled the 1900s with a simply outstanding vintage.

Well-spaced rainfall occurred throughout the 1999 spring, which is when it is most needed but rarely comes. Although there was a very active cyclone season in the tropics and rain depressions threatened, the heavy rain that so often mars January and February didn't eventuate in 2000. Thunderstorms caused localised hail damage. The summer overall was quite cool and vintage started slightly early.

Semillon and shiraz were the great successes, apart from a few vineyards, which had suffered from downy mildew and never fully ripened their grapes. I can't remember trying so many ripe, full-flavoured semillons from so many companies. In fact, the difficulty some winemakers faced was identifying the finer, tighter wines for release as aged wines. Chardonnays were merely very good. Timing was all-important with shiraz. Those who picked early made good but unexceptional wines. Those who waited too long, perhaps for over-cropping vines, were caught by heavy rain in early March. Those who picked just before that rain made wines of wonderful depth and structure, certainly the best since 1991 and probably for many years before that.

1999

The Hunter had had unusually good rain over winter and the wet weather continued through September and October. There was a little downy mildew. Scattered rain continued throughout November, but the weather then turned dry. January was hot, and rain towards the end of the month and early February renewed the threat of rot in whites.

Picking started in early February and the difficult weather persuaded most winemakers to pick early, rather than take risks. The semillons were of very good quality and, although a little lighter than in 1998, had a very attractive softness about them. Chardonnays, while sound, generally lacked weight, but made attractive, early maturing wines. The shiraz wines had very good colour and flavour and a lovely softness. Pat Auld of Lindemans likened them to the '87s.

1998

The Hunter had no really good rainfall between the 1997 vintage and September and irrigation started early in those vineyards that had water available. Beautifully timed rains in August prompted a good start to the year. There was useful follow-up rain in October and November, but a hot period with bushfires in early December left vineyards badly in need of top-up rain.

Heavy rain in January caused problems in early vintage and some chardonnay was picked earlier than ideal. However, the weather became drier and most fruit was delivered in very good condition. Semillons were excellent – the best since 1995 – but chardonnays were less even.

Most have developed quickly and should be drunk by 2002. During vintage, shiraz looked merely good, but the wines have since improved out of sight in wood and are now mostly of top quality – full flavoured, round and soft, and suitable for long cellaring.

1997

Budburst was uneven, but good follow-up rain gave the Hunter the best start for many years. A massive hailstorm caused widespread damage to buildings and cars at Singleton in early December and growth on one vineyard was completely destroyed. Repeated bursts of rain during late January and February caused widespread bunch rot in white varieties and most grapes had to be picked before they were ripe. (Phillip John of Lindemans said that the whites were 'the worst he had seen', which got the wine press calling local winemakers, who strongly denied the accusation. The weak 1997 classes in the Hunter Wine Show later that year completely vindicated Phillip's comment.)

Verdelho beat the rain and most of these wines were good. The semillons and chardonnays either were rot affected, so already deep in colour and over-developed, or were quite lean and are now aging slowly. The weather turned fine later in vintage and shiraz grapes came in very well.

These wines have great colour and flavour, but have quite strong tannins. Some lack the usual Hunter softness and balance, and can even seem hollow. They're well worth keeping, all the same, and there will undoubtedly be great wines amongst them.

1996

Winter and early spring were very dry, but there was good rainfall in October. Scattered rainfall through the summer caused some concern and vintage started in cool, damp weather until dry, hot days speeded ripening. Fine weather throughout most of February saw a slightly below-average crop of good-quality grapes delivered. Sugar levels were satisfactory, although the cool summer and early onset of autumn conditions in the vineyards prevented high baumés being achieved.

Overall it was a good year for both whites and reds. There'll be debate for some years about whether 1996 or 1995 was better for semillon. The chardonnays were mixed – the riper ones good, but some lacking depth and richness. The shiraz wines had good colour and fruit, with medium weight and soft tannins. They were not as big as the '95s, but many had better balance and softness. They should age very well and develop more typical Hunter style than the '95s.

1995

A very dry winter contributed to relatively poor growth after budburst and strong, hot westerly winds were common in spring. However, things improved greatly with good rain in November and December. Overall there was a disease-free growing season and the harvest took place in ideal, dry weather. Yields were generally below average.

Semillon was the outstanding white variety, with the best wines seen for many years. They are developing slowly, and clearly have great long-term potential. Shiraz was also superb, challenging the quality of the 1991 vintage.

The wines have quite high tannin levels – some are even a bit too dry and firm – and will live for many years.

1994

Overall this was a cool year, with adequate rainfall spread over the growing season. However, there was extreme heat during early January, with major bushfires in the Sydney and Hunter areas. Rain from mid-February spoilt what would otherwise have been a high-quality vintage. White wine quality was a bit uneven but the best wines were still very good, chardonnay generally performing better than semillon.

The 1994 reds have turned out much better than was originally expected. They have strong fruit and are ageing very well.

1993

In spite of low winter and spring rainfall, budburst was the best for several years. The growing season was generally cool, and scattered summer rain produced some pressure from downy mildew. Vintage was later than average and further wet weather caused some fruit to be picked early to beat the rot. The riper chardonnays were quite good, but semillon was a bit green and disappointing. Reds were relatively poor, lacking colour and showing green, under-ripe flavours.

1992

The 1991 drought continued into this growing season, with only 100 mm of rain from April to December. Stored water, where available, ran out and vine growth was poor. Then, at the start of the vintage, 250 mm of rain fell in a week, creating havoc with the harvest. In spite of this, some parcels of riper chardonnay turned out very well and some semillons were good. However, the reds were mostly poor and diluted, lacking ripeness and flavour. Yields were generally low.

1991

This was a very dry year throughout the whole growing season and yields were about half the average. The reds were rich and strong and have since aged brilliantly in bottle, although some are on the tough side. Many still need bottle age to show their best. The whites were big, rather broad, wines that developed early. The odd semillon will still take some bottle age, but most should be drunk.

1990

A wet vintage, but some good, medium-weight reds and whites were made. Most should be drunk by 2002.

1989

There was some rain at vintage, but quite good reds and moderate whites were made. In fact, shiraz turned out better than anyone would have predicted at the time. The best will still last into the early 00s.

1988

A wet summer and vintage generally produced ordinary wines.

A few semillons still open well and the best reds will last, but shouldn't require further cellaring.

1987

This was a relatively cool year and, in spite of rain near the start of vintage, both reds and whites were excellent.

The best semillons are still drinking well and will last. The reds are of medium weight, with very elegant flavours and are developing slowly. The best still have several years ahead of them into the 00s.

1986

This was a very good year in the Hunter for both whites and reds. The reds had very good depth and structure.

The best semillons reached their peak around 2000. Some of the reds will age further.

1985

A hot, dry summer produced very firm reds that have lasted well. Some of the semillons were rather tough and lean when young and seemed to lack fruit but have, surprisingly, come round well with cellaring.

1984

There was heavy rain early in vintage and follow-up showers never allowed the vines and soil to dry out. The semillons picked before the rain affected them turned out brilliantly. Some Rothbury, Tyrrell's and Mount Pleasant wines are still excellent at the turn of the century. The reds were badly rain-affected and light in flavour.

1983

The summer was generally hot and dry and there was extreme heat mid-vintage. The reds were excellent, with deep colours and higher tannin levels than usual. The whites were full flavoured from the start; this was a year when you could get semillon very ripe if you wanted to.

The best of the reds are still drinking brilliantly some two decades on, although they still show some firmness. The best of the semillons still drink well but lack charm.

1982

The Hunter had a one-year respite from a four-year drought. The vintage period was quite cool, apart from one very hot spell in mid-February. The whites were very good but the reds were of average quality and lacked weight. Some semillons still drink well but most of the reds have now passed their best.

1981

This was an exceedingly dry year with a hot summer. I remember wide cracks in the soil in many vineyards. Yields were simply pathetic in vineyards that did not have water and even in some that did. The whites were coarse and matured early. Many reds were massive and too tannic to be balanced. Others, surprisingly, lacked flavour. The outstanding wine was the Saxonvale Show Shiraz off the Happy Valley vineyard.

1980

The growing season was generally dry and the summer hot. The whites were mostly rather plain and broad, and have not lasted, but the reds were very good and the best still drink well.

1979

A cool year that produced some exceptional semillons, the best of which still drink well. The reds have mostly not lasted as well as was originally expected.

1978

As there had been the year before, there was a dry growing season spoilt by torrential rain at the beginning of vintage, with follow-up showers. Most grapes were picked early to beat the weather and few wines still open well.

1977

A generally dry year with flood rain in the middle of vintage. The whites that came in beforehand were good but generally not great. The weather fined up later and some good reds were made, many with quite strong tannins.

1976

Semillons were very good and lasted well. The reds had good flavour and balance, but most have passed their best.

1975

A dry and very late vintage – some blamed the nearby aluminium smelter and fluoride fall-out – apart from a late-vintage deluge. Semillons were good, without being exceptional, although some have lasted well. The reds were mostly good.

1974

A very wet vintage produced uneven whites and thin, diluted reds. A few semillons were exceptional and have lasted well.

1973

A warm, fairly dry year produced some very good, if fairly big, whites. There were also good reds, but few have lasted.

1972

An excellent white year but the reds were rather light.

1971

Extremely wet. Most wines were badly rot affected. 'The worst year in living memory', according to Murray Tyrrell.

1970

Largely a good, but not great, year. Some whites, particularly from Lindemans, were exceptional. Reds were mostly soft and medium bodied.

1969

A drought year with bushfires. Coarse whites and rather plain, though big, reds.

1968

Wet vintage. Some exceptional semillons. Most reds were light, but there was the occasional very good wine.

1967

Coolish year with some rain. Exceptional semillons – one of the great Lindemans years – but these have now declined. The reds were medium bodied and well balanced and a few still open brilliantly.

1966

Dry, warm year. Some good semillons but lacking finesse. Quite big reds which have lasted well.

1965

Drought year. Exceptional for both whites and reds. With rare exceptions, the whites have now gone too far, but the best reds – and there were plenty – will live for many years. Tyrrell's, Tulloch and Lindemans wines are still worth looking for. They have simply extraordinary quality.

1964

Good middle-ranking wines that have mostly faded. There was the occasional exceptional white.

1963

Medium weight, soft reds that were beautiful at ten to fifteen years, but have not lasted. Even the best semillons have faded.

1962

Hail reduced crops, but there were some high quality, lighter reds and magnificent semillons.

1961

Appalling hail damage, but those reds that were made were excellent.

1960

Warm, hail-affected year, with a small amount of high-quality wine.

1959

An exceptional year for both whites and reds, the latter ranking with the 1965s as the best in a half-century.

The *Wineries*

Most of the information given in the following profiles is pretty much self-explanatory, but some things are perhaps worth clarifying.

Most of the Pokolbin wineries are also shown in the tourist guide *Hunter Valley Wine Country* published by the Cessnock City Tourist Board. For the Broke Fordwich area, look for the Singleton Visitors' Guide published by the Singleton Shire Council. The Muswellbrook Information Centre can provide you with a map of the Upper Hunter wineries.

Where it says that a winery cellar door is open on public holidays, this does not include Christmas Day or Good Friday. On any other public holiday, you'll be fine.

Where a winery has a mailing list, and you discover you like that winery's wines, I strongly recommend you put your name down. Mailing list customers are often offered new releases before the wine trade, and are sometimes offered special releases that the trade doesn't get. Some wineries' newsletters can also be quite entertaining.

Where relevant, the name of the winery's wholesale distributor is also listed. Details about these distributors can be found towards the end of the book. If you are after a particular wine in your home state, and can't get in touch with the winery, the distributor should be able to point you in the direction of a retailer near you.

I found that a small number of wineries acted as if they didn't want anyone to know they were there. As far as possible, I have given you as much information as I can. But if I haven't been able to taste the wines and can't make any recommendations, I'm sorry ... perhaps you can let me know.

Tasting Notes

With almost all wineries, I have given short descriptions of some of the wines – either the wines I like or the wines that best represent the vineyard or 'house style'. I tasted many of the wines in a big tasting in the Pokolbin Community Hall in mid-2000, and was joined by some of the winemakers who also wanted to try them. Others, I tasted at home later or when I called at the cellar doors myself.

Wherever possible, the vintages of the wines I describe are as close as I could manage to currently available at the time of publication. Where the vintages have changed, the tasting notes should still give you an idea of that winery's style and strengths.

The prices quoted with the wines are from several sources. In most cases they are cellar door prices as at May 2000, before the introduction of GST. A few prices may have crept up slightly, but they should still be a good guide. A few are 'recommended retail'

– more what you're likely to find in a bottle shop. When you call at cellar door, you may get a pleasant surprise. Some prices are not shown – either because they are museum wines or pre-release wines, or because prices were unavailable at the time of going to press. Given the various ways of pricing wine, all prices sould be read as indicative.

The information in the book is correct at time of going to press, but the wine industry is moving quicky – so, by the time you read this, anything might have happened.

Allandale

ADDRESS: Lovedale Road, Allandale 2320
TELEPHONE: (02) 4990 4526
FAX: (02) 4990 1714
E-MAIL: wines@allandalewinery.com.au
WEB: www.allandalewinery.com.au
ESTABLISHED: 1978
CELLAR DOOR: 9am–5pm Mon–Sat, 10am–5pm Sun
OWNERS: Wally and Judith Atallah
VITICULTURIST: Bill Sneddon
WINEMAKERS: Bill Sneddon and Steve Langham
1999 PRODUCTION: 15,000 cases
MAILING LIST: Yes
DISTRIBUTED: Aria Wine Co. (NSW and Qld); Vintners (Vic.); Winter Wines (Tas.)
FEATURES: Barbecue and picnic facilities; Lovedale Long Lunch, May; Jazz at Budburst, October; Strings in the Winery, November.

Allandale is an important name in Hunter history, as this area, between Lochinvar and Pokolbin/Cessnock, was the centre for many vineyards in the 1800s. The original Allandale winery also housed the local distillery. The present Allandale was one of the first new wineries in the Hunter, founded by Ed Jouault and colleagues in 1978. The property was the site of George Kime's vineyard in the late 1800s and near the original Allandale winery of that century. Ed was a studious yet inventive winemaker and established a very good reputation in a short time. Some of his wines were magnificent and some technically questionable, but they were always interesting.

Ed died tragically in a car accident a few years later and since then ownership has passed to Wally and Judith Atallah. Bill Sneddon, an early graduate of the Riverina College (now Charles Sturt University), has been the winemaker for the last fifteen years and has become strongly identified with the company. He also oversees sales and marketing, which looks to me like two full-time jobs, and yet I've never seen Bill flappable.

Initially Allandale had no vineyards but specialised in agreements with contracted local grape growers. Later it planted a vineyard of its own, which now totals about 7 hectares of pinot noir, chardonnay and semillon, but Bill still gets good parcels of fruit from Hilltops (Young), Mudgee and McLaren Vale.

In Bill's time the wines have always been of very good quality and in recent years Allandale has been one of the most consistent producers in the Hunter. It deservedly has a very loyal following.

The '99 Verdelho is quite fine on the nose but is a full-bodied wine with good varietal flavour.

The 1998 McLaren Vale Shiraz is a big, soft wine that's packed with plenty of rich, sweet fruit.

1995 Semillon

I have seen this wine several times and it always impresses. (It won the trophy as best semillon at the Cowra Wine Show in 1998 and has won many awards elsewhere.) The nose is beautifully complex, with nutty developed characters and great richness. The palate is round and soft, with lovely depth of flavour, grilled nuts and toast to the fore. A simply delicious wine that will continue to gain character for several years yet.

1998 Chardonnay ($18)

Hunter chardonnay doesn't come much better than this. The nose has wonderful depth of fruit, which has a real sweetness to it (not in the sugar sense) without being overly ripe. It's a very complex wine, some of that complexity beginning to come from bottle age. The palate is rich and well balanced, showing what you can achieve with great fruit and sensitive winemaking. A beautifully crafted wine that will develop further in the short term.

1997 Chardonnay

This is also a brilliant wine and a surprise from this difficult white wine vintage. It has a really fabulous nose, with some bottle age adding complexity to ripe, peachy fruit. The palate is round and full bodied, with very good balance. It was close to its best in 2000, but should hold until 2001/2.

ADDRESS: Lovedale Road, Lovedale 2320
TELEPHONE: (02) 4930 7387
FAX: (02) 4930 7900
E-MAIL: winemasters@allanmere.com.au
WEB: www.allanmere.com.au
ESTABLISHED: 1984
CELLAR door: 9am–5pm 7 days
OWNERS: Greg Silkman, Gary Reed, Steve Allen and Craig Brown-Thomas
VITICULTURIST: Jenny Bright
WINEMAKER: Greg Silkman
1999 production: 10,000 cases
MAILING LIST: Yes, and Allanmere Wine Club
DISTRIBUTED: Direct from vineyard plus export
FEATURES: Lovedale Long Lunch, May.

When Dr Newton Potter and his wife Ginnie bought land on Lovedale Road, they had not intended to build a winery, but build one they did, in 1984. They planted no vineyard, but instead took grapes from local growers, which Potter made into wine with the assistance of Geoff Broadfield, previously a winemaker with Wyndham Estate. Broadfield also used the Allanmere winery for his contract winemaking.

Allanmere burst on to the scene with very successful chardonnays, which had considerable show success and rapidly established Allanmere as one of the 'must visits' amongst the Hunter cellar doors. Trinity, a blend of chardonnay, semillon and sauvignon blanc, was also very successful. A concession to vineyards has since been made, with the planting of 2.5 hectares of chardonnay.

The Potters sold to a group of four winemakers who had also set up the Monarch Winemaking Services in the old Hungerford Hill/McGuigan winery on the corner of Broke and McDonalds roads. Greg Silkman had been one of the partners in Tamburlaine,

Steve Allen and Craig Brown-Thomas came from Saddler's Creek and Gary Reed came from Calais. After two years in bottle, the '97 Hunter Mudgee Shiraz was in that 'in-between' stage: no longer youthful and fruity but not yet complex and mature. The fruit was good and there was well-handled oak. Give it another year or two to come round. It will develop for several years yet.

1999 Semillon

Very intense, lifted, lemony fruit on the nose. The palate is fresh, with good citrus flavour and nice length. It has the fruit to drink well early, but would be so much better with some age. Great potential.

1999 Verdelho ($16)

This is a very typical Hunter verdelho, with heaps of ripe, tropical fruit and a full-bodied palate, where a light tannin grip is balanced by a trace of sweetness. There's plenty of alcohol, which makes the wine very full and round in the mouth. Enjoy it while it's young and fresh. The next vintage is knocking on the door.

Arrowfield

ADDRESS: Denman Road, Jerrys Plains 2330
TELEPHONE: (02) 6576 4041
FAX: (02) 6576 4144
E-MAIL: arrowine@hunterlink.net.au
WEB: www.arrowfieldwines.com.au
ESTABLISHED: 1969
CELLAR door: 10am–5pm 7 days
OWNERS: Hokuriku CCBC (Japanese Coca-Cola Bottling Co.)
VITICULTURIST: Ruth Sutherland
WINEMAKERS: Blair Duncan and Derek Fitzgerald
MAILING LIST: Yes
DISTRIBUTED: Young and Rashleigh, NSW; The Wine Co., Vic.; Wine 2000, Qld; Moss Stirling Vintners, WA; David Johnstone & Assts, Tas.; and export
FEATURES: SJ's Restaurant, lunches Wed–Sun. Barbecue and picnic facilities, children's playground.

This, in its day, was the largest vineyard ever established in the Hunter, but it wasn't so for long. In common with many other new vineyard ventures in the 1970s, reality was a lot tougher than the dream.

In 1969, W R Carpenter and Company bought an extensive property at Jerrys Plains, between Singleton and Denman. In the next few years, the company planted more than 480 hectares of grapes, 280 of them red. At the time, the red wine boom was at its peak and it wasn't long before the new wine drinkers joining the market started clamouring for white. Arrowfield did at least have a substantial area of whites, which was more than some of the new companies had, and the wines were very good.

During the six years with Gary Baldwin as winemaker, Arrowfield produced a string of show successes and built a strong reputation for quality in the industry. The trouble was that its disposing of large quantities of cheap, ordinary red wine had tarnished Arrowfield's name and after that the marketing became a struggle. However, the surplus was relatively shortlived, as a radical re-structuring of the vineyards reduced grape production to such an extent that Arrowfield began to source fruit from other areas. Under winemaker Simon

Gilbert, Arrowfield began to develop a good name for Cowra Chardonnay; and its Show Chardonnay, mostly from its own vineyards at Jerrys Plains, was a frequent medal and trophy winner.

Carpenters sold to ARABS – not a teetotal group from the Middle East, but Australian Racing and Breeding Stables. (The Upper Hunter is an important horse-breeding area.) For all ARABS' success, they might just as well have been teetotal, as Arrowfield still struggled in the market.

When ARABS sold to a syndicate involving Andrew Simon, the founder of Camperdown Cellars, and banker Nick Whitlam, they retained the name Arrowfield. To avoid confusion, and probably leave behind the baggage attached to the old name, the winery's name was changed from Arrowfield to Mount Arrow. (This seemed similar to changing your name from Goldstein to Goldberg.) Simon and Whitlam had already been partners in the vineyard Simon Whitlam, which later became an Arrowfield-owned brand and which has now been withdrawn from the market.

Then, in 1991, Arrowfield was sold again, this time to the Japanese Coca-Cola brand holder, Hokuriku CCBC. Since then, not surprisingly, export has been a strong focus for Arrowfield, which had by then resumed its previous name.

The whites continue to be the main successes, as far as Hunter grapes are concerned, although the reds can surprise. I thought the 1997 Shiraz was a fantastic wine – soft, full and rich, with wonderful developing earthy flavour; and the 1998 is a good follow-up.

Hunter Valley Semillon Chardonnay 1999

This wine shows how well these two varieties work together. The flavour is largely semillon, with some nice lemony characters, but the chardonnay gives extra body and some fresh melon notes. The wine was probably at its best in 2000, although the toastiness that will appear a couple of years hence will give it more complexity, if that's what you're after.

Hunter Valley Verdelho 1999 ($13.20)

The nose is quite complex, more so than many verdelhos, with ripe rockmelon and pineapple fruit and also an intriguing nuttiness. In the mouth, the wine shows a rather lighter touch than I'd expected, although it still has plenty of tropical flavour. Enjoy it while it's young.

Hunter Valley Shiraz 1998 ($15.60)

This is a relatively firm red, with very good flavour, but more 'claret' in style than the traditional Hunter shiraz. The nose is complex and spicy, showing some new oak and an intriguing, rather funky character suggesting barrel fermentation. Charred oak and fruit mingle on the palate, which is well balanced in a firm sort of way. It has very good depth of ripe flavour and the wine should develop well for many years.

Audrey Wilkinson

ADDRESS: De Beyers Road, Pokolbin 2321
TELEPHONE: (02) 4998 7411
FAX: (02) 4998 7303
RE-ESTABLISHED: Early 1970s (as Oakdale)
CELLAR DOOR: 9am–5pm weekdays, 9.30am–5pm weekends & public holidays
OWNER: James Fairfax
VITICULTURIST: Carl Davies
WINEMAKER: Chris Cameron
1999 PRODUCTION: About 25,000 cases
MAILING LIST: Yes, and wine club
DISTRIBUTED: Cellar door only
FEATURES: Magnificent views from bright, airy new cellar-door building incorporating old restored winery.

In recent years, this vineyard has had a chequered career – an unjustified fate, as it is truly historic in the Hunter and lies in one of the most beautiful, secluded valleys of the region. Audrey Wilkinson was the last in a line of well-known family of winemakers who had been involved in several seminal Hunter vineyards, including Côte d'Or, Mangerton, Ivanhoe and Coolalta (later bought by Lindemans). He was revered as a great gentleman, and Max Lake's interview with him (reproduced in *Hunter Winemakers*) is compelling reading for anyone with a love of history and wine – and compulsory for those with both. He must also have been an extraordinary diarist, as the Mitchell Library in Sydney has forty-five of his diaries, plus five of his father's and two of his grandfather's.

Wilkinson's Oakdale wines were famous, but the fates gave him difficult years in which to make his last wines and the vineyard fell into disrepair on his death in 1962. It was re-established less than ten years later and provided grapes for many well-known Hunter wineries. (Curiously, Wilkinson never drank wine himself, an identical stance to another renowned winemaker, Bill Redman at Coonawarra.)

In 1994 the property was bought by the Pepper Tree Wines group, which upgraded the vineyards – now 49 hectares of mostly chardonnay, semillon and shiraz – and the old Wilkinson winery. The remaining parts of this now feature in a very smart and reasonably sympathetic building at the top of the hill. Two dates are inscribed above the old winery's entrance door: 'Established 1866' and 'Built 1917'.

It's a mind-numbing thing to walk across the dirt floor amongst the old round concrete fermenters, some of them engraved 'Cummowaborren Monier, Alexandria 1902' and with the initials of the workmen who had cast them; to touch the old receival bin through which would have passed so much wonderful fruit from long-forgotten vintages; to see the old single-cylinder petrol engine that drove the belts for all the equipment (there would have been no electric power then). Wilkinson and his fellow winemakers must have had a hard life, fighting the downturn in demand for Hunter wines and without the modern equipment we now take for granted.

The view from the building is spectacular, north down the Wilkinson vineyards and across to Brokenback, south over Côte d'Or,

Lindemans and Mount Pleasant and east over just about everywhere. But there's something I have to get off my chest.

Here is a heritage site, famous vineyards (admittedly replanted), a wealth of photographs, historical documents, family memorabilia and some originally labelled bottles, which together form a wonderful record of a winemaking dynasty. All credit to the current owners for assembling this. So why on earth do they sanction labels that look like a Technicolour version of 'Footrot Flats', and, what's more, without the dog? I found the packaging downright insulting. And, practically, a label more sympathetic to the vineyard's past would have distanced the wines further from the Pepper Tree wines. It doesn't make sense.

There, that's over. So what are the wines like?

The 1998 Traminer has plenty of flavour, the varietal fruit now combined with some curiously smoky complexity from bottle age. The 1999 Semillon showed some SO2 – it may have been bottled recently – with light lemony fruit and very tight acidity. This is a semillon for the long haul. On the other hand, the '96 Shiraz was fully ready at four years of age – a nicely balanced, mature red with soft, earthy characters. My pick of the wines is the chardonnay.

1998 Chardonnay

Good depth of peachy fruit on the nose, with well-integrated new oak. The palate is soft and round, the overall balance and flavour making it a very attractive wine. It should gain some toasty complexity over another year or two in bottle.

Bacchus Estate

ADDRESS: 381 Milbrodale Road, Broke 2330
TELEPHONE: (02) 65791069
FAX: (02) 65791069
E-MAIL: bacchus.fine.wines@hunterlink.net.au
WEB: Under development
ESTABLISHED: 1993
CELLAR DOOR: 11am–4pm weekends. Other times by appointment.
Also Broke Village Store.
OWNERS: Theo and Maria Poulos
VITICULTURIST: Bill Oliver
WINEMAKER: Andrew Margan (contract)
1999 PRODUCTION: About 1100 cases
MAILING LIST: Yes, and Bacchus Club Boutique
DISTRIBUTED: Currently direct from vineyard
FEATURES: Broke/Fordwich Harvest Festival 'Spirit of the Vine'.

Theo and Maria Poulos are restaurateurs in Macquarie Street, Sydney. When they bought their Milbrodale Road property, it already had 7 hectares of old semillon and chardonnay planted, to which they have added shiraz. There are plans to extend further with cabernet sauvignon, verdelho, chambourcin, grenache and merlot, which will bring the area to 32 hectares. There may also be a winery.

Currently the Pouloses sell most of their grapes but take back some as finished wine under the Bacchus Estate label. Vines and olives go hand in hand almost everywhere in Broke nowadays and Theo and Maria have close to 1000 olive trees which will soon be yielding oil.

ADDRESS: 700 Yarraman Road, Wybong 2333
TELEPHONE: (02) 6547 8118
FAX: (02) 6547 8039
WEB: www.barringtonestate.com.au
ESTABLISHED: 1994 (as Barrington Estate)
CELLAR DOOR: By appointment
OWNERS: Gary Blom and family
VITICULTURIST: Chris Messerle
WINEMAKER: Dan Crane
DISTRIBUTED: Hill International
FEATURES: Weekend and holiday accommodation in fully restored,
self-contained workers cottages.

When Penfolds vacated the Lower Hunter in 1963 and sold Dalwood Estate (later to become Wyndham Estate), it planted vineyards and built a winery on an 1100 acre property in the Upper Hunter near Wybong, which it called Wybong Estate. But the new vineyards didn't deliver what Penfolds wanted and, in an extraordinary about-face less than twenty years later, it sold the property to the rapidly expanding Rosemount Estate. In 1994 Rosemount sold to Gary Blom and family and the winery has been Barrington Estate ever since. Blom is a successful Sydney businessman who, amongst other things, is the developer of the Imax cinema chain that has now moved beyond Australia to several other countries.

Simon Gilbert made the first Barrington wines on contract. Then, in 1998, Barrington built a new winery and was joined by English winemaker Dan Crane who, with a degree in politics and history and another in winemaking from Roseworthy, must be one of the more broadly experienced winemakers around. Like many Englishmen in the UK trade who became fascinated by Australian wine, Crane had his enthusiasm fired at retail chain Oddbins.

Barrington had expanded the vineyard area to 70 hectares by 1999 and is still planting. Varieties cover the mainstreams – chardonnay, shiraz, semillon, merlot, cabernet sauvignon, traminer – as well as chambourcin and a few less common ones.

Top of the list is Yarraman Road, which includes the Millennium Series, while the Pencil Pine range includes semillon, chardonnay, chambourcin and a blend of shiraz, cabernet and merlot. Lower priced brands include Heelers Folly Station and Narrambla 'The Banjo'.

I must say the early Barrington Estate wines lacked some excitement for me. Possibly the cropping levels were too high to give intense flavours. At least, with its own winery and winemaker, Barrington now has complete control of its destiny, so I was looking forward to seeing how much had changed. I found less difference than I had expected.

The '99 Pencil Pine Chambourcin has plenty of flavour and some of the fleshy balance I look for but it also showed distinct volatility.

1999 Pencil Pine Gewürztraminer ($15.95)

The nose is typical of this variety, with perfumed lychee fruit. On the palate, the wine's quite delicate and light bodied. It has intense varietal flavour but achieves this with a light, delicate touch and finishes quite dry. Drink it now for pristine fruit or over four years or so for more softness and complexity. Very attractive.

Yarraman Road Millennium Semillon *1999* ($39.95)

This is a fresh, quite undeveloped semillon with light vanilla character to the fruit. It lacks some volume of flavour at present but is well structured and the fruit lingers, giving the wine some length. It's a fresh young semillon that's currently a bit demure but will age well. Nothing special, I hear you say. But what is special is that the wine is sealed under a Stelvin closure – that is, a screw cap without a cork. This seal is simply the best if you want your wine to age slowly and gracefully over many years (and want to avoid the risk of a corked bottle at the end). I've tried several whites aged under Stelvin since the 1970s and they have all been brilliantly fresh. If you're serious about freshness and complexity in bottle-aged semillon, cellar a few of these. The back label guarantees the freshness of the wine after '5, 10 or 25 years'. I believe it.

1999 Heeler's Folly Chardonnay ($14.95)

The packaging is a lot of fun, but I think the designer caught a glimpse of Devil's Lair's Fifth Leg label first. Botrytis seems to be boosting the fruit character, giving the nose quite a distinct perfume and the flavour some tropical/guava characters. It also brings a very full, viscous body and a grip to the finish. This is a full-flavoured chardonnay that will fill out quite quickly in bottle.

ADDRESS: Branxton Road, Pokolbin 2321
TELEPHONE: (02) 4938 1556
ESTABLISHED: 1963
CELLAR DOOR: By appointment
OWNERS: The Roberts family
WINEMAKER: Bob Davies, with John Roberts
MAILING LIST: Yes
DISTRIBUTED: Direct from vineyard
FEATURES: Stone winery built with materials from the original
George Wyndham homestead, 'Dalwood'.

When geologist Jim Roberts planted vines on his large grazing property in 1963, he was only the second, after Lake's Folly, in living memory to start a new wine business in the Hunter. Roberts was extremely innovative, designing and building a field crushing unit to process grapes as quickly as possible in the vineyard. He also used carbonic maceration when fermenting some of his wines and pioneered the use of small new oak barrels for whites when other winemakers had barely thought of it. The labels he designed, each one portraying his impressions of the wine, were groundbreaking in their time and would even be thought so now.

His white wine style was unique, relying on very high levels of new oak flavour and considerable development in barrel before bottling. They couldn't be judged using the accepted parameters of the time but nevertheless built a cult following. After Jim's untimely death, his son John took over the reins, maintaining his father's approach.

Over the years, we seem to have seen less and less of Belbourie. The once bright and familiar barrel on the Branxton Road has faded and is cracking open, the gateway looks unused and the family appears to have become reclusive, at least as far as wine is concerned. Part of their vineyard was sold to Molly Morgan next door several years ago. John Roberts didn't respond to several requests for information, although John's wife did tell me they have wine available for sale but that they are currently not making any. It seems that time is, for the present, standing still at Belbourie.

This is all a bit sad. Although I was one of those who didn't enjoy the Belbourie whites, I'll still champion anyone who wants to work outside the mainstream, particularly if there are people who like what they do.

Beyond Broke Vineyard

ADDRESS: Cobcroft Road, Broke 2330
TELEPHONE: (02) 6026 2043
FAX: (02) 6026 2043
E-MAIL: kennerob@albury.net.au
WEB: www.worldwidewine.com
ESTABLISHED: 1996
CELLAR DOOR: No. Tastings at Broke Village Store.
OWNERS: Robert and Terry Kennedy
VITICULTURIST: Ken Bray
WINEMAKER: Peter Howland, from 2000 (contract)
MAILING LIST: Yes
DISTRIBUTED: Wine Works

This vineyard was originally planted by Lindemans in 1974 but was put on the market during a rationalisation of Lindemans' vineyards in the Hunter. Bob Kennedy bought it in 1996 and, with his wife Terry, has been reworking the vines. Of the 31 hectares, chardonnay is in the majority, followed by semillon and verdelho. Nearly one hectare of shiraz was added in 1998. As if this wasn't enough, the Kennedys bought another ex-Lindemans block in May 1999, bringing them more shiraz and semillon plus a little pinot noir, and their total holding to 40 hectares.

Their first semillon, made by Andrew Margan, won two trophies at the Hunter Valley Wine Show later that year – one for best 1997 semillon and one as the best white of that vintage – a great start. (I was judging that year, and the wine certainly deserved the win, although it didn't have much opposition. But the lack of good '97 whites makes their success all the more significant.) The Kennedys have some reserve stock of this semillon for release as an aged wine. The verdelho won a bronze at the same show.

I thought several of the 1998 wines – Verdelho, Semillon and Chardonnay – were developing quickly and getting a bit fat. They are full flavoured and complex but need drinking up.

1997 Sparkling Semillon ($190 per case)

This is an unusual line, but it works well and has had some show success. The nose has very attractive toast and straw characters and the palate is full flavoured, soft and balanced. It's holding its freshness well and tastes exactly of what it is – Hunter semillon.

1999 Chardonnay ($150 per case)

There's a lot happening in this wine. Firstly there's plenty of oak, which adds slightly resiny overtones to the more usual vanilla, and bacony malolactic characters give further complexity. The palate is medium bodied, with all those complexities working. The wine should settle down after a little time in bottle, with an intriguing, if idiosyncratic, result.

Beyond Broke Shiraz *1997*
($220 per case)

When you lift the glass, you can smell that this is a very complex wine. There's rich, sweet fruit, some earth and a hint of tar. The flavour has great depth and is beginning to mature very well, and the tannins are already quite soft and palatable. All the same, the strength of the wine shows that it has several years of development ahead. Give it some time.

ADDRESS: Lot 21 McDonalds Road, Pokolbin 2321
TELEPHONE: (02) 4998 7585
FAX: (02) 4998 7732
E-MAIL: office@bimbadgen.com.au
WEB: www.bimbadgen.com.au
ESTABLISHED: 1996
CELLAR DOOR: 10am–4.30pm 7 days, longer during daylight saving time
OWNER: Alan Jones
VITICULTURIST: Thomas Jung
WINEMAKER: Kees van de Scheur
1999 PRODUCTION: 38,000 cases
MAILING LIST: Yes, and Club Bimbadgen
DISTRIBUTED: Dilettare, Vic.
FEATURES: Esca – 120-seat restaurant plus private dining room.
Accommodation in Bimbadgen Homestead – a four-bedroom house
with full facilities – and a two-bedroom cottage.

There would be no contenders with this winery for the most sorry history in the last thirty years. Built by Jock McPherson in 1968, the winery operated as a cooperative, taking grapes from about 120 hectares of vineyard divided into several 'projects' – vineyards that were separately owned by groups of investors. Jock's son Andrew, now a successful wine exporter to the USA, was the first winemaker. The wine quality was often disappointing and there were problems marketing the wines. A few years later the venture folded, most of the vineyards were sold and the winery became reborn as Tamalee.

In the succeeding years, the winery passed through several hands, at various times being Pindari, Sobels and Parker Estate. In the Parker years, David Lowe was winemaker and used the winery as his production base, during which period it underwent considerable renovation. It was at this time that Stan Parker bought the Bimbadgen Vineyard, which gave the winery its current name.

Colgate Palmolive chairman John Alder had planted the Bimbadgen Vineyard on Palmers Lane in the 1960s and for many years supplied grapes to Tyrrell's. I remember that the Vat 12 Shiraz was usually made from Bimbadgen fruit.

In 1996, Alan Jones, the managing director of Mulpha Australia, bought the winery and vineyards. For the first time I can ever remember, the winery has a prosperous look to it. The various vineyards now total 44 hectares, across semillon, chardonnay, pinot noir, shiraz, cabernet sauvignon and verdelho. Bimbadgen also has a 40 hectare vineyard at Yenda, in the Riverina, which provides fruit for the Grand Ridge range.

If you've known the winery for a while, just a brief look will show you how much has changed. Beautiful gardens frame the top entrance to the building, which leads to the restaurant. The winery floor below can be viewed through glass panels. There were always wonderful views across to the Brokenback Range and north to the Barrington Tops, but those views are now even better, with the gardens and the restored vineyards in the foreground.

The winery's bell tower is still there but has also been transformed by the surroundings. That same tower now features widely in an advertising campaign – Seen in all the right places – where it appears as a tattoo on some rather attractive, unclad torsos. After all, sex sells. (The 'Signature' ad is my pick, by the way.)

There are three ranges under the Bimbadgen umbrella: the Signature wines (at the top), Bimbadgen Estate and Grand Ridge.

The 1998 Shiraz didn't appeal to me greatly, thanks to some tarry, swampy overtones, although it does have considerable flavour and will age for several years.

1998 Semillon ($22.50)

The Semillon is a better wine, albeit in a very full, forward style. Ripe, intense, tropical fruit on the nose suggesting some botrytis. The palate is quite full flavoured, with fruit-salad and lime juice characters, and finishes with a light tannin grip. This is a full-flavoured semillon for those who don't want to wait. If you do give it some age, it should develop quickly to give a full-bodied, richly flavoured wine.

ADDRESS: Turanville Road, Scone 2337
TELEPHONE: (02) 6545 3286
FAX: (02) 6545 3431
ESTABLISHED: 1994
CELLAR DOOR: 11am–4pm. Coaches by appointment.
OWNERS: Merilyn and Michael Eagan
VITICULTURIST: John Almond
WINEMAKER: Greg Silkman and Gary Reed
1999 PRODUCTION: about 50,000 cases
MAILING LIST: Yes
DISTRIBUTED: Red Rock Beverages (NSW)
FEATURES: Annual October concert by 70-piece orchestra
from Newcastle Conservatorium.

'Macbeth will never vanquished be until Great Birnam wood to high Dunsinane hill shall come against him.'

Unfortunately for Macbeth, Macduff's army cut branches from Birnam Wood as a disguise when it advanced on Dunsinane Castle, where he was holed up.

The moral? Listen more to witches and less to your wife, if she's homicidal.

Macduff was eventually crowned at Scone, so it was an amazing coincidence that in the 1800s another, and presumably more stable, Macbeth family took up a property near Scone, in the Upper Hunter, and called it ... Dunsinane.

Dunsinane was bought by the Eagan family in 1988. Michael Eagan had owned a motor car dealership in Sydney but the bush called and he bought the property as a horse stud. However, a conversation with winemaker Simon Gilbert got him thinking about vines. The result's in your glass.

Mike and Min planted vines in 1994 – and quickly, too. They now have 32 hectares across chardonnay, semillon, verdelho, sauvignon blanc and shiraz. But sales growth has been so rapid that the Eagans have been buying grapes from other growers to fill the gap. Others in the family have become involved, too, with son Daniel, daughter Rebecca and Rebecca's husband Philip. Together they have developed Dunsinane as a 'luxurious rural retreat', with tree-lined drives and gardens, cattle, horses and (of course) the vineyards.

Birnam Wood is the premium label, while Birnam Estate markets the more commercial wines, under names that continue the Shakespearian theme – the Witches Brew, The Bard's Tipple and The King's Cup.

I admit that the size of the Birnam Wood brand came as a complete surprise to me. It's quite an achievement to build such success in such a short time. The wines are beautifully packaged – individual and smart, without being gimmicky. The first Birnam Wood wine I tried was a year or two back, the '98 Verdelho, which had very attractive, ripe, perfumed fruit. I haven't tried the '99, but their other wines were pretty good.

1998 Birnam Estate Chardonnay
'The Witches' Brew' ($10)

This has full, ripe fruit on the nose, with attractive peach and melon characters. It's still quite fresh, too. The palate has medium weight, well-combined fruit and subtle oak, and fresh acidity. There's surprising complexity for a wine of this price. I don't know how they do it. Great value.

47

Birnam Wood

1998 Birnam Wood Premium Reserve
Chardonnay ($16)

The nose is much fuller, rounder and more complex than the junior version, with excellent oak handling and some nice malolactic complexity. A lovely soft mouthfeel is the main feature of the palate, which is full bodied and round in the mouth, with very good depth of flavour. Again, great value at this price.

1998 Birnam Wood Premium Reserve
Shiraz ($13)

Fresh nose with nice red berry fruit and well-handled sweet oak. The palate is medium bodied, with very attractive flavour and soft tannins. It's not particularly rich in flavour, but will give a lot of drinking pleasure till about 2002. Once again, very good value.

ADDRESS: Coulson Road (off McDonalds Rd), Pokolbin 2321
TELEPHONE: (02) 4998 7295
FAX: (02) 4998 7296
E-MAIL: blueberryhill@hunterlink.net.au
WEB: www.blueberryhill.com.au
ESTABLISHED: 1970
CELLAR door: 9am–5 pm 7 days
OWNERS: John and Wendy Howarth
VITICULTURIST: Vin Con Viticultural Consultants
WINEMAKER: Monarch Winemaking Services
1999 PRODUCTION: 45 tonnes
MAILING LIST: Yes
DISTRIBUTED: Direct from vineyard
FEATURES: Self-contained accommodation, with tennis court and swimming pool.

This vineyard was originally established as part of the McPherson Estate in 1970. For many years the grapes were sold to other winemakers, notably Pepper Tree Wines and Tyrrell's. Blueberry Hill was one of the sources of the Peppertree Merlot that received great international recognition. The vineyard now contains six varieties – chardonnay, sauvignon blanc, merlot, pinot noir, shiraz and cabernet sauvignon.

In April 1999 the Howarths opened their cellar door for the first time, selling their wines under the Blueberry Hill label.

The '98 Chardonnay is drinking well, with well-married fruit and oak and good balance but, surprisingly for the Hunter, I preferred the sauvignon blanc.

1999 Sauvignon Blanc ($210 per case)

This is quite a full-flavoured sauvignon, with plenty of ripe, tropical fruit, and contrasts the grassier styles from cooler areas. The palate has a full body and is soft and round in the mouth, assisted by a touch of sweetness. Drink it while it's young and fresh.

1998 Shiraz

This is quite a firm style of shiraz, with plenty of extract and tannin, but the whole thing's a bit tight and undeveloped at present. With a few years in bottle it should blossom beautifully to give a full-flavoured, mature Hunter of the firmer style. Give it at least five.

Boat Shed Vineyard

ADDRESS: 703 Milbrovale Road, Broke 2330
TELEPHONE: (02) 9876 5761
FAX: (02) 9876 5761
ESTABLISHED: 1989
CELLAR DOOR: No
OWNERS: Mark and Helen Hill
VITICULTURIST: Trevor Tolson (contract)
WINEMAKER: Mark Davidson (contract)
1999 PRODUCTION: 60 tonnes
MAILING LIST: Yes
DISTRIBUTED: Direct from the vineyard

Rowing has been a major part of Mark Hill's life, so the choice was easy when he wanted to rename the vineyard he bought in 1998. As a schoolboy, Mark had rowed at Abbotsford – and the boatshed, which had been built in 1925, was almost as familiar as home. From 1990 to 1998 he coached the senior IVs and saw his three sons row for the school during the same period. The boatshed, naturally, features on the label and Mark must be hoping there are a lot of thirsty rowers out there.

The chardonnay vines had been planted in 1989 by the previous owners, the O'Loughlin family, and to these the Hills have added verdelho, chambourcin, cabernet sauvignon and merlot. About half of the 25 hectare property is now planted.

The vineyards are managed using sustainable viticulture and organic principles, and insecticides have not been used on the vineyard for ten years.

1999 Chardonnay ($15)

Obvious new, vanilla oak is the main feature of this wine at present. However, the fruit has been picked only moderately ripe and the palate has a reasonably elegant weight, so the wine should develop quite well over a couple of years, coming into better fruit/oak balance and filling out in flavour. If you're drinking it now, you'd have to enjoy the oak.

ADDRESS: Lot 12 Lindsay Street, Belford 2335
TELEPHONE: (02) 6574 7172
FAX: (02) 6574 7172
ESTABLISHED: 1996
CELLAR DOOR: 10am–5pm
OWNERS: Robyn and Graham Renfrew
VITICULTURISTS: Robyn and Graham Renfrew
WINEMAKER: Graham Renfrew
MAILING LIST: Yes
DISTRIBUTED: Direct from the winery

Cellar door after cellar door getting mono-tonous? Feel like a stop with a difference? Then try Bramblewood, where the vines aren't vines – they're boysenberry canes.

Graham Renfrew went for a holiday to New Zealand in 1964, stayed for fourteen years and came back to Australia with a wife, Robyn. While they were there they grew boysenberries commercially; and so, on arriving in the Hunter Valley in 1990, that's what they decided to do. However, after several years, they were barely getting anywhere. 'Once you've paid the pickers,' Graham said, 'there's not much left for you.' Being in the Hunter, they decided wine might be the go, and made their first vintage in 1996.

So far, all their wines sold have been made from boysenberries, which they release under the name Patiena, but the Renfrews have been making small batches with other fruits. They have a very old grapefruit tree on their property which horticulturists can't reconcile with current varieties and which seems to have great heritage value. It also makes wonderful wine. The bad news is that it will be a few years before the cuttings have given the Renfrews enough fruit to make their grapefruit wine commercial.

Graham is very passionate about his wines. His stainless steel fermenters and gleaming tanks are just a means to an end. 'You've got to feel it,' he told me. 'It's not all science; you have to love the wine, to understand it.'

Forget any images you may have of sickly-sweet fruity drinks. These are seriously good, well-made wines. They just have very different flavours. They also have some bottle age and the complexity that comes with it. And as for when you would drink them, I can only repeat the Renfrews' blurb, 'with ... soft cheeses or with dessert'.

1997 Patiena ($20)

Deep red colour. Rich, quite complex nose, not unlike a very ripe zinfandel. The palate is full bodied – it has 15 per cent alcohol! – with rich flavour, distinct sweetness and plenty of soft tannin to balance it. This would go beautifully with soft cheeses and dried fruit.

1998 Patiena ($20)

Deep purple–red. A fresher version of the '97, with the same intensity and soft tannin, but rather drier and without the same alcoholic impact. (It's only 12.2 per cent.) There's still a little sweetness, but at the sort of level that would make the wine enjoyable with roasted duck or pork with a fruit glaze.

1999 Grapefruit

Just to whet your appetite for things to come ... Fresh, very aromatic nose with grapefruit and tropical fruit characters reminiscent of a ripe sauvignon blanc. The palate has great depth of flavour, full body, balanced sweetness and fresh acidity. Delicious.

ADDRESS: Mount View Road, Mount View 2325
TELEPHONE: (02) 4990 3670
FAX: (02) 4990 7802
E-MAIL: indulge@briarridge.com.au
WEB: www.briarridge.com.au
ESTABLISHED: 1970 (as Squire Vineyard), 1987
CELLAR door: 9.30am–5pm, 10am–5pm Sunday
OWNERS: John Davies and Neil McGuigan
VITICULTURIST: Derek Smith
WINEMAKER: Neil McGuigan, with guest winemaker Karl Stockhausen
1999 PRODUCTION: 20,000 cases
MAILING LIST: Yes, and Vintage Club
DISTRIBUTED: Estate Wines (Sydney & Canberra); Premier Estate Wines (NSW, Qld);
and export.
FEATURES: Various Mount View festivals.

Neil McGuigan is a rogue. I could tell you about various activities he got up to in previous jobs (but I won't). He's also greatly entertaining, in that hearty way that must be a McGuigan genetic trait, and he makes some fantastic wines.

Briar Ridge started as The Squire Vineyard, established in 1970 by Murray Robson, a partner in the men's clothing store The Squire Shop in Sydney's Double Bay. Murray is one of the industry's best communicators and promoters, so it was not long before the vineyard's name changed to recognise its great asset. The early wines were rather uneven, but the reputation of the best of them, and Murray's great personal attention (which saw him hand-sign every label), ensured a dedicated following – here and overseas.

However, the winery began to suffer financial woes and, following Robson's departure in 1987, it was eventually bought by a partnership including John Scott and Cessnock businessman John Davies, who had previously bought the Pokolbin Creek vineyard from Seppelt. Long-time winemaker Kees Van de Scheur stayed for a while, but left later to start his own venture. Neil McGuigan then joined Briar Ridge as a partner and winemaker, after a short period with his brother Brian in McGuigan Brothers.

A great coup for both the winemaking and marketing of Briar Ridge was the appointment of ex-Lindemans winemaker Karl Stockhausen as consultant. Karl has particular input into the two wines in the Signature series that bear his name.

The quality and consistency of the Briar Ridge wines are excellent and this is borne out by frequent awards in the Hunter Valley Wine Show. This a 'must visit' for anyone who loves the Hunter mainstreams – semillon, shiraz and chardonnay.

The '98 Neil McGuigan Chardonnay is typical of that overall quality, combining good depth of fruit and a little vanilla oak in a very stylish wine. But I think the semillons and shirazes are the really impressive wines.

1999 *Early Harvest* ($17.50) and
1999 Karl Stockhausen Semillon ($23)

The semillons are the real stars of Briar Ridge. I thought the '98 wines were outstanding and both these '99s are excellent examples of young Hunters, too. Both have a fresh, lemony intensity and a crisp acid balance. The Early Harvest is the slightly fuller of the two. You can enjoy them now as light, fresh whites but their real destiny is with five to ten years' bottle age.

1998 Karl Stockhausen Shiraz ($24.50)

Good deep, youthful colour. Rich fruit and oak on the nose, which shows excellent depth. The palate is quite firm and closed at present, and clearly needs time to soften and open out. When it does, you'll have a wonderfully rich, mature Hunter. It may take five to ten years.

1998 Old Vines Shiraz ($18.50)

Ripe, chocolatey fruit has been well married with a touch of new oak in this wine. The overall balance is beautiful and there's plenty of soft tannin, but the wine does need time to develop. Try at least five years.

ADDRESS: Broke Road, Broke 2330
TELEPHONE: (02) 6579 1065
FAX: (02) 6579 1065
E-MAIL: broke@ryanwines.com.au
WEB: www.ryanwines.com.au
ESTABLISHED: 1988
CELLAR DOOR: Sat, Sun 11am–5pm. Other times by appointment.
OWNERS: The Ryan family
VITICULTURIST: Matthew Ryan
WINEMAKER: Monarch Winemaking Services (contract)
1999 PRODUCTION: 21,000 cases
MAILING LIST: Yes, plus e-mailed newsletter
DISTRIBUTED: Bacchant Wine Merchants
FEATURES: Annual Yabby Broil in April, Budburst Festival in August.

Bill Ryan had had a successful business in hotel management when he and his wife Bliss decided to diversify. In 1988 they bought land just to the north of Broke, near the intriguingly named Monkey Place Creek, and planted vines. At an early stage, Bill recognised the potential for his site to grow vines of great vigour, so he sought advice from viticultural consultant Dr Richard Smart, one of the first Hunter vignerons to do so.

The good doctor prescribed the Scott Henry trellising system. You can see this in operation from the road on their cabernet sauvignon vines, their canes held vertically up and down by foliage wires. (A piece of trivia for boring dinner parties. This method was developed by an American, Scott Henry, who, in his day job, was a rocket scientist.) This vine training method was a controversial choice and viewed with great scepticism in the conservative Hunter, as it can produce huge crops of grapes that have difficulty ripening. However, it has worked well for the Ryans, who have had good show success with their wines, particularly the 1991 Cabernet Sauvignon.

In 1994 the Ryans bought Minimbah, near Singleton. Duncan Forbes McKay, a wealthy grazier, built this magnificent house in the 1870s. The house contains a staggering forty-five rooms and the sweeping staircase is made from Australian hardwood which McKay sent to Germany to have carved. The Minimbah Vineyard, planted in 1998, brings the Ryans' total area under vine to 28 hectares. The varieties include chardonnay, shiraz, cabernet sauvignon, cabernet franc and sauvignon blanc.

More recently, sons Matthew (in the vineyard) and William (who, with wife Fiona, manages various aspects of the company) have joined Bill and Bliss.

The premium range is Broke Estate on Monkey Place Creek, with a second label – Ryan.

Broke Estate Chardonnay 1998 ($19)

This is a very big chardonnay indeed. The colour is already quite golden and the nose shows very ripe, tropical fruits – guava, in particular. The palate has developed quite quickly, giving further complexity to the sweet fruit and oak, but the wine still has life. If you're not concerned about subtlety in your chardonnay, this one's for you. I wouldn't cellar it, though.

Ryan Basket Pressed Shiraz 1998 ($13)

Ripe fruit on the nose with strong, coconutty American oak. The palate has big flavour and slightly chewy tannins but finishes with overall balance. It should develop some cedary complexity over three years or so.

Broke Estate Cabernets *1998* ($26)

The nose is quite latent and undeveloped but has very dense, concentrated fruit smouldering away. The palate matches this, with typically firm, drying cabernet tannins and really big flavour. (Take note, sceptics: this wine is fully ripe and not overcropped.) It may lack delicacy, but it certainly has impact and should age for many years.

Broke Estate Cabernets *Moussant 1995* ($38)

Hunter reds develop wonderful mellowness and perfume with age, so it's no surprise that they make great base wines for sparkling reds. I wouldn't have picked this wine as cabernet rather than shiraz, but that's not the point. It has lovely flavour and softness. The nose is mellow, with complex, slightly earthy notes and the palate beautifully balanced and almost creamy. It's not greatly intense but is simply deliciously drinkable.

ADDRESS: McDonalds Road, Pokolbin 2320
TELEPHONE: (02) 4998 7559
FAX: (02) 4998 7893
E-MAIL: graveyard@brokenwood.com.au
WEB: www.brokenwood.com.au
ESTABLISHED: 1970
CELLAR DOOR: 10 am–5 pm 7 days
OWNERS: A private syndicate
VITICULTURIST: Keith Barry
WINEMAKER: Iain Riggs and Peter Charteris
1999 PRODUCTION: over 50,000 cases
MAILING LIST: Yes
DISTRIBUTED: Tucker Seabrook all states except Chace Agencies in SA

Appearances can be deceptive. Walk in to the fairly small, kind of cosy, thoroughly lived-in cellar door at Brokenwood, with its walls plastered in memorabilia, (wine, cricket and banqueting), its welcoming staff and well-known labels, and the overall impression is of a boutique vineyard run by a bunch of fun-loving mates. You just don't get the impression that this is actually a relatively sizeable operation, producing over 50,000 cases of wine a year, and with vineyards not only in the Hunter but also in McLaren Vale, South Australia (the Rayner and Jelka vineyards, both of which are bottled under the Brokenwood label) and the Yarra Valley, Victoria (Brokenwood bought the controlling share of the extremely well-regarded Seville Estate in 1997).

This has a lot to do with the fact that, since the beginning, thirty years ago, when three Sydney lawyers, James Halliday, Tony Albert and John Beeston bought a small block on McDonalds Road and planted vines, Brokenwood has attracted the kind of people who will ensure that, no matter how big the winery gets, it will always retain its sense of fun and high ideals of quality.

For most of the 1970s, Brokenwood was a very small player, a tiny vineyard effectively run by people in their spare time because it was fun, and who were able to sell most of their production to their mates.

In 1978, though, with the purchase and subsequent planting of the Graveyard block next door, and the arrival a couple of years later of a 'proper' winemaker in the form of Roseworthy-trained Iain Riggs, Brokenwood came of age and started both its slow, moderate expansion and the development of some seriously legendary wines.

The winemaking ethos and laid-back culture of Brokenwood have attracted many winemakers over the years: a list of 'graduates' from the winery's vintage 'university' reads like a who's who: Wayne Donaldson (currently Vice President winemaking at Chandon in California), Fiona Purnell (currently at St Huberts, Yarra Valley), Dan Dineen (now at Tower Estates, just down the road in the Hunter), along with many others from both here and overseas. Indeed, for the last few years, Brokenwood has actively fostered the learning process by sponsoring a vintage position to the dux of the second year winemaking course at the University of Adelaide and taking on young Italian winemakers keen to learn about Australian techniques.

You'd be hard pressed to find a bad wine at Brokenwood. The Cricket Pitch range of red

Brokenwood

and white multi-district blends is always reliable easy drinking in the under-$20 category; the Brokenwood semillon is usually one of the valley's most immediately appealing on release, with exaggerated crisp fruit flavours and a juicy palate; the Graveyard chardonnay is often a good example of regional Hunter style; and the 'standard shiraz' (traditionally a blend of Hunter and McLaren Vale fruit) is usually rich, round and deceptively easy to drink.

It's the top shelf wines, though, that really forged Brokenwood's reputation, and they continue to do so. The ILR reserve semillon, first released a couple of years ago, has quickly made its way into many critics' top ten lists for Hunter semillon – the 1994, still available (only just) at the time of writing was a lovely, tangy, toasty white wine just beginning to hit its straps. The Rayner vineyard shiraz is a magnificently fleshy, rich, powerful red with years of cellaring potential (the 1998 being a particularly strong example). And the Jelka botrytis-affected riesling (sold in striking, tall, 500 ml bottles) is brilliantly intense and fragrant dessert wine (perfect with passionfruit tart).

Top position, however, still goes to Brokenwood's best wine, the Graveyard shiraz. As shown by a June 2000 vertical tasting of every Graveyard made (1983 to 2000), at its best, this is simply one of the Hunter's outstanding wines – and one of very few Hunters to appear in the Langtons Classification of Australian wine.

At the time of writing, the current (hard to procure) Graveyard was from the excellent 1998 vintage and displayed all the hallmark qualities of the mature (20 year old) vineyard and the growing season: incredibly ripe, bold, supple purple plummy fruit flavours wrapped up in a blanket of supremely stylish toasty oak. It's not a big wine, though: like all the best Hunters there is an almost ethereal lightness of perfume and softness of structure that will see it age into a great old wine. (The 1983 is still drinking very well indeed, with classic spice and leather and earthy flavours; the 1986 is approaching its peak and should last for a while yet, and younger vintages like '91 – atypically big and tannic – '93, '94 and '96 will evolve for years.) Unlike other Hunter shirazes, though, the Graveyard often has an alluring, gamey, highly perfumed quality that reminds me of red wines from the northern Rhone Valley.

(This entry was written by Max Allen, as Nick Bulleid is a member of the syndicate that owns Brokenwood, and is therefore perhaps a little too emotionally involved to be critical – although Max is obviously a bit of a fan.)

ADDRESS: 725 Milbrodale Road, Broke 2330
TELEPHONE: (02) 6579 1165 or 9906 7698
FAX: (02) 9438 4985
E-MAIL: janemarquard@brokespromise.com.au
WEB: www.brokespromise.com.au
ESTABLISHED: 1996
CELLAR DOOR: By appointment. Also Broke Village Store.
OWNERS: Dennis Karp and Jane Marquard
VITICULTURIST: Trevor Tolson (contract)
WINEMAKER: Andrew Margan (contract)
1999 PRODUCTION: 1800 cases
MAILING LIST: Yes
DISTRIBUTED: Southwell and Garrett (NSW and ACT)
FEATURES: Large olive grove planted with four varieties of Tuscan, Spanish and kalamata olives.

In 1996 Dennis Karp and Jane Marquard bought a block of land between Milbrodale Road and the Wollombi Brook about 5 kilometres north of Broke, and planted vines and olives. The inspiration was a six-month stay in Italy, during which they took part in grape and olive harvests. Since returning, Dennis has studied organic farming at TAFE in the evenings after his day job in banking – sounds much more interesting to me – and more recently Jane has given up her part-time work as a lawyer to develop the business.

Their soil is largely river-derived sandy loam suitable for whites, with smaller patches of red clay loams. They now have semillon, chardonnay and shiraz in production and are adding merlot and barbera. Their first chardonnay was made in 1998 and not long after the 2000 vintage they pressed their first extra virgin olive oil, which will be on the market soon.

1999 Chardonnay *The Singing* ($215 per case)

Pale–medium gold colour. The nose has lots of ripe, even exotic fruits, with peach and tropical characters mingling with understated oak. The palate continues with full body and rich fruit-salad flavour. There's also an impression of sweetness. The balance is good, with softness and length. Here's a chardonnay for those who want lush flavour and drinkability. It will probably be at its best young, so drink it while it's fresh.

1998 Chardonnay *The Dance of Anna* ($181.50 per case)

A big contrast to the '99. The colour is a little paler and the nose is also less evolved, with fresh melon fruit and a chalky overtone. The palate is leaner and tighter than the voluminous '99, with moderate depth of flavour and a little flinty hardness on the finish. The wine needs a year or two in bottle to soften and fill out. So, unusually, I'll say drink the young wine and keep the older one.

1999 Shiraz ($181.50 per case)

Mid purple–red. Ripe, juicy fruit on the nose, showing red berries and a little oak. There's pleasant softness in the mouth, with a slightly leafy edge to the fruit and mild tannins. The wine's a little simple at present, but it does have flavour, and should build complexity over three years or so. When the vines get older, this might be one to watch.

Brush Box Vineyard

ADDRESS: 40 Rodd Street, Broke 2330
TELEPHONE: (02) 6579 1250, (02) 9913 1419
FAX: (02) 9913 1419
ESTABLISHED: 1991
CELLAR DOOR: No
OWNERS: Paul and Suzanne Mackay
VITICULTURIST: Neil Orton
WINEMAKER: Peter Howland (contract)
MAILING LIST: Yes
DISTRIBUTED: Direct from vineyard

In 1997, Paul and Suzanne Mackay bought a young vineyard not far from the Wollombi Brook, near Broke. Planted in 1991, it contained cabernet sauvignon, merlot, chardonnay and verdelho. The previous production had been sold to Tyrrell's, but from the 1998 vintage the Mackays started to keep grapes for their own wine.

The three years since have enabled the Mackays to discover all those intriguing little details of wine production that you usually don't hear about, like the number of merlot vines that weren't really merlot and the row of cabernet vines in the verdelho block ...

They have reworked part of the vineyard, replacing some of their chardonnay with shiraz and extending the area to 6.5 hectares.

Only one Brush Box wine has come my way.

1998 Verdelho ($13)

The nose is quite full, with some attractive pineapple character. In the mouth, the wine is round and balanced, with moderate flavour and length. It's pleasant drinking now.

ADDRESS: Palmers Lane, Pokolbin 2321
TELEPHONE: (02) 4998 7654
FAX: (02) 4998 7813
ESTABLISHED: 1987 (as Calais)
CELLAR DOOR: 9am–5pm 7 days
OWNER: Richard Bradley
VITICULTURIST: Ross Drayton
WINEMAKER: Adrian Sheridan
MAILING LIST: Yes, and Corporate Club
DISTRIBUTED: Classical Wines of Australia
FEATURES: Undercover barbecue and picnic area.

Calais started life as Wollundry, when Ron and Kay Hansen planted it in 1971. From the start, the wines were very uneven in quality and eventually sales became so slow that over-age was added to the faults, including hydrogen sulphide, that were already in the wines. After a family break-up in 1987, the Hansens sold to Colin Peterson, the son of Ian and Shirley Peterson who had established Petersons at Mount View.

When I was putting these tasting notes together, Colin Peterson presumably had other things on his mind, like selling his winery, as he several times avoided the temptation of sending me anything. However, Calais' information is reasonably well documented and a trip to the cellar door showed me the wines. The 10 hectare vineyard contains semillon, chardonnay, shiraz and cabernet sauvignon. Colin has developed the winery into a contract winemaking facility where previous Calais and Peterson winemaker Gary Reed, and now Adrian Sheridan, make wine for several smaller vineyards in the Hunter.

Calais was sold as this book went to print, the purchaser being Richard Bradley, who owns a computer software company in Sydney.

I found the quality of the wines a bit uneven and several are on the expensive side. The '97 Semillon ($25) is one of the better wines I've seen from that year. It has good, lemony fruit and quite a delicate, fresh palate and will clearly develop well for many years. Calais has some mature semillons for sale; the '91 ($32) is now very full, honeyed and toasty, but was almost sold out when I tasted it. I'm sure there'll be another mature wine to replace it. The '98 Reserve Chardonnay ($25) is a very big wine, with ripe tropical fruit, heaps of oak and a distinct furry texture. I don't need words like 'delicate' or 'restrained' here.

1998 Reserve Chambourcin ($35)

This has very good depth of berry fruit on the nose and well-handled oak. In the mouth, the wine's rich and flavoursome, with lots of berry character (red and black) and that typically supple tannin you expect from the variety. Good drinking until 2001 or so. I didn't like the '98 Estate Chambourcin, which was quite porty.

1998 and 1997 Reserve Shiraz (both $35)

Two good wines of rather different style. The '98 has the richer, sweeter fruit and the better palate structure. The oak is obvious, but well handled and the tannins, while firm, will clearly soften with age. The '97 has very strong, charred oak characters. It has good depth of fruit to match, but is quite dry and firm on the finish – typical of the year. Both will age well, developing more complex flavours and softening, but my money's on the '98 as the better prospect. It's recommended. I liked less the '98 Estate Shiraz ($19.50). The green flavour and 13.5 per cent alcohol show that you can still get unripe flavours in wine when the grapes were sugar-ripe.

ADDRESS: Londons Road, Lovedale 2325
TELEPHONE: (02) 4990 2904
FAX: (02) 4991 1886
E-MAIL: capercaillie@hunterlink.net.au
ESTABLISHED: 1995
CELLAR DOOR: 9am–5pm weekdays, 10am–5pm Sun
OWNERS: Alasdair and Trish Sutherland
VITICULTURIST: Keith Holder (contract)
WINEMAKER: Alasdair Sutherland
1999 PRODUCTION: 6000 cases
MAILING LIST: Yes, and The Clan vintage wine club
DISTRIBUTED: Rutherglen Wine and Spirit Co.
FEATURES: Regular displays of fine art and crafts, plus Lovedale region activities.

Alasdair and Trish Sutherland are long established in the Hunter. Al started at Arrowfield in 1975 and then moved to Saxonvale, where he made some out-standing wines in the late 1970s and 80s. Trish, in the meantime, ran her own catering business and also worked in Hunter restaurants. After Saxonvale had been sold to Wyndham Estate, they spent a while running restaurants at Yamba and Port Macquarie, but then returned to the Hunter and bought the Dawson Estate vineyard.

Alasdair's tall and hearty, with a generous smile that matches his wines. It was great to see him back in the Hunter.

Already they have had great success with Capercaillie and the wines have been frequent medal winners in the Hunter Valley Wine Show.

Individual vineyards often show quite individual fruit characters. When I told Alasdair his '99 Chardonnay showed passionfruit aromas, he wasn't the least surprised. 'Absolutely typical,' he said. 'It's the vineyard that does it.'

The '99 Gewürztraminer ($17) shows good fruit in a light, crisp style that's completely unlike the Alsace model but a reminder of how well the variety can sometimes perform in the Hunter. The '98 Dessert Gewürz ($18.00, 375 ml) has similar fruit intensity but isn't really luscious enough for desserts. Capercaillie also makes a very good chambourcin. Look out, too, for the wines they are making from Orange – that's the region, not the fruit!

1999 Chardonnay ($19)

This is a lovely wine, in quite a fresh, lively style with sensitively handled new oak. That intense passionfruit character is really individual and the wine's delicacy suggests it will improve with some bottle age. If you like huge, full-bodied, peachy chardonnays, look elsewhere, but if you like really good flavour with an elegant touch, this will be for you.

1999 Semillon ($17)

Delicate, lemony fruit on the nose, showing good intensity. The palate has good flavour and length, and a light tannin texture doesn't upset the balance. A very good young semillon with great potential for bottle development. The '98 is of similar style and quality, but is already moving down that development path that will eventually see both wines at their best. I strongly recommend them both.

Capercaillie

1998 Shiraz ($22)

Ripe berry fruit is slightly dominated by new
oak at present, but the depth of character is
considerable and the wine will clearly
develop beautifully. Those firm tannins
should soften quite soon, to give a richly
flavoured wine with cigar-box complexity.
(The 1997 Shiraz was excellent, too.)

ADDRESS: Palmers Lane, Pokolbin 2321
TELEPHONE: (02) 4998 7665
FAX: (02) 4998 7665
E-MAIL: sales@carindalewines.com.au
WEB: www.carindalewines.com.au
ESTABLISHED: 1975
CELLAR DOOR: 10am–4.30pm Fri–Mon
OWNERS: Brian and Judy Walsh
VITICULTURIST: Brian Walsh
WINEMAKER: Colin Peterson (contract)
1999 PRODUCTION: 1600 cases
MAILING LIST: Wine Club
DISTRIBUTED: Direct from vineyard
FEATURES: A large range of German clocks. Facets gallery in the loft
of the cellar door, featuring exhibitions of textile arts and ceramics.
A champagne garden opening in spring 2000.

'We're really very small. Are you sure you want to write about us?' Brian Walsh had wine to sell, so, yes, I wanted to. Some of that wine may not have sold all that quickly, as they still have several vintages of older wine available. However, Brian told me he likes to sell his wine with some age.

Brian was a teacher in electrical trades at a local TAFE college when he and his wife Judy bought their Palmers Lane property in 1975. Since then they have planted 4.5 hectares of chardonnay, cabernet franc and merlot, with a small amount of muscat. Brian has plans for a sparkling merlot.

A great attraction was the espresso machine; a coffee and muscat would be mandatory on a cold winter's trip round the cellar doors.

Blackthorn is a blend of cabernet sauvignon, cabernet franc and merlot. The 1997 was ready for drinking at three years of age, with mature, cedary flavour and soft tannin. The 1997 Chardonnay was fully developed and getting quite fat in flavour. I preferred the less forward '96.

1996 Chardonnay ($25)

The nose is very complex, with ripe fruit, oak and toasty development marrying well. These same characters mingle on the palate, which has a full body and plenty of flavour. It's a good example of bottle-aged Hunter chardonnay and I think it was at its best when I tasted it in 2000.

Catherine Vale Vineyard

ADDRESS: 656 Milbrodale Road, Bulga 2330
TELEPHONE/FAX: (02) 6379 1334
E-MAIL: catherinevale@hotmail.com
WEB: www.catherinevale.com.au
ESTABLISHED: 1993
CELLAR DOOR: 10am–5pm weekends & public holidays. Other times by appointment.
OWNERS: Bill and Wendy Lawson
VITICULTURISTS: Bill and Wendy Lawson with Graham Doran
WINEMAKER: John Hordern (contract)
1999 PRODUCTION: 66 tonnes of grapes
MAILING LIST: Yes
FEATURES: The new vintage launched on the last Sunday in March,
and special events advised by newsletter.

Bill and Wendy Lawson were teachers in Sydney when they planted semillon and chardonnay on their 40 hectare block right under the bush-clad slopes between Broke and Bulga. Bill was the sports master at Knox College in Sydney, where he had coached the first XV rugby and athletics and swimming teams. They named the property after Bill's aunt, Catherine Lawson, who was a noted Sydney writer and court reporter. A year later, the lure of country life proved too strong (ah! the empathy) so they took early retirement and joined their vines. They also moved house, literally, having bought the old Uniting Church Manse at Singleton, which now looks over the vineyard at Catherine Vale as it accepts their restoration.

The original 3 hectares of whites have been supplemented with nearly a hectare of barbera and dolcetto, some of the first plantings of Italian red varieties in the Hunter.

Their first crop was entirely lost to birds – they are very close to the bush – but now the fruit is split two ways (and the birds get none): the best parcels of fruit identified in the vineyard for the Catherine Vale label and the balance for John Hordern, their contract winemaker.

1998 Semillon ($12.80)

Some straw-like development characters are beginning to show on the nose, over good semillon fruit. The palate is light and crisp, in the style that will welcome bottle age. It's a pleasant glass of wine now, but will be better once that development has run its course by about 2004.

1998 Chardonnay ($14.50)

Complex nose, with ripe fruit, a little new oak and some toasty development. The palate has good flavour, is medium bodied and is drinking close to its best.

ADDRESS: Broke Road, Pokolbin 2320
TELEPHONE: (02) 4998 7548
FAX: (02) 4998 7805
ESTABLISHED: 1969
CELLAR door: Weekends or by appointment
OWNER: Dr Don François
VITICULTURIST: Dr Don François
WINEMAKER: Dr Don François
MAILING LIST: Yes
DISTRIBUTED: Direct from vineyard

Don François was the director of the New South Wales State Fisheries Department and, even while he still lived in Sydney, dabbled with winemaking in his Sydney garage. He wrote the chapter 'Observations on Home Winemaking' in Len Evans' *Complete Book of Australian and New Zealand Wine* in 1973. Eventually his garage proved to small – and possibly the crates of Riverina grapes from the market unsatisfactory – so in 1969 he planted vines on a beautiful east-facing slope at the foot of the Brokenback Range just north of Tyrrell's. The bush at the base of the range starts right at his back door and he has a spectacular view east over the valley.

Don planted shiraz, semillon, chardonnay and pinot noir and these now total 2.4 hectares. He made his cellar from huge square-section stormwater culvert, partly underground, which gives him excellent temperature control. He also has a beautiful kitchen garden alongside the cellar.

Don, like many smaller vignerons, used the help of friends at weekends to get the chores done – picking, bottling etc. – and the friends were entertained with good food (Don is a great cook) and wine. In a very individual touch, Don would also entertain them with his banjo playing and songs, many of them American folk songs – Don was originally from the States – and many hysterically funny. One such friend, Rod Laing-Peach, kindly gave me a bottle of Don's 1981 Shiraz, which I had told him won the trophy for best museum red in the 1997 Hunter Wine Show. We drank it in March 2000 and it was still magnificent.

A few of us wrote a song, 'Don François' pinot noir', to the tune of 'Edelweiss', which was extremely uncomplimentary, but Don had the good grace to join in many times.

Some of Don's early reds suffered from 'the dreaded', a dose of the old Hunter sulphide, but the wines are now more consistent. Certainly, he has always been able to get plenty of generous flavour into them. His semillon has also been successful in shows, particularly with a bit of bottle age. The 1989 Chardonnay was still looking good at eight years of age, too.

Unfortunately Don suffered a stroke a few years ago and his speech has not fully recovered. This hasn't slowed him down, however. He described his frustration at being able to think but not vocalise the words he wanted. 'But I can still work like fury,' he added.

I tried several of his reds in barrel and thought his '99s were tremendous.

The shiraz has very concentrated, berry fruit – one of the richest '99s I've tried. 'You think that's keen?', Don asked. I agreed it was. 'Nice fellow on that,' he added. I didn't think his 2000 reds had the flavour of the 1999s. Don's pinot noir in future will be made as a sparkling red and his first batch was looking good.

1996 Mallee Semillon ($11)

This simply has to be the greatest bargain in the Hunter. It's a silver medal winner in the Hunter Show and will inevitably do better as it ages. The nose is still remarkably fresh, with intense vanilla and lime characters. It looks like a two year old. The flavour is fabulous, too, with great varietal fruit and soft acidity. I kept on thinking I'd made some mistake, but the more I tasted it, the better it looked. Just get some.

1995 Shiraz Pinot Noir ($11)

Soft, fragrant nose showing beautifully complex, earthy, developed fruit. The palate is soft and round and has lovely smoothness, with very complex, thoroughly Hunter flavours. It looks fully mature, but will continue to live for many years. For those who love developed Hunter reds, another bargain.

ADDRESS: Thompsons Road, Pokolbin 2320
TELEPHONE: (02) 4998 7634
FAX: (02) 4998 7860
E-MAIL: chateaupato@hotmail.com.au
ESTABLISHED: 1981
CELLAR DOOR: By appointment
OWNERS: The Paterson family
VITICULTURIST: Nick Paterson
WINEMAKER: Nick Paterson
1999 PRODUCTION: 150 cases
MAILING LIST: Yes
DISTRIBUTED: Boutique Wine Centre, Pokolbin, and direct from the vineyard

The late and greatly lamented David Paterson was a tremendous bloke and one of the most cheerful characters around Pokolbin in the 1980s. David died in the late 90s but the vineyard he started with his wife Helen lives on. David was an announcer and broadcaster with ABC radio in Newcastle when he and Helen bought their property on Thompsons Road in 1979. They gradually planted just over 2 hectares of the 16 hectare property with shiraz, but they could hardly have known that they had planted in one of the worst droughts in living memory, so their first crop was a while coming. This was the 1984 vintage which, as fate would have it, was very wet. They supplemented their grapes with some unwanted shiraz from over the fence in Brokenwood's Graveyard and this wine won their first show award – a silver.

They added a small block of gewürztraminer and malbec across the road, bought from Hungerford Hill in 1985, but only five years later this was acquired to become part of the Cypress Lakes golf course.

The vineyard is now managed, and the wine made, by their son Nick, 'The Dog', who was assistant winemaker at Brokenwood but later moved to Tyrrell's for the 2000 vintage.

1998 Shiraz ($25)

Packed with very concentrated fruit, this wine cries out to be cellared. Rich, blackberry shiraz has been given just a touch of sympathetic oak. A little volatility does nothing to detract. There's a considerable amount of tannin in the wine, but this is quite soft, so it could be drunk soon by lovers of 'big reds'. However, its real destiny is to be kept for as long as you care to.

ADDRESS: 1 Gillards Road, Pokolbin 2320
TELEPHONE: (02) 4998 7887
FAX: (02) 4998 7887
E-MAIL: conshers@one.net.au
WEB: www.constablehershonwines.com.au
ESTABLISHED: 1981
CELLAR DOOR: 10am–5pm 7 days
CHIEF EXECUTIVE: Michael America
VITICULTURIST: Vinecare Australia Pty Ltd (contract)
WINEMAKER: Neil McGuigan (contract)
1999 PRODUCTION: 3000 cases
MAILING LIST: Yes
DISTRIBUTED: Direct from the vineyard
FEATURES: Landscaped gardens in four themes – Traditional English Secret Garden, Herb and Knot, Rose, and Sculpture. Garden tours take place at 10.30am each weekday. Music in the Hunter Festival, November.

Wonderful name isn't it – Constable and Hershon? It conjures up visions of an old-world English wine merchant, purveyor of fine claret and vintage port; or perhaps of landscape gardeners, in the tradition of Capability Brown.

As it happens, Constable and Hershon is a bit of both. You can taste the wine and view the gardens.

The land was previously part of Hungerford Hill but in 1982 was bought by two families related to the current chief executive Michael America. The vineyard totals about 6 hectares, planted to chardonnay, cabernet sauvignon, semillon and merlot. Pinot was also tried, but was subsequently replanted with semillon. In 1984 work began on four formal gardens and, amazingly, for the next eleven years the owners waited while the gardens grew and matured, and sold the wines only by mail order. In April 1995 the gardens were opened to the public for the first time.

As open gardens go, these are not extensive, but they are impeccably maintained and lie within a broad sweep of beautifully grassed north-facing hillside. They provide a tranquil spot which allows reflection, far from the busy roads and tourist buses. And they do have some

individual features. The sculpture garden has some excellent pieces, both classical and modern, and the herbs in the Herb and Knot garden, growing in neatly clipped hedges, are far from your usual kitchen garden mix. The rose garden has largely modern (hybrid tea) roses, but it would have been nice to see some older varieties, like Damasks or Gallicas.

The wines are as well presented as the gardens.

1999 Semillon ($19.95)

Palish yellow colour. Full, soft fruit on the nose with nice lemon overtones. The palate is fresh and crisp and quite fine in style, with good balance. A benchmark Hunter semillon, which drinks well now and will fill out in flavour over several years. The 1998 was an outstanding wine when it was young, so there seems to be good consistency.

1999 Unwooded Chardonnay ($19.95)

I'll have to revise my opinion of unoaked chardonnay if I have many more wines like this one. It has beautifully ripe, melon fruit and a full, round palate. There's a suggestion of sweetness – whether from fruit, alcohol or sugar, I'm not sure. Delicious drinking now, while it's fresh.

1998 Chardonnay ($21.50)

This is a medium-weight chardonnay with good peachy fruit and well-married new oak. The palate is soft, round and well balanced. Very good drinking before 2002.

1998 Cabernet Merlot

Attractive berry fruit on the nose, with sweet new oak. The palate has good flavour and a touch of elegance, with nice, fine tannins. The wine's beginning to drink well and should develop more complexity over the next five years.

ADDRESS: 556 Hermitage Road, Pokolbin 2320
TELEPHONE: (02) 6574 7120 or 9387 1100
FAX: (02) 9387 6688
ESTABLISHED: 1991
CELLAR DOOR: No
OWNERS: Carol and Neal Crisford
VITICULTURISTS: Carol and Neal Crisford
WINEMAKER: David Hook (contract). Steve Dodd from 2000.
1999 PRODUCTION: 340 cases
MAILING LIST: No
DISTRIBUTED: Available from the Hunter Valley Wine Society, The Wine Society and direct from the vineyard

Neal Crisford has a special interest in wine. He was the producer/director of a series of educational videotapes for the Open Training and Education Network that have been extensively used by TAFE colleges. He also made videos for the Australian Society of Wine Education; you may have seen these at the ASWE's Taste Theatres at Wine Australia in Sydney in 1996 and Melbourne in 1998. He's currently completing a video on the Hunter.

With his wife Carol, Neal has planted two hectares of grapes on the brown to red loams at their family property on the Hermitage Road. The varieties are cabernet franc and merlot – perhaps they like St Emilions – although they are uncertain over the exact proportion of each. (The two varieties have been somewhat confused in Australian vineyards.) The vineyard's name is derived from the synergy that these two varieties show in parts of the Bordeaux region. The Crisfords have plans to build a small winery, but for now they oversee the fermentation in other wineries.

I'm not sure how typical the '98 Cabernet franc/Merlot is of their other vintages. It has the suppleness you'd expect from these varieties, but already seems quite mature and shows some swampy characters.

ADDRESS: 2656 Wybong Road, Wybong 2333
TELEPHONE: (02) 6547 8149
FAX: (02) 6547 8144
E-MAIL: johnc@nobbys.net.au
WEB: www.cruickshank.com.au
ESTABLISHED: 1973
CELLAR DOOR: 9am–5pm 7 days
OWNER: John Cruickshank
VITICULTURISTS: John Cruickshank and Hartley Smithers
WINEMAKER: Hartley Smithers
1999 PRODUCTION: 5000 cases
MAILING LIST: Yes, and the Callatoota Club
DISTRIBUTED: Direct from vineyard

Management consultant John Cruickshank had been interested in wine for several years when, in 1973, he took a big step and bought the homestead block of an old property called Callatoota, not far from Sandy Hollow. He planted 4 hectares of cabernet sauvignon and in 1981 added a winery. I seem to remember that, in those early days, Callatoota was the only winery making entirely cabernet sauvignon – certainly in the Hunter, and perhaps in Australia. It's no longer their only wine as, with a rush of blood to the head, the Cruickshanks have since planted cabernet franc and, very recently, shiraz. Nevertheless, you have to admire their single-mindedness. They now have 7.4 hectares of cabernet sauvignon, 2 hectares of cabernet franc and 2 hectares of shiraz. This fruit seems to satisfy their needs, as they buy no grapes from elsewhere.

When you enter the Callatoota winery, you feel as if you're in a time warp. Almost all the storage is large oak – either 1500 to 2000 litre casks or large vats. No big stacks of new barrels, no ranks of stainless steel tanks, apart from some (largely hidden) Potter fermenters. The label stays in sympathy; it hasn't changed since the first wines were released and features an early photograph of the winery and vineyard. John is currently planning a new label, although he's had mixed messages about the current one. The buyer of a major retail chain told him they wouldn't stock the wine because of the label, while an executive from the same company said approvingly 'why would you want to change it?'

The Callatoota reds are very individual. They are big wines with plenty of tannin and extract – and yet, from the older examples I have tried, they develop mature flavours quickly. The 1995 Cabernet Sauvignon ($14) has developed earthy and fruitcake flavours already. There's no new oak used – virtually no small oak at all, in fact – so if you're tired of over-oaked reds, you could take refuge here. However, I did find myself wishing the wines showed more freshness.

What I'd recommend is, if you enjoy 'big reds' with plenty of flavour and tannin and no new oak, buy them and drink them now.

Rosé ($11)

If you like slightly sweet, fruity rosés, skip a couple of lines. This is a complex, developed rosé akin to the Provence style, with plenty of mature flavour, and finishes very dry with a light touch of tannin. It's a rosé for food, including steak, and not for a gentle aperitif.

Cabernet Sauvignon *Pressings 1998*
(not released at time of publication)

This was my pick of the reds. It has a deep colour and the big, pungent berry fruit to match. The palate has heaps of intense flavour and very firm tannins to dry the finish. This is a big mouthful of wine for those who mourn the passing of the old-style Rutherglen red.

ADDRESS: Pothana Lane, Belford 2335
TELEPHONE: (02) 6574 7164
FAX: (02) 6574 7209
E-MAIL: davidhook@hunterlink.net.au
ESTABLISHED: 1985
CELLAR DOOR: By appointment
OWNERS: David Hook
VITICULTURIST: Jade Apthorpe
WINEMAKER: David Hook
1999 PRODUCTION: About 18,000 cases
MAILING LIST: Yes
DISTRIBUTED: Prime Wines

David Hook's main activity is as a contract winemaker for others in the district, but he also has his own vineyard, Pothana, not far from the famous Elliott semillon vineyard at Belford. David has 8 hectares of vines, including semillon, chardonnay, pinot noir and shiraz. For many years his wines appeared under the vineyard name, but he has recently been releasing some under another label – The Gorge.

The flavour of The Gorge '99 Chardonnay seems to have some assistance from botrytis and there's distinct volatility lifting the nose. However, if you enjoy very big, guava/pawpaw flavours in your wines, you may enjoy it.

1999 The Gorge Semillon Sauvignon Blanc ($15)

This wine combines Hunter semillon with sauvignon blanc from Orange. It's a clever blend and works well. The sauvignon blanc gives the wine some tropical fruit characters and a hint of grassiness, while the semillon contributes to the overall balance on the palate and fills out the flavour. The overall impression is of fresh, lively flavour and soft acidity. Enjoy it now.

1999 The Gorge Semillon ($15)

This is a beautiful young semillon with great potential for bottle age. The fruit on the nose is very fresh, with lovely vanilla and lemon characters. The palate's round and full, with the appearance of just a little straw from development. The wine has the flavour to drink young but give it four years or more and you'll have a cracker of an aged wine.

1999 The Gorge Shiraz ($16.95)

Mid purple–red colour. Soft shiraz fruit on the nose, with attractive sweet berry overtones. There's also some sweet new oak. The palate is medium bodied, with good flavour and a little stalkiness, and finishes with a bit more tannin grip than I'd expected. This won't be a long keeper, but will gain some more complexity over the next three or four years.

De Iuliis

ADDRESS: Lot 1 Lovedale Road, Rothbury 2321
TELEPHONE: (02) 4967 5611
FAX: (02) 4968 8192
E-MAIL: dewine@wareng.com.au
WEB: www.dewine.com.au
ESTABLISHED: 1987
CELLAR DOOR: Opening late 2000 at Butterflies Gallery, Broke Road
OWNERS: The De Iuliis family
VITICULTURIST: Keith Holder (contract)
WINEMAKER: Michael De Iuliis with David Hook
1999 PRODUCTION: About 6000 cases
MAILING LIST: No
DISTRIBUTED: Direct from the vineyard

There was a delicious irony when the De Iuliis family bought land at Keinbah in 1987 and started planning their vineyard. Celeste De Iuliis' first destination on arrival in Australia had been the Greta migrant camp, fifteen minutes from the block that was to become the family vineyard. His son Joss, who started an engineering company in Newcastle, used to drive past the vineyards on his way to the coalfields and dreamt that one day the family might start its own. That happened in 1990, when Celeste and Joss planted semillon, verdelho, chardonnay, merlot and shiraz on the block they had bought a few years before.

Their first vintage was in 1992. The family and friends picked the first grapes, made the wine and drank the results.

Celeste's grandson Michael was beginning to take an interest. 'Most of the 1993 harvest was sold to Tyrrell's,' he explained, 'but we kept a small quantity aside for the family, which David Hook made for us. We entered it in the Singleton (Hunter Valley) Wine Show and won a silver.' Michael is now the winemaker and is finishing post-graduate studies in oenology at Adelaide University.

In 1999 the family bought the Butterflies Gallery and Mallee's Cafe on Broke Road, near Oakvale, and will be developing a cellar door tasting and sales area.

The '99 Semillon is a pleasant young wine with ripe fruit flavour. It's just beginning to pick up a little straw character from bottle age. The '99 Chardonnay looks as if it has been made with some skin contact, as it has distinct tannin which dries the mouth. The fruit is quite full and peachy and there's also a suggestion of sweetness. All of this means that it gives you a big mouthful of wine and will probably develop quite quickly in bottle.

1999 Verdelho

Verdelhos don't come much bigger than this. It has ripe, fruit salad characters on the nose, which is lifted by alcohol and some volatility. The palate is full-bodied and full-flavoured to match. If you like really big whites, this is for you, although you'd have to accept that volatility. All it lacks is restraint.

1998 Show Reserve Shiraz

This is a tremendous red. The nose is a bit closed at present, but there's concentrated blackberry fruit lying there latent, ready to burst out with time. It's complemented by sweet American oak. I loved the rich fruit and balance of the wine. It has considerable depth of flavour and will respond very well to long bottle age, although the tannins are balanced enough for you to drink it right away.

ADDRESS: Oakey Creek Road, Pokolbin 2320
TELEPHONE: (02) 4998 7513
FAX: (02) 4998 7743
E-MAIL: drink@draytonswines.com.au
WEB: www.draytonswines.com.au
ESTABLISHED: 1853
CELLAR DOOR: 8am–5pm Mon–Fri, 10am–5pm weekends & public holidays
OWNERS: Several members of the Drayton Family
VITICULTURIST: Greg Drayton
WINEMAKER: Trevor Drayton
1999 PRODUCTION: 100,000 cases
MAILING LIST: Yes
DISTRIBUTED: Halloran Manton (NSW and Vic.); Wine Source (Qld);
Decanted Liquor Merchants (WA) and export.
FEATURES: Winery tours, Wine Club, barbecues. Bulk wines available.

The Draytons are the greatest surviving wine dynasty in the Hunter and have spawned several wine companies, of which Drayton's Family Wines is the largest and longest established. Joseph Drayton arrived from England in 1853 after an horrific voyage during which he lost his son Charles and, in quarantine shortly after, his wife and newborn daughter. Shortly after arriving in the Hunter Valley he met and married Mary Chick – the Chicks were to become important vignerons in their own right – and eventually cleared land at Pokolbin just beneath Brokenback, calling the land 'Bellevue'. Although wheat was the first crop Joseph planted, he added vines in the late 1850s and the Draytons have been in continuous production ever since, surviving many lean times.

Joseph and Mary's son William expanded the property and established the company W Drayton and Sons, which changed its name to Draytons Family Wines not long ago. Those sons totalled nine, and there was a solitary daughter, so it's no surprise that there are plenty of Draytons around. (And please don't ask me how the various branches of family are related. I've never been able to follow it.) A long while back they bought land to the west of Bellevue which had been the site of the original Ivanhoe

Vineyard, a famous property in the 1800s. Stephen and Tracey Drayton now own this.

Draytons Family has 82 hectares under vine, including semillon, chardonnay, shiraz, verdelho, merlot and cabernet sauvignon. Their chardonnay vineyard was, for a while, one of the largest in Pokolbin and their first chardonnay, made in 1979, was exceptional and drank well for many years. The winemaker since the late 70s has been Trevor Drayton, a Dux at Roseworthy.

Over the years, Draytons seem to have had bursts of innovation followed by periods of inactivity. Their new-oak matured semillon, I think from the 1967 vintage, was the first of its type in the Hunter. Some wines have been truly remarkable, while others slip easily from the memory. Recently they have had great show success with two wines, William Shiraz and Joseph Shiraz, which commemorate their founders. Joseph Shiraz won a trophy as the best red at the 1995 Melbourne Wine Show. There are several ranges at Draytons, with the widely distributed Oakey Creek wines the most familiar. These are made from grapes sourced from the Hunter and elsewhere and are competitively priced. The Hunter wines lie largely in the Premium and Limited Release ranges.

Draytons Family Wines

1997 Bin 5555 Shiraz ($15.80)

This has been a familiar label for some time. I particularly enjoyed the 1987, which I am still keeping, and there were some outstanding 5555s from earlier years, but the 1997 is a bit short, with under-ripe fruit. I expect the '98 will show more richness. I enjoyed the 1997 Vineyard Reserve Shiraz more. It has good balance and softness and attractive light berry flavour.

1999 Verdelho ($15.80)

Full, tropical fruit on the nose, with some banana overtones. There's plenty of flavour on the palate, which is full bodied and finishes with a light grip. Good drinking over the next couple of years.

1998 Vineyard Reserve Semillon ($18)

This semillon is made in a big, forward style. Enjoy it young, but don't expect a really long-term keeper. The fruit is quite ripe and tropical, with a suggestion of botrytis giving complexity. The palate is full, even a touch oily, with intriguing smoky overtones. A big wine, contrasting the mainstream Hunter style, that should appeal greatly to those who want flavour in their whites.

1998 Vineyard Reserve Chardonnay ($18)

My pick of the Drayton wines. It shows you can get flavour without going for super-ripeness in the grapes. The nose is very complex, with a little oak and some yeast lees adding character. The palate shows real finesse, with delicate flavours and lovely balance. This style of Hunter chardonnay ages well, so if you want toastier, developed flavours, put some away.

ADDRESS: 558 Wollombi Road, Broke 2330
TELEPHONE: (02) 6579 1062
FAX: (02) 6579 1062
E-MAIL: graemegibson@yahoo.com.au
ESTABLISHED: 1992
CELLAR DOOR: By appointment. Also at Broke Village Store.
OWNERS: Graeme Gibson & Jennifer Burns
VITICULTURISTS: Graeme Gibson & Jennifer Burns
WINEMAKER: David Lowe (contract)
1999 PRODUCTION: 200 cases
MAILING LIST: No
DISTRIBUTED: Direct from vineyard

Graeme Gibson was a solicitor in Sydney before he gave the rat race away and moved to the Hunter, buying a block of land near the Wollombi Brook just south of Broke. He planted chardonnay, merlot and sangiovese, some of which he sells as grapes, with the rest made into wine for the Drews Creek label. Graeme was one of the main drivers of the Broke Fordwich area's submission to become a Geographical Indication. This defines the area as a unique and controlled region for grape production. He was also mayor of Singleton for a year or so. 'He just got elected, did what he wanted to do and got out' one of the locals told me.

The only Drews Creek wine I have tasted was the 1998 Unoaked Chardonnay (late in 1998), which I found a bit plain and hard.

Duck Hollow Winery

ADDRESS: 103 Deasys Road Pokolbin
TELEPHONE: (02) 9415 6656
FAX: (02) 9415 6656
E-MAIL: duckhollow@chasclarkson.com.au
ESTABLISHED: 1988
CELLAR DOOR: By appointment
OWNERS: Ellen and Peter Clarkson
WINEMAKER: Andrew Spinaze (contract)
1999 PRODUCTION: 200 cases
MAILING LIST: Yes
DISTRIBUTED: Direct from vineyard
FEATURES: Country style self-contained homestead available for weekend stays, sleeping up to ten people.

Duck Hollow is another of those small-holdings that are springing up all over the Lower Hunter, with accommodation to let in a house or cottage and a few acres of vines. The block of vines on the hill behind the house was planted in 1988 and another block below it added later. For several years the grapes were sold, but since 1997 the Clarksons have retained enough for a hundred cases of each under their own label. I was unable to arrange a meeting to try the wines, but they are made by Andrew Spinaze at Tyrrell's, who knows more than a bit about chardonnay and pinot noir, so, provided the vineyard delivers, the wines should be worth trying.

ADDRESS: 657 Milbrodale Road, Broke 2330
TELEPHONE: (02) 6579 1344
FAX: (02) 6579 1355
E-MAIL: cjbe@hunterlink.net.au
ESTABLISHED: 1995
CELLAR DOOR: By appointment
OWNERS: Christopher and Belinda Elsmore
VITICULTURIST: Bryan Hubbard
WINEMAKER: Gary Reed and Tony Bainton (contract)
1999 PRODUCTION: 1090 cases
MAILING LIST: Yes
DISTRIBUTED: Fergus Hurley
FEATURES: Broke Fordwich festival 'The Spirit of the Vine' and Broke Fordwich
tastings at Chatswood Chase, Sydney.

Chris and Bindy Elsmore have planted their Caprera Grove vineyard with about 3 hectares of chardonnay and nearly 1 hectare of shiraz and will be adding other reds, semillon and perhaps verdelho over the next few years. Some of their wine is made locally in Broke but, in the case of the oak-matured wines, they hand the grapes over to Gary Reed to make.

The labels are very striking, featuring elegantly enquiring geese, and have been chosen for entry in design awards.

1999 Chardonnay ($15.99)

This was my pick of the Elsmore chardonnays. (Both the 1999 Unwooded and the 1998 seemed to be quite advanced in their development.) It has ripe, peachy fruit on the nose, with just a little oak. The palate has good flavour and balance and is medium bodied. It was close to its best in 2000.

ADDRESS: 393 Milbrodale Road, Bulga 2330
TELEPHONE: (02) 96642368; (02) 6579 1061
FAX: (02) 96642368
E-MAIL: victoria_foster@uow.edu.au
ESTABLISHED: 1990
CELLAR DOOR: By arrangement
OWNER: Dr Victoria Foster
VITICULTURIST: John Tulloch
WINEMAKER: Tyrrell's (contract)
1999 PRODUCTION: 250 cases
DISTRIBUTED: Direct from vineyard
FEATURES: Accommodation, including a private pool and heated outdoor spa
and unique Gourmet Wine Education weekends.
For information, write to 4/15 Baden Street, Coogee 2034.

Victoria Foster works in the Education Department at the University of Wollongong – the wrong direction for the Hunter, so she must clock up the miles. When she replanted her land with vineyard in 1990, it had lain fallow for thirty years, although a cottage on the property, made from sixty-year-old iron-bark, had survived. Since then, she has been supplying grapes to Tyrrell's for their Verdelho.

Elysium wines are available from the Broke Village Store and from the vineyard by appointment. The sandwich board outside the property when I called read '1994 Reserve Verdelho tasting', suggesting that there are older wines available, too, but unfortunately there appeared to be no one at home.

ADDRESS: Wilderness Road, Lovedale 2321
TELEPHONE: (02) 4998 7734
FAX: (02) 4998 7209
ESTABLISHED: 1986
CELLAR DOOR: 10am–5pm weekends & public holidays. Other times by appointment.
OWNERS: Rob and Toni Powys
VITICULTURIST: Keith Holder (contract)
WINEMAKER: Contract
DISTRIBUTED: Direct from vineyard
FEATURES: Emma's Cottage – three-bedroom, fully self-contained farmhouse
with its own vineyard. Complimentary bottle of wine for guests.

Rob and Toni Powys have been growing grapes since 1986 but initially sold the fruit and didn't release wine under their own label until 1994. They have about 3 hectares of vines – shiraz, merlot, chardonnay and semillon.

Several older vintages are available, although I found the whites and reds had aged quite differently. The whites are still youthful and fresh, the semillons in particular, and will take further age with ease. There aren't many opportunities to taste and buy older semillons of this quality, so take the chance. The older reds are fully mature and shouldn't be kept much longer. The Cabernet Merlots from 1997 and 1996 are even a bit tired already.

1996 Semillon ($15)

This is a tremendous example of bottle-aged semillon yet a wine that will age gracefully and fill out in flavour for many years. It has a quite undeveloped, fresh nose with fresh, lemony fruit. The palate has wonderful length of flavour, very good balance and a beautiful soft finish, with fresh acidity. Good value. I'll be getting some of this myself.

1995 Semillon ($16)

This wine is in the same mould as the '95, with fresh fruit, delicacy and crisp acidity. There's also a hint of greenness, not unpleasant in the least, which makes me think the wine may have started with some grassy characters. For me, the '96 has the edge, but this is still recommended.

1996 Unoaked Chardonnay ($16)

This wine has aged very well, possibly thanks to a lack of oak. The nose and flavour have become quite complex, with very attractive toastiness from bottle age, and the palate is soft and balanced. It's not the big, peachy style of chardonnay that gets too big with age, but shows full flavour with restraint. (I thought the 1998 Chardonnay too oaky for the amount of fruit.)

1998 Shiraz ($20)

Berry fruit, sweet vanilla oak and a hint of liquorice on the nose. The palate has full flavour and is well balanced and round in the mouth, with soft tannins. The oak's a bit obvious at present, but this should marry in well over the next year or two. This '98 will age better than the earlier vintages.

ADDRESS: Marrowbone Road, Pokolbin 2320
ESTABLISHED: 1985
CELLAR DOOR: No
OWNERS: Peter Doyle and family
VITICULTURIST: Ian Tinkler
WINEMAKER: Philip Ryan (contract)
1999 PRODUCTION: 1100 cases
MAILING LIST: No
DISTRIBUTED: Sold in Doyles fish restaurants

There's no cellar door you can visit here, but it's a vineyard you should know about. In 1985 Peter Doyle – the fish one, not the Cicada one – bought a small block in the shadow of Mount Bright, not far from the Mount Pleasant winery. He planted chardonnay, semillon and a small amount of merlot. The semillon and merlot grapes are sold at present, but the chardonnay is bottled and sold at the various Doyles restaurants at Watson's Bay, Circular Quay and the fish markets.

'It was only ever meant to be a hobby,' Gayle Doyle told me. Some hobby! At the 1999 Sydney Wine Show, the 1999 Endless Summer Chardonnay won the trophy as best white wine from a named vineyard. This was a wonderful thing to happen. Peter Doyle has been in poor health for the last few years, a tragedy for someone who was once so generously hearty, so it was great to see him at the Sydney Showground receiving his trophy.

1999 Chardonnay

You can see why this wine won its trophy. It has very intense, peachy fruit with extra complexity from carefully handled oak. The flavour's rich and ripe and really fills the mouth. This is a lovely, full-bodied wine that probably can't get any better with time.

ADDRESS: Palmers Lane, Pokolbin 2320
TELEPHONE: (02) 4998 7333
FAX: (02) 4998 7798
E-MAIL: evansfamilywines@bigpond.com.au
ESTABLISHED: 1977
CELLAR DOOR: By appointment
OWNERS: Len Evans AO OBE and family
VITICULTURIST: Alan Townley
WINEMAKER: Keith Tulloch
MAILING LIST: Yes
DISTRIBUTED: Tucker Seabrook
FEATURES: Quirky cellar door building in classic Evans style.

Not long after he started The Rothbury Estate, Len Evans spotted a ridge of land off Palmers Lane looking over Rothbury and across to Brokenback. This was the site of the Pinchin home and vineyard, planted in the 1860s. Only a doorstep and the water tank remained of the house. Just off this ridge, behind a row of ancient pepper trees, Len built his extraordinary house 'Loggerheads'. 'If my guests are asked what they did, they can say they spent the weekend at loggerheads.' Before this, Len had planted a small vineyard of chardonnay below the house. Later he added more chardonnay plus gamay and pinot noir on the slopes back to Palmers Lane.

Why did Evans, the staunch promoter of semillon and shiraz in the Hunter, want to plant pinot, chardonnay and (for heaven's sake!) gamay? 'I had Rothbury, then,' he replied. No other explanation seems necessary.

The wines were initially made at The Rothbury Estate but, after this fell to Mildara Blass, ex-Rothbury winemaker Keith Tulloch continued to make the Evans wines elsewhere. Recently, they have added wines made from other vineyards, notably Ivan Howard's Somerset Vineyard on Oakey Creek Road.

Those who used to frequent Evans' restaurant and cellar at Bulletin Place will recognise some of the interesting paraphernalia that adorns the walls of the cellar door building – old photographs, wine advertisements, prints. I've had many a drink at that table in the middle of the room.

St Ignatius keeps a scholarly watch over the courtyard. (I'll admit that at first I thought this was St Peter, in a time-share arrangement with Château Petrus.)

Throughout his career, particularly as a show judge, Evans has always promoted style over sheer size, and he's followed his own advice with all his wines, particularly the '98 Chardonnay. Lovers of big, peachy chardonnays may find the wine lean. I don't. The '98 Pinot Noir takes a similar approach, with softness and complexity the main features. It already has really interesting fungal and earthy notes and should mature over several years, becoming a soft, earthy Hunter red rather than a mature varietal pinot.

1998 Chardonnay ($20)

This has all the flavour intensity you'd want, the fruit and oak beautifully married, but achieves this within a very fine, stylish

Evans Family Wines

palate that finishes with tight acidity. It will take a couple of years' age with ease.

1998 Howard Shiraz ($25)

Rich, complex fruit on the nose, showing excellent depth and nicely married oak. The palate is richly flavoured, yet medium bodied and quite stylish, with soft tannins and all the makings of a lovely, soft Hunter 'Burgundy'. A beautifully styled wine that will develop superbly.

1997 Howard Shiraz ($25)

The nose is still a little closed, but shows lovely Hunter shiraz character. The palate is rich, round and soft, surprisingly so for a 1997, with beautiful earthy complexity developing. A brilliant young wine with great potential – a classic in the making.

Farrell's Limestone Creek Vineyard

ADDRESS: Mount View Road, Mount View 2320
TELEPHONE: (02) 4991 2808
FAX: (02) 4991 3414
E-MAIL: farre49@ibm.net
ESTABLISHED: 1980
CELLAR DOOR: 10am–5pm Fri–Mon & public holidays. Other days by appointment.
OWNERS: The Farrell family
VITICULTURIST: Roger Dixon (contract)
WINEMAKER: Neil McGuigan (contract)
1999 PRODUCTION: 3000 cases
MAILING LIST: Yes and wine club
DISTRIBUTED: Direct from the vineyard and via Kieran Farrell
FEATURES: Wine club, offering especially reserved quantities of older vintages.

Farrell's is one of the highest vineyards in Mount View, and therefore in the Pokolbin area. It's at the top of the slope below Mount Bright, in a simply beautiful position below the bush and the cliff face. As you leave your car, the sound of bellbirds wafts through the trees and comes close to distracting you from the breathtaking view.

The vineyard was established in 1980 by Sydney endocrinologist Dr John Farrell and his wife Camille. The 8 hectare vineyard is planted with sauvignon blanc, semillon, chardonnay, pinot noir, merlot, shiraz, cabernet franc, cabernet sauvignon and verdelho. For a while the Farrells sold part of their fruit and took only some for themselves, but in 2000 they began bottling all under their label for the first time.

I have previously liked their '97 Merlot, which is quite a complex wine, with berry and earthy notes and a lovely supple palate. The '97 Chardonnay appealed to me less, as it has developed quite quickly, to give a very full, tropical flavour and a broad palate.

1999 Semillon ($17)

This is a very fine example of young semillon, with fresh, zesty fruit on the nose and a taught, steely palate. You can enjoy it now for its crispness and youth, or keep it for five years to develop more softness and complex, toasty flavours.

1999 Cabernet Merlot ($18)

Fresh, berry fruit on the nose, showing pleasant lift and life. The palate has medium weight, with those same berry characters, and finishes with fine, balanced tannin. This can be drunk now, so easy is the balance, or kept for short-term cellaring to develop cedary complexity.

1999 Shiraz ($20)

The nose has good depth of rich, blackberry fruit. The palate is quite stylish, with good varietal flavour and finishing with rather tight tannin. This is best kept for a couple of years to loosen up, after which it will drink well or keep further for more softness and complexity.

ADDRESS: Lot 222 Marrowbone Road, Pokolbin 2320
TELEPHONE: (02) 4928 2544
FAX: (02) 4928 2405
ESTABLISHED: 1990
CELLAR DOOR: By appointment
OWNER: Robert Fernance
WINEMAKER: Contract
MAILING LIST: Yes
DISTRIBUTED: Direct from vineyard and The Cricketers' Arms, Newcastle

Bob Fernance's forebears farmed the Yarramalong Valley south of Cessnock, although they never planted vines. Those of you familiar with the Wollombi Road between Peate's Ridge and Wollombi will have seen the floodway Fernances Crossing, after you come down from the hills and enter the valley. ('Are Fernances marsupials?', a friend in my car once asked.)

Bob and his family now live in Newcastle, where he owns and manages the Cricketers' Arms in Bruce Street, Cooks Hill. He needed a supply of wine for the pub, so bought a 30 hectare block planted with not quite 2 hectares of shiraz and chardonnay. However, this hasn't been enough to satisfy demand, so he now buys additional fruit.

I haven't tried the wines. So, if you're in Newcastle, drop in to the Cricketers' Arms and let me know what they're like.

Foate's Ridge

ADDRESS: 241 Fordwich Road, Broke 2330
TELEPHONE: (02) 6579 1284
FAX: (02) 9922 4397
E-MAIL: tony@foate.com.au
WEB: www.foate.com.au
ESTABLISHED: 1991
CELLAR DOOR: No. Mail order and via website.
OWNER: Tony Foate
VITICULTURIST: Neil Grosser (contract)
WINEMAKER: Trevor Drayton (contract)
MAILING LIST: Yes
DISTRIBUTED: Direct from vineyard

In 1991 Tony Foate and family bought a 36 hectare block of land just outside the Broke township. This stretches from the sandy loam flats of the Wollombi Brook to the red clay loams on the slopes, spanning both white and red wine country. They planted 2 hectares of chardonnay the following year and produced their first wine in 1994. Verdelho followed in 1995, along with more chardonnay. Merlot and cabernet sauvignon were added later, bringing the vineyard to 6 hectares. They have a good source of water from a natural spring on the property and from the Wollombi Brook, if needed.

The vineyard has been set up on a Scott Henry canopy system – quite a popular method in the Broke area – under the supervision of consultant Dr Richard Smart. This tries to contain the natural vigour of the Broke soils and gives good fruit exposure to sunlight, encouraging ripe flavours, particularly in reds.

Helen Mitchell of Mantis Design designed the striking, not quite garish, black and gold label. No likelihood of getting lost on the shelf here! However, at present the bottles are yet to meet a shelf, as the wines are available only via the website or mail order. The website has an unusual feature: a cellar management page, where you can set up and maintain the details of your own wine cellar.

I tasted two of the 2000 wines before they were bottled.

2000 Verdelho

Ripe pineapple fruit on the nose, showing very good depth. The palate is soft and full bodied, with excellent flavour. A flavoursome verdelho suitable for drinking over its first couple of years.

2000 Chardonnay

I tasted this before it had received much in the way of oak maturation, so the wine was only part-made. It showed ripe fruit on the nose, a soft, medium-bodied palate and reasonable length. Again, it will probably be suited to early drinking.

ADDRESS: 185 Fordwich Road, Broke 2330
TELEPHONE: (02) 6579 1197
FAX: (02) 6579 1197
ESTABLISHED: 1990
CELLAR DOOR: Not yet. Broke Village Store.
OWNERS: Warren and Julia Moore
VITICULTURIST: Warren Moore
WINEMAKER: Monarch Winemaking Services (contract)
MAILING LIST: Yes
DISTRIBUTED: Direct from vineyard

Warren Moore had worked in his family printing business in Sydney for many years before he sold out in the 1980s. After working in other businesses, Warren and his wife Julia bought land near Broke and, in 1990, planted chardonnay, merlot, shiraz, cabernet sauvignon and verdelho. They also added a fairly substantial grove of olive trees.

The land had been part of the original grant to explorer John Blaxland in 1824, which Blaxland named after his birthplace, Fordwich, in England. Warren and Julia discovered that the name Fordwich Estate, which had been owned by Saxonvale, was now available, so Fordwich Estate their place became. Since then, Warren has gradually learnt the art of viticulture, while Julia has been able to return, in part, to her previous profession of commercial art; she designed the maps on the current Broke/Fordwich vineyards brochure and the Singleton tourist booklet.

(Disclosure: Since starting this book, I have begun to give some marketing advice to the Moores.)

The two Fordwich Estate whites from 1998 are both big, full-flavoured wines with very ripe flavours. They should be drunk soon. They are now being replaced by the 1999s, which are fresher and more delicate.

1999 Verdelho ($15)

The nose is fresh and has ripe, tropical fruit with some pineapple overtones. Full-bodied palate with plenty of ripe flavour and a suggestion of sweetness. A touch of light tannin dries the finish. This is a typically rich Hunter verdelho that's suited to immediate drinking, while it's young and fresh.

1999 Chardonnay ($16)

Ripe, peachy fruit on the nose, with sweet vanilla character from new oak lending complexity. The palate is medium to full bodied and has plenty of flavour, the oak and lees maturation giving further complexity. The balance is good and the wine finishes soft and creamy. I reckon it was at its peak in 2000 and will continue to be for another year or so.

1998 Cabernet Merlot ($17.50)

Medium–deep purple red colour. Complex nose with ripe berry fruit and subtle new oak. The palate is full and round, with very good depth of flavour and firm, balanced tannin. The wine needs a couple of years to soften and gain more complexity and has at least six years' development ahead of it.

1998 Cabernet Sauvignon ($18)

Medium–deep purple red colour. Good depth of red and black berry fruits on the nose, with obvious but well-handled new oak. The palate has very 'correct' cabernet style – good depth of varietal fruit, a tight balance and firm tannins. This is quite a firm but well structured wine that actually needs a little time to come together, for the fruit and oak to marry and develop complexity. It will live for many years.

ADDRESS: Deaseys Road, Pokolbin 2321
TELEPHONE: (02) 4998 7630
FAX: (02) 4998 7603
E-MAIL: gabrielspaddocks@hunterlink.net.au
WEB: www.gabrielspaddocks.com.au
ESTABLISHED: 1970
CELLAR DOOR: 9am–5pm Thurs–Mon
OWNERS: Chris and Gabriel Anderson
VITICULTURIST: Graham Doran (contract)
WINEMAKER: To be appointed
1999 PRODUCTION: 7500 cases
MAILING LIST: Yes
DISTRIBUTED: Direct from the vineyard

After the demise of the McPherson Pokolbin Cooperative, the vineyards were sold off in separate parcels, one of which was bought by Neil and Caroline Sutherland in 1979. At the time Neil was head of a scientific instrumentation company but studied oenology at Charles Sturt University and took to winemaking with ease. His laboratory was, naturally, one of the best equipped of any small winery in the Hunter.

Nicholas Sutherland was gradually taking over the winemaking duties from his father when a family split-up brought the vineyard on to the market, to Nicholas's great distress. In 1999, the business was bought by Chris Anderson, a senior executive with a tele-communications company, and his wife Gabriel.

The vineyard had become somewhat run down, but the Andersons are rejuvenating it and have also done a great job with landscaping the gardens. They have 22 hectares of chardonnay, chenin blanc, shiraz, semillon, pinot noir and cabernet sauvignon, and they are planting some merlot.

The current wines, from the 1999 and 1998 vintages, were made by Nicholas Sutherland.

1999 Chenin Blanc ($17)

This was the Sutherlands' signature wine. It has quite full, tropical fruit on the nose and a round, soft and well-balanced palate. It's not greatly distinctive of the variety, but is a very drinkable, mildly flavoured wine that you can enjoy until 2001.

1999 Chardonnay ($17)

Those who tire of full-bodied, oaky chardonnays can take some refuge here. The nose has good depth of peach and melon fruit, with just a little understated oak. The palate is fairly light in weight (for chardonnay) yet has all the flavour you'd want and an attractive, soft balance. It will develop well for a couple of years if you'd like some more toasty complexity.

1998 Shiraz ($17)

This is not a wine for the faint-hearted. The nose has very ripe fruit, with some spice and plum characters and cinnamon from new oak. It doesn't quite prepare you for the palate, which is very big and alcoholic. While it has big flavour to match, my impression is one of fire and heat, so some may find it almost uncomfortable. The wine will live for many years and should appeal to those who mourn the passing of the 'big red'.

ADDRESS: Lovedale Road, Lovedale 2321
TELEPHONE: (02) 4930 7113
FAX: (02) 4930 7114
E-MAIL: sales@gartelmann.com.au
WEB: www.gartelmann.com.au
ESTABLISHED: 1972
CELLAR DOOR: 10am–5pm 7 days
OWNERS: Jorg and Jan Gartelmann
VITICULTURIST: Steve Gell
WINEMAKER: Gary Reed
1999 PRODUCTION: 93 tonnes
MAILING LIST: Yes
DISTRIBUTED: Direct from the vineyard, plus some local and Sydney shops and restaurants
FEATURES: Vineyard and olive grove tours available. Bookings essential. Picnic facilities.

Jorg Gartelmann had a computer business in Sydney when he and his wife Jan decided that a country life was the way to go. In 1996 they bought 53 hectares of land, which had been part of the George Hunter Estate, from Sydney businessman and restaurateur Oliver Shaul. Shaul had planted George Hunter in 1972 and, at its peak, the vineyard reached 60 hectares, a very large area in those days. The majority of the fruit was sold to other producers, although some made its way into the George Hunter label and the Shaul restaurants, which included The Summit and The New York Grill.

The vineyard now totals 16 hectares and is planted to chardonnay, semillon, chenin blanc, shiraz and merlot. Some of this fruit is sold, but since the 1998 vintage all varieties have appeared under the very striking Gartelmann label (referred to by some locals as 'the mad magpie').

The 1998 Chardonnay has heaps of flavour, although highly toasted, smoky oak tends to dominate the fruit at present.

I preferred the '99 Chardonnay Semillon blend, which is medium bodied and has fragrant, tropical fruit.

1999 Chenin Blanc ($13)

Chenin's not usually particularly positive in the Hunter in terms of flavour, so this was a pleasant surprise. It has a full body and fresh, tropical flavour. Not long ago I tried the 1983 George Hunter Chenin, made from this vineyard, which was still in good shape. However, I still think Hunter Chenin is best when it's fresh, so enjoy this 1999 as soon as you can.

1998 Diedrich Shiraz ($29) and
1998 Shiraz ($25)

These are two quite different wines. The Diedrich is very ripe-flavoured, even a little porty, with, curiously, a slightly herbaceous overtone. It's already developing complex earthy Hunter overtones. I preferred the standard '98 Shiraz, with more mainstream fruit flavours, some nice earthy development appearing and a touch of sweet, smoky oak.

ADDRESS: Milbrodale Road, Broke 2330
TELEPHONE: (02) 4998 7474
FAX: (02) 4998 7974
E-MAIL: glenguin@bigpond.com
ESTABLISHED: Early 1990s
CELLAR DOOR: Boutique Wine Centre, Pokolbin, 9am–5pm 7 days
OWNERS: The Tedder family
VITICULTURIST: Klaus Hahn
WINEMAKERS: Rhys Eather (contract) and Robin Tedder
1999 PRODUCTION: 15,000 cases
MAILING LIST: Yes
DISTRIBUTED: Wine Source (NSW, Vic., Qld) and export

The Glenguin vineyard was started by Robin Tedder, with the assistance of his brother Andrew. It takes its name from the Scottish whisky distillery where their grandfather Arthur Tedder was born. Arthur became Deputy Supreme Allied Commander in the 1939–45 war and subsequently Baron of Glenguin. (Robin appears reluctant to flaunt his title, Lord Tedder, which sounds rather like an aristocratic bear.)

Both Glenguin vineyards are at Broke – the River Oaks Vineyard, which was bought with some chardonnay already planted; and the Gravel Terrace Vineyard, which was established shortly after. Robin also takes grapes from contracted growers in Broke, Orange and Pokolbin and in 1998 was lucky enough to get shiraz from the fifty-year-old Tallawanta vineyard.

Robin spent many years in investment banking and is one of Australia's thirteen Masters of Wine. This requires, amongst other things, a detailed understanding of the international wine trade, and Robin combines his experience in these different fields in a small consulting business, principally on the financial and business management of wineries. He has also built up successful exports to four countries. The Glenguin label design was taken from a painting by friend, wine auctioneer and fellow Master of Wine Andrew Caillard.

1999 The Old Broke Block Semillon ($18.90)

This is a classic Hunter semillon in the finer, 'chablis' style. It has intense citrus fruit on the nose, with a hint of hay. The palate is fresh and delicate, with good balance and zingy acidity. You can enjoy it now as a light, crisp white or keep it for many years of toasty development.

1998 Individual Vineyard Shiraz ($28)

Yet another brilliant '98 Hunter shiraz. The nose shows very concentrated, ripe fruit, but is still quite closed. There are rich berry and chocolate flavours on the palate, with wonderful depth and plenty of soft tannin. An outstanding young wine with huge cellaring potential. Strongly recommended.

Golden Grape Estate

ADDRESS: Oakey Creek Road, Pokolbin 2320
TELEPHONE: (02) 4998 7588
FAX: (02) 4998 7730
ESTABLISHED: 1985
CELLAR DOOR: 10am–5pm 7 days
OWNERS: WIV (formerly Pieroth)
WINEMAKER: Michael Jantzen
MAILING LIST: Yes
DISTRIBUTED: Direct from cellar door and mailing list
FEATURES: Restaurant, open 9am–5pm 7 days, plus dinner at weekends. Wine museum, gift shop, picnic areas and wine trail. October Winefest.

This property was originally settled in the mid-1800s by George Wills, who operated the Clayton Winery, a name that has a delicious irony now. The land and winery were bought by Wesley 'Johnny' Drayton in about 1918 and from him passed to Barry Drayton, who named it 'Happy Valley'. Barry made wine here for several years before selling and moving to a new property on Marrowbone Road, which he named 'Hillside'. Tragically, he died in 1979 while cleaning a fermenter – news that I heard, by some strange twist of fate, when I was myself inside a fermenter and cleaning it.

Happy Valley briefly became the Pokolbin Cooperative before being bought by Saxonvale in 1972. Saxonvale's restaurant, in what had been the winery building, was operated by a recent arrival from France, Robert Mollines who, with his wife Sally, introduced the first great food Pokolbin had ever seen. He's since gone on to start spectacular restaurants at The Cellar and currently Robert's in the Pepper Tree complex.

Saxonvale moved its operations to Broke and in 1985 the old winery/restaurant complex was bought by the Pieroth organisation – now known as WIV International – and tastefully renamed Golden Grape Estate.

(Pieroth specialises in direct-to-the-public sales of pedestrian German and other European wines.)

To the surprise of local pundits, who were initially horrified at Pieroth's arrival in the Hunter, it remains Golden Grape today and, apart from having a very steady stream of customers, seems to have made little impact on the Hunter ambience.

The vineyard below the winery was the source of many outstanding wines in the past, including the 1981 Saxonvale Show Shiraz, so it was with great interest that I visited Golden Grape to find where that shiraz now appeared. The company had told me that some of its wines are made on contract in South Australia, Rutherglen and overseas, so I was quite surprised to find that most on offer were from the Hunter.

I told the attendant I was interested only in Hunter wines and asked for some guidance. Was there anything he thought that Golden Grape did particularly well? 'Do you like Bailey's?' he replied. 'We do some pretty good creams.'

While generally sound, the wines were mostly rather plain and seemed expensive for what they were. I find it difficult to recommend anything. The 1998 Semillon ($15.95) had plenty of flavour but was quite broad and lacked delicacy. The '99 Sauvignon Blanc ($18.95) had lightly tropical fruit but was quite dull. The '99 Chardonnay ($22.95) was my pick of the whites, with melon fruit, well-handled oak and a nice touch of malolactic. But the big companies are making such wine for around a tenner.

'Can you tell me where the shiraz from that block just outside ends up now?' I asked. I was shown the 1999 Cabernet Hermitage ($19.95), which had pleasant berry and earthy flavour and soft tannins, but lacked depth and was hardly what I expected.

I was the last customer that afternoon and the staff were clearly fidgety. I left, and the doors were hurriedly locked behind me, ten minutes before 5pm.

Golden Grape has been a successful business for some time now and is clearly giving some of the public what they want. I obviously don't represent its target market.

Grimm's Domain

ADDRESS: Broke Road, Pokolbin 2320/
3/130 Raglan Street, Mosman 2088
TELEPHONE: (02) 9969 2575, 0411 479 041
FAX: (02) 9969 2575
ESTABLISHED: 1996
CELLAR DOOR: No
OWNER: Wolfgang Grimm AM
VITICULTURIST: David Lowe
WINEMAKER: David Lowe and Jane Wilson
1999 PRODUCTION: 530 cases
MAILING LIST: Yes
DISTRIBUTED: TBA and export

'Here is the humble beginning of a new Grimm's Tale in a nutshell.' So read the reply from Wolfgang Grimm about his new vineyard.

Wolfgang is best known in Sydney as the past manager of the Hotel Inter.Continental in Macquarie Street, a position he was brought out from Germany to fill. During his time there, he built made hotel into one of Sydney's finest, managing it with great efficiency and always with an impish sense of humour.

Perhaps encouraged by the discovery that the hotel stands on the site of the first vineyard in Australia, Wolfgang became determined to develop the Inter.Continental as the 'wine hotel' of Sydney. He did this by encouraging wine company dinners and functions, an excellent wine list, support for the New South Wales Wine Experience each October and numerous other events, often at 'friendly' rates. Each year he generously shouted a magnificent dinner for the judges at the Sydney Wine Show. He was awarded an Honorary Order of Australia for his eight years' contribution to tourism and culture.

Wolfgang left the hotel for a more senior position with the Inter.Continental group in Hong Kong, but clearly Australia and wine tugged hard at him. In 1992 he had bought land on Broke Road, between Tyrrell's and Oakvale, and planted nearly a hectare of semillon there in 1996. In early 2000 he returned to Sydney and is now working for Bass Hotels and Resorts Asia Pacific.

I tried his 1997 Semillon (presumably made from bought grapes) at his 2000 Sydney wine judges' dinner and it was very good indeed. The 1999 is being held back to give it more bottle age and the 2000 was due for release as this book went to print. He has just recently planted shiraz but, to tide him over, took some grapes from another vineyard in 1999, and this wine was released with the 2000 Semillon.

Wolfgang told me his vision was 'to make the best authentic Hunter Valley wines possible and to promote NSW wine's excellence both in Australia and overseas.' Knowing Wolfgang, he'll have no trouble with either, and he'll have great fun doing it, too.

ADDRESS: 940 Milbrodale Road, Broke 2330
TELEPHONE: (02) 6579 1193
FAX: (02) 6579 1269
E-MAIL: contact@hollyclare.com.au
WEB: www.hollyclare.com.au
ESTABLISHED: 1989
CELLAR DOOR: By appointment
OWNERS: The Holdsworth family
VITICULTURIST: Bill Holdsworth
WINEMAKER: Tamburlaine (contract)
1999 production: About 2000 cases
MAILING LIST: Yes
DISTRIBUTED: TBA. Currently direct from vineyard.
FEATURES: Accommodation at vineyard will be developed.

John Holdsworth started planting Hollyclare in 1989 and released his first wine with the 1991 vintage. The vineyard nestles into the slope and under the bush to the west of the Milbrodale Road. Its name came from his mother and mother-in-law, Holly and Clare. Since Bill's death, the vineyard has been managed by his sons Jason and Bill and their families.

The 10 hectare vineyard currently has chardonnay, semillon and shiraz, and the Holdsworths have also planted aleatico to see how that fares.

1998 Shiraz ($18)

Rich fruit and smoky oak intermingle in this wine. There's also a slight Hunter pong that clears away with a bit of breathing. This is a medium-bodied red, with plenty of flavour and soft tannins, that should fill out well in the medium term – say, five years.

ADDRESS: 16 Gillards Road, Pokolbin 2321
TELEPHONE: (02) 4998 7693
FAX: (02) 4998 7693
E-MAIL: honeytree@bigpond.com
WEB: www.honeytreewines.com
ESTABLISHED: 1970
CELLAR DOOR: 10am–5pm Fri–Mon, Tue–Thurs by appointment
OWNERS: Robyn and Henk Strengers
VITICULTURIST: Ken Bray
WINEMAKER: Gary Reed (contract)
2000 PRODUCTION: about 3700 cases
MAILING LIST: Yes
FEATURES: Accommodation in a two-bedroom, fully self-contained cottage.

The Honeytree Vineyard was first planted by Maurice Schlesinger in 1970 and supplied grapes to several wineries in the Pokolbin area. The Littles bought the vineyard in 1985 to augment their own vineyards, but this didn't last long, and eventually Henk and Robyn Strengers bought it in 1997. The varieties now include semillon, shiraz, cabernet sauvignon and clairette.

The Strengers have made a particular feature of the clairette, which is more familiar to long-term Hunter visitors as blanquette. This used to be widely grown in the Hunter, and Tyrrell's' Vat 3 Blanquette Shiraz was a favourite of many. Clairette has quite a broad varietal character that quickly develops honeyed overtones, but it also tends to be a bit grippy. The 1999 Honeytree Clairette shows all these characters, but those tannins should be less obvious with food. The star amongst the Honeytree wines is currently the shiraz.

1998 Old Vines Shiraz ($20)

This is a beautiful, full-bodied Hunter red. It has wonderful complexity from sweet, soft shiraz fruit and well-married oak. There are plenty of tannins but these are even and soft. There is already a little Hunter earthiness appearing, but the complexity will clearly build for several years yet. A real pleasure.

Hope Estate

ADDRESS: Cobcroft Road, Broke 2330
TELEPHONE: (02) 6579 1161. Freecall 1800 222 176
FAX: (02) 6579 1373
E-MAIL: hope@hunterlink.net.au
WEB: www.hopeestate.com.au (under construction)
ESTABLISHED: 1994
CELLAR DOOR: 10am–4.30pm 7 days. Groups and tours by appointment.
OWNERS: Michael and Karen Hope and family
VITICULTURIST: Neil Orton
WINEMAKER: Peter Howland
MAILING LIST: Yes
DISTRIBUTED: The Wine Company (NSW); Trinity Wine Agency (Qld); and export.
FEATURES: Wollemi Restaurant, open 10am–3pm for morning tea, lunch and afternoon teas. Also available for pre-booked functions.

Michael Hope is a pharmacist with several businesses in Lithgow, Sydney and the Hunter area. I've always thought that winemaking is like chemistry on a grand scale, so it's no surprise that they hold similar attractions. In 1994, Michael and his wife Karen bought 15 hectares of vineyard near Broke and immediately started to extend this further. Not content with just growing grapes, the Hopes bought the Saxonvale winery, which had been inactive for several years after it had been sold to Wyndham Estate. Saxonvale had been making really excellent wine in the 1970s, in turn under winemakers Mark Cashmore and Alasdair Sutherland (now at Capercaillie), but had become caught up in the Gollin crash in 1974 and after that had gone through several changes of hands. While the wines remained excellent, the marketing suffered and with each change the wines sold ever more poorly than they deserved.

Initially the Hopes called their venture Hill of Hope, a name that had particular significance to those who knew the winery's history. They later changed this to Hope Estate lest the Henschke family show interest. (Since then, Hill of Gold in Mudgee has successfully defended its name against

accusations of confusion with Hill of Grace, so that fear probably wasn't justified.)

The vineyards now total 90 hectares, making this one of the larger properties in the Hunter and, I think, the largest in the Broke area. They are planted with semillon, chardonnay, pinot noir, merlot, shiraz, cabernet sauvignon and verdelho.

The wines have largely fulfilled that early promise. Of the large range, the only wines that didn't appeal to me were the '98 Cabernet Merlot, which is a bit aldehydic, and the Unwooded Chardonnay, which is simply a bit plain. The other wines had plenty to recommend them and some were excellent.

The '98 Verdelho has plenty of ripe fruit and the 1997 Blanc de Noir, made from pinot noir, is full flavoured and dry, with a good mousse and plenty of developing toasty flavour.

1999 Semillon ($15)

This is a good example of young Hunter semillon in the classic 'best with bottle-age' style. It has distinct hay and lemon characters on the nose and a fresh, crisp palate with medium body and good balance. It would drink well now with delicate foods like fish, but should develop brilliantly over five to ten years in bottle, filling out with lovely toasty flavour.

1998 Chardonnay ($17)

To really enjoy this wine you also need to enjoy new oak. That oak is French and of excellent quality, so the overall effect is still very attractive. There's good depth of ripe fruit on the nose, with that lemony oak overlay, and the palate is medium bodied, well balanced and quite stylish. The oak and fruit should marry together well over the next year or two to produce a very complex wine.

1998 Shiraz

I'm not sure which vineyard this fruit came off, but the wine bears an uncanny resemblance to the Saxonvale wines of the early '80s, which is a great sign. The nose has very good depth of ripe fruit, showing both black and red berries, with beautifully handled new French oak. The palate's of medium weight but has wonderful flavour and plenty of soft tannin. It hides its 14 per cent alcohol admirably and is so well balanced it drinks pleasantly already. Keep it for ten years or more and you'll have a brilliant, mature Hunter red.

1999 Merlot ($20)

Ripe plums, berries and a little earthiness combine on the nose with a touch of new oak. The palate is plump, soft and well balanced – just what merlot's structure should be and not a cabernet look-alike. The tannins are fine and soft, so you could drink this very young. It would be so much better with about four years in bottle, however. Very good.

Horseshoe Vineyard

ADDRESS: Horseshoe Valley, Denman 2328
TELEPHONE: (02) 6547 3528
FAX: (02) 6547 3548
E-MAIL: horseshoe@hunterlink.net.au
ESTABLISHED: 1986
CELLAR DOOR: 10am–4pm Sat, Sun & public holidays
OWNERS: John Hordern and family
VITICULTURIST: John Hordern
WINEMAKER: John Hordern
2000 PRODUCTION: 10,000 cases
MAILING LIST: Yes
DISTRIBUTED: Fine Wine Specialist (NSW);
Australian Boutique Premium Wines (SA); and export

In 1966, grazier David Hordern planted grapes on his property 'Brogheda' north of Denman in the Upper Hunter. The following year, together with Bob Smith, he planted a further vineyard nearby and not long afterwards they were making wine. This, and the huge Penfolds Wybong Estate vineyard nearby, didn't go unnoticed by David's brother Robert, who planted his own vines on his property in the Horseshoe Valley, to the south of Denman. For many years, he was content to sell the fruit to others, but in the meantime son John had been getting experience at local wineries and studied oenology at Roseworthy Agricultural College, now Adelaide University. And so, from 1986, they have been making wine under the Horseshoe Vineyard label.

The vineyard now has 10 hectares of vines, including semillon, chardonnay and shiraz. Whites are the main focus, as John reckons he can only make the reds he wants about four years in ten from Upper Hunter fruit. He supplements his red crush with grapes from Mudgee and Orange.

The actual company name is Anthony Hordern and Sons Pty Ltd, which dates from the department stores that past members of the family once owned. The stores were bought by Waltons and eventually passed into the Bond empire. When this came tumbling down, John was pleased to find that the old family company name was again available, and grabbed it.

For the last few years, John has been making his wines in the old Oak milk factory in Muswellbrook, which he shared with Simon Gilbert. With Simon moving to a new winery at Mudgee, John will have the winery to himself and is starting a joint venture with Rex D'Aquino from Highland Heritage in Orange, whose wines he has been making for several years. His contract winemaking goes further still, with grapes coming from Tenterfield and Canowindra.

Wandering around the winery with John, we tried some great youngsters from 2000, including three contrasting semillons. The Horseshoe Vineyard wine has very intense, ripe fruit and really classic Hunter semillon structure; a Merriwa wine was grassier and a bit sauvignon blanc-like, but not lean; and the example from Broke was the fullest, with great depth of ripe, apricot fruit. This was obviously one of those 'on-years' John spoke of, as the 2000 shiraz in wood was also very good.

John has some different approaches with his whites. He is one of the few to use oak maturation for semillon – and American oak, what's more. There's an unoaked version as well, which often develops very well in bottle. The 1989 was excellent when I last tried it in 1997 – a beautifully rich, soft wine with nutty developed flavour. Also, he releases his chardonnay with bottle age, both the oak-matured and unoaked versions. He even has a re-release of his 1991 Chardonnay. The wines below show the contrasts.

1998 Unwooded Semillon ($14.50)

Full, straw-like characters on the nose, showing distinct development, suggesting the wine is evolving quickly. However, the palate still has freshness and crisp acidity and that development has added complexity. The wine should fill out further, over another three years or so, into a complex, nutty wine.

1997 Classic Hunter Semillon ($16.50)

The nose shows plenty of vanilla from new American oak. Full, round palate with plenty of body and flavour, the oak again quite apparent, and with fresh acidity on the finish. The wine's in very good shape for a three year old (particularly from a difficult year) and should develop further into a big 'Hunter white burgundy' style. ('Classic' to me usually implies an unoaked wine but, provided you enjoy new oak and know it's there, I wouldn't worry.)

1996 Classic Hunter Chardonnay ($18.50)

The nose is still quite fresh, with nutty characters beginning to develop and some vanilla from new oak. The palate is medium bodied, with a very attractive, soft balance and quite complex flavour. When many other chardonnays would be looking too fat and over-developed, this one still has freshness and life. All the same, it's fully ready to drink.

Horseshoe Vineyard

ADDRESS: Heddon Street, Kurri Kurri 2327
TELEPHONE: (02) 4936 0300
FAX: (02) 4936 0360
ESTABLISHED: 1995
CELLAR DOOR: By arrangement
OWNERS: The Hunter Institute of Technology
VITICULTURISTS: Peter Went and Steve Gell
WINEMAKER: Rhys Eather (contract)
1999 PRODUCTION: 1800 cases
MAILING LIST: Yes
DISTRIBUTED: Direct from the Kurri Kurri campus

The Hunter Institute offers diploma courses in various aspects of wine production for industry trainees, interested amateurs and professional grape growers and winemakers. It teaches these courses at several campuses across the Hunter region, but the main centre is Kurri Kurri. The Institute's vineyard has been planted with semillon, chardonnay, verdelho, shiraz, cabernet sauvignon and chambourcin, and the grapes are vinified at the Institute's new winery by the students under the watchful eye of local winemaker Rhys Eather from Meerea Park. Sales of wine from the Kurri campus support the teaching and research activities.

I have tried two of their wines. The '98 Hunter Valley Dry White has pleasant, lightly tropical fruit, while the '97 Semillon shows stronger characters.

1997 Semillon

This is an intriguing wine, with bigger fruit – almost verdelho-like – than I would have expected from this vintage. The fruit is quite ripe and tropical, and the palate full bodied, with a hint of oiliness. (In retrospect, there may be some botrytis there.) A full-flavoured semillon that's ready for drinking.

ADDRESS: Hermitage Road, Pokolbin 2320
TELEPHONE: (02) 4998 7500
FAX: (02) 4998 7211
WEB: www.brlhardy.com.au
ESTABLISHED: 1997 (under BRL Hardy)
CELLAR DOOR: 9.30am–5pm 7 days
OWNERS: BRL Hardy – listed public company
VITICULTURIST: Luke Wormald
WINEMAKERS: Red – Steve Pannell, White – Glenn James
1999 PRODUCTION: 7000 cases
MAILING LIST: No
DISTRIBUTED: BRL Hardy
FEATURES: Brokenback Trail 'Weekend Affair'.

Hardys was one of the first companies to recognise the synergy between Hunter Valley and McLaren Vale shiraz and, under their brilliant winemaker Roger Warren in the 1950s, Hunter shiraz was an important component of some of the company's top reds, particularly St Thomas Burgundy. I have shared many bottles of St Thomas from various vintages in the 50s and most still drink beautifully. The wine for these was usually bought from Draytons and Elliotts, but these purchases seemed to cease around the early 1970s.

Hardys made two forays into the Hunter, as shareholders in both Hollydeen and Arrowfield, but otherwise their interest in the Hunter waned. If you include Seppelt's brief period in the Hunter in the 1970s, Hardy's is one of the few large companies not to have owned vineyards there.

That sentiment seemed to change in 1996 when, in a brief but intense flurry of activity, the now BRL Hardy tried to take over The Rothbury Estate but were beaten on the line by Mildara Blass. As if in self-consolation, they turned around and bought the Hunter Ridge brand and leased the Richmond Grove winery and cellar door facilities from McGuigan Wines in 1997. They also took some of the Richmond Grove stock.

Apart from the obvious branding of the cellar door area on Hermitage Road, there seems to have been little action. I must confess that I don't really understand what Hardys is doing at Hunter Ridge. I can only suppose that the move is part of some unannounced plan. It is a highly professional company, but the wines and activity to date seem very half-hearted. The '96 Shiraz, which was presumably made in the McGuigan era, has some flavour and a nice balance, but seems a bit plain, with a dank overtone. I preferred the '99 Chardonnay which, although slightly reserved at present, has really fine fruit and a nice touch of vanilla oak. It has good balance and should fill out well over a year or two.

1999 Verdelho ($13.95)

Ripe, tropical fruit on the nose, with quite good depth. The palate is round and full-bodied with good balance. A pleasant, flavoursome wine for early drinking.

Inglewood Vineyards

ADDRESS: Yarrawa Road, Denman 2328
TELEPHONE: (02) 6547 2556
FAX: (02) 6547 2546
E-MAIL: inglewood@hunterlink.com.au
ESTABLISHED: 1988
CELLAR DOOR: By appointment
MANAGING director: Ross Pitts
VITICULTURIST: Brett Keeping
WINEMAKER: Monarch Winemaking Services (contract)
1999 PRODUCTION: About 19,000 cases
MAILING LIST: Yes
DISTRIBUTED: Inglewood Wines Pty Ltd

Inglewood is one of the only vineyards in the Hunter that actually has the Hunter River run through the property. It lies just downstream from the main Rosemount vineyards and winery and near the junction of the Hunter and Goulburn rivers. During its establishment, the company relied heavily on the guidance of John Muddle, who had managed the development of the nearby Richmond Grove vineyard in the 1960s.

The 161 hectare vineyard is planted in two sections: Inglewood to the west of the river and Dalswinton to the east. The varieties are chardonnay, semillon, pinot noir, merlot, shiraz, cabernet sauvignon, ruby cabernet, cabernet franc, marsanne and verdelho, the last being one of the largest plantings in New South Wales. About a quarter of the fruit is sold under the company's brands, Inglewood and Two Rivers, the balance being sold on contract to other winemakers.

To date the Inglewood wines have been made by Simon Gilbert or Monarch, but the company is planning to build a winery in time for the 2001 vintage.

The labels have just gone through a substantial re-design and now look very smart indeed. Inglewood is the premium range and Two Rivers the more affordable one.

The Inglewood Reserve Chardonnay has plenty of rich flavour but, like many others from the '98 vintage, is developing quite quickly. If you like big, peachy chardonnay, give it a try.

Two Rivers Hidden Hive Verdelho *1999* ($12.80)

This is a pretty good verdelho, in the big, ripe style. The nose has plenty of pineapple and rockmelon character and the palate has the richness and full body to match. It's soft and well balanced, helped by a little sweetness from either alcohol or a trace of residual sugar. Very good drinking and probably peaking around 2000.

1999 Two Rivers Stones Throw Semillon ($12.80)

A beautifully balanced, soft young semillon. The nose has lovely vanilla and hay characters, with some estery, tropical overtones. The palate is full and round, with very good varietal flavour and soft acidity. The wine was drinking very well in 2000 and should fill out quite quickly to be a richly flavoured, complex wine. Good value.

1998 Inglewood Reserve Shiraz ($24.70)

This has plenty of raspberry fruit on the nose, with subtle oak and a little lift from volatility. The palate has good depth of flavour, with rich red berries, and finishes with slightly raw tannin astringency. Give it a little time to soften.

ADDRESS: Marrowbone Road, Pokolbin 2320
TELEPHONE: (02) 4998 7325
FAX: (02) 4998 7848
E-MAIL: ivanhoewines@bigpond.com.au
ESTABLISHED: 1860s, re-established 1966
CELLAR DOOR: 10am–5pm
OWNERS: Stephen and Tracey Drayton
VITICULTURIST: Stephen Drayton
WINEMAKER: Monarch Winemaking Services (contract)
1999 PRODUCTION: 6500 cases
MAILING LIST: Yes
DISTRIBUTED: Lewis Fine Wines, NSW
FEATURES: Wine education classes for groups, by appointment. Function/dining room in cellar under winery. Chocolate festival in April, featuring major brands such as Ferrero and Cadbury, the launch of new product lines, medieval jousting (I didn't think they had chocolate in those days), fudge making demonstration, pipe bands and line dancing.

Ivanhoe is one of the famous vineyards of the nineteenth century, which went out of production – it's thought in the 1920s – before the Drayton family replanted it in 1966. It was first planted in the 1860s by Mrs George Stephens, who was related to the Wilkinson family by marriage. When Reg and Pam Drayton split from the rest of the Drayton business in 1989, Ivanhoe and two other vineyards went with them. (See the entry under Reg Drayton Wines.) After the tragic death of Reg and Pam in the Seaview air disaster, children Stephen and Robyn continued to run the company together but, in 1996, they went their separate ways, Stephen and wife Tracey taking Ivanhoe.

Their 32 hectares of land, 22 hectares of them under vine, are in a magnificent position on an east-facing slope of Mount Bright. Only grapes from the vineyard are used under the Ivanhoe label. Stephen says that at Ivanhoe they are 'trying to get the true flavours of the region' and use as little winemaking intervention as possible. They certainly have one of the best pieces of dirt in the Hunter on which to practise that philosophy. Their house nestles into the bush at the top of the slope with a great view over Pokolbin and across the valley towards the Barrington Tops. The blue and silver Ivanhoe label, in part designed by the Draytons, draws on the heraldic associations of the vineyard's name, which was taken from the novel by Sir Walter Scott. The cellar door building, designed by Susie Lochhead as a replica of the original Ivanhoe homestead, uses the same colours.

It's difficult to know where to start with the wines, as so many of them are so good. The 1998 Verdelho ($17.90) is their first release of the variety and is a great start, with very intense pineapple and apricot fruit characters and a rich, full-bodied palate, yet without obtrusive sweetness or tannin. The '98 Chardonnay is also very good and still quite fresh, with rich melon flavour, although I would have preferred French to American oak. The '98 Traminer ($15.90) is fresh and quite delicate, with roses and lychees on the nose and a soft, almost dry finish. There's also a Late Picked Traminer, from 1999 ($20), which is fresh and lively, with excellent varietal fruit and moderate lusciousness.

1995 Semillon ($17)

Pale, quite undeveloped colour. Very fresh nose with beautiful vanilla semillon character and just a little development appearing. The palate is delicate, yet intense, with really wonderful flavour and balance, and a lovely soft finish. This is a simply brilliant young semillon – yes, it's young at five years of age – that will continue to develop for many years. It's also exceptional value.

1998 Shiraz ($19.50)

Very complex, fragrant nose, with beautiful sweet, spicy fruit and a nice touch of new oak. The palate is medium bodied, yet quite round and plump, and has very good depth of flavour, with distinctly firm but balanced tannin. A wonderful young Hunter shiraz that will develop for many years into a classic. Strongly recommended.

1998 Shiraz *Pressings* ($22)

This is a slightly more raw version of the previous wine. It certainly has rich flavour, but the strong tannins create an impression of hollowness. Lovers of 'big reds' may prefer this, but I'll go for the simple – and cheaper – seduction.

1998 Cabernet Sauvignon ($22)

You may have gathered by now that I'm not always a big supporter of Hunter cabernet, but here's one that works. The fruit on the nose shows really distinct, varietal berry notes. The palate is quite firm and very 'correct', in cabernet terms, but without the green, unbalanced tannins and gum-leaf characters shown by less fortunate Hunter wines. It should age well, but will probably develop more Huntery characters than varietal ones as it ages.

ADDRESS: Lot 38 Mount View Road, Mount View 2330
TELEPHONE: (02) 4990 1273
FAX: (02) 4991 3233
E-MAIL: Jackson'sHill@bigpond.com.au
WEB: www.jacksonshill.com.au
ESTABLISHED: 1987
CELLAR DOOR: 10am–5pm 7 days
OWNERS: The Winborne family
VITICULTURIST: Michael Winborne
WINEMAKER: Michael Winborne
1999 PRODUCTION: 18 tonnes
MAILING LIST: Yes
DISTRIBUTED: Direct from vineyard
FEATURES: Olive grove, with olives available for sale.

Jackson's Hill has a beginning that's very familiar to all do-it-yourself winemakers. The Winbornes bought an 18 hectare block of pasture at Mount View in 1983 and for the next four years travelled from their home in Singleton to plant cabernet franc (in 1984) and semillon (in 1985) and to build their large earth-brick house (in 1987). During this period, they camped in the earth-floored shed that was to become their temporary winery, where they made their first wine in 1987. A winery building went up in time for the 1992 vintage.

The vineyard now totals just 3 hectares, comprised of 1.5 hectares of cabernet franc, 1 hectare of cabernet sauvignon and 0.5 hectares of semillon. These yield about 750 cases of red each vintage and 250 of white. The Winbornes find that the vines grow well on their deep soils without irrigation. They use largely organic principles in their grape growing and winemaking, with herbicides the only concession to more conventional wine production.

The '99 Semillon is relatively full, with good fruit intensity and a hint of coarseness on the finish. It's a full-flavoured wine now and should become quite big with age.

The choice of cabernet franc is an intriguing one, as this has been an erratic variety in most parts of Australia and I've seen few attractive wines made from it. But having tried the Jackson's Hill I find it difficult to argue with their choice.

1998 Cabernet Franc ($216 per case)
It's rare to see this as an unblended variety and the result is very successful. There's ripe, plummy fruit on the nose, which also suggests suppleness and softness. The palate delivers, with good depth of flavour and a really charming balance and softness. It should take a few years' age quite easily … but why wait? – it's delicious now.

1998 Cabernet Sauvignon
The nose has good berry fruit, with a hint of capsicum and a little sweet oak. The palate is richly flavoured and quite supple, suggesting merlot (which the wine apparently doesn't contain). The overall flavour and balance are very good and the wine should develop well for several years.

ADDRESS: Rylstone Road, Baerami, via Denman 2333
TELEPHONE: (02) 6547 5168
FAX: (02) 6547 5164
E-MAIL: info@jamesestatewines.com.au
WEB: www.jamesestatewines.com.au
ESTABLISHED: 1982
CELLAR DOOR: 10am–4.30pm 7 days
OWNER: David James
VITICULTURIST: Stephen Bottomley
WINEMAKER: Peter Orr
MAILING LIST: Yes, and wine club
DISTRIBUTED: Direct from vineyard and export.

James Estate started its life as Serenella, when Giancarlo Cecchini planted vines on his 1100 hectare farming property in the Upper Hunter. The first few vintages were made elsewhere, but a winery was built in time for the 1987 vintage. The wines were made by Giancarlo's daughter Tish, who had studied winemaking in Italy. Serenella had success in various wine shows and I particularly remember a couple of chardonnays in the 1990s that had very good flavour.

Unfortunately, ill health in the family forced them to put the property on the market and, in 1997, they sold to Newcastle businessman David James, who renamed it James Estate. (But the effervescent Tish is not lost to the Hunter. See 'Serenella'.)

The vineyards now total 53 hectares and are planted to sauvignon blanc, semillon, chardonnay, pinot noir, merlot, shiraz, cabernet franc, cabernet sauvignon and (exotically) sylvaner.

As often happens with the Upper Hunter, I thought the whites were the stars. The '98 Shiraz didn't appeal to me.

The '98 Reserve Chardonnay is a relatively tight, higher acid style that actually needs a little time in bottle to come around. The flavour's good, but will fill out further by 2001 or 02.

1999 Semillon ($16)

This has a beautifully fragrant nose with fresh, lemon zest overtones. The palate has good intensity and medium weight – more like a Lower Hunter white than a fuller Upper Hunter one. It's a good each-way bet: it has the flavour to drink well young and should develop beautifully over a few years.

1999 Verdelho ($16)

This is a full-flavoured wine with plenty of richness and character. There's very good depth of tropical fruit, and the fruit is pretty ripe, so there's quite high alcohol, too, giving the wine considerable fullness and body. The wine achieves all this and yet retains balance and avoids the matty tannins you often get with verdelho. Enjoy it while it's young.

ADDRESS: De Beyers Road, Pokolbin 2320
TELEPHONE: (02) 4998 7528
FAX: (02) 4998 7370
E-MAIL: jytwine@hunterlink.net.au
ESTABLISHED: 1989
CELLAR DOOR: 10am–5pm 6 days (closed Wed)
OWNERS: Jay and Julie Tulloch
VITICULTURIST: Jay Tulloch
WINEMAKER: Jay Tulloch
MAILING LIST: Yes
DISTRIBUTED: Inglewood Wines (NSW)

You don't have to read far into this book to know that there have been many ebbs and flows of company and family fortunes in the Hunter valley. Few of the great winemaking families have survived in the Hunter – the Draytons and Tyrrells are exceptions – while most of the early names have passed into history, such as the Wilkinsons, Phillips, Kelmans and Campbells. So it's good to see that the passing of old family wineries like Tullochs into corporate hands hasn't meant the departure of the Tulloch family from the scene.

Jay Tulloch was the manager at his family company while it underwent several changes of ownership, eventually coming to rest with Southcorp. He was the third generation at Tulloch, which was founded in 1895 when his grandfather, a Branxton storekeeper, accepted the land and vineyard in settlement of a bad debt. Jay took over from his father Hector and eventually became the manager of Southcorp's operations in the Hunter, before taking early retirement in 1997. His wife Julie had done great work in supporting the Tulloch brand, hosting functions for the trade in their home. They had started their new venture some years before, in 1991, when they planted vines along De Beyers Road not far from Tulloch and opposite Lindemans' Cawarra Vineyard. Their 3 hectares of grapes –

chardonnay, semillon and verdelho – are augmented with fruit from local growers.

Jay is a skilled horse and cattleman, has a simple country directness and is a man of few words, but what he doesn't know about the Pokolbin area isn't worth knowing.

All the JYT wines rely on finesse and drinkability rather than sheer opulence. You won't find big, over-ripe wines under this label. The '98 Chardonnay is typical, with good fruit flavour and a fine, medium-bodied palate that's halfway between semillon and the bigger chardonnays in weight. That delicate touch should help it age over three years or so.

1999 Verdelho ($18)

This follows the successful style of the Tulloch wine, with fresh, pineapple fruit and a full, round palate softened by a trace of sweetness. Attractive drinking while it's young and fresh.

1998 Semillon ($18)

Good fruit on the nose, with slightly tropical overtones and developing some smoky complexity. The palate is finely constructed and has very good flavour and balance. It should develop well over the next five or six years to become a beautiful, mature, toasty semillon.

Kester

ADDRESS: Lilywood Farm, O'Connors Road, Pokolbin 2325
TELEPHONE: (02) 4990 7867, 0418 685 664
FAX: (02) 4990 7867
E-MAIL: perdiem@hunterlink.net.au
WEB: www.perdiem.com.au
ESTABLISHED: 1997
CELLAR DOOR: No. Available from Small Winemakers Centre.
OWNERS: Keith and Amanda Tulloch
WINEMAKER: Keith Tulloch
1999 PRODUCTION: 4800 cases
MAILING LIST: Yes
DISTRIBUTED: Direct from the vineyard

Keith Tulloch had been the winemaker for The Rothbury Estate for four years when it was bought by Mildara Blass. Keith had been making Evans Family wines at Rothbury and continued the working relationship with Len Evans by making his wines in other wineries. Soon, he started making wine for his own brand, Kester, to which he has recently added another range, Per Diem.

Kester wines are made from the main Hunter varieties and Keith describes them as 'Hunters for long-term development'. Per Diem, as the name suggests, are wines for 'now'.

1999 Per Diem Verdelho

You'd expect Keith to deliver a flavoursome verdelho, after his experience at Mount View, and so he does. This has rich, tropical fruits and is quite fresh and undeveloped. The palate is lighter than I had expected and finishes quite dry with a little hardness, although this does give the wine some structure and keeps that big fruit in check. 'Per Diem' it may be called, but it should loosen up over a few months.

1999 Kester Chardonnay

Keith certainly goes for big flavours. This wine is big and peachy, and seems to be quite forward in its development. It's also very complex, with well-married oak and some attractive lees overtones. If you like plenty of flavour in your chardonnay, give it a try, although I'd drink it before 2002.

1998 Kester Shiraz

This is a pretty big shiraz, with very rich, ripe fruit and overtones of chocolate. The flavours really fill the mouth with sweet fruit, alcohol and a little oak. The tannins are also mouth filling, but they're soft and balanced. There's a rather old-fashioned complexity to the wine, but in an attractive way. It needs a little time to come together and will live for years.

ADDRESS: Cnr Broke Road and Halls Lane, Pokolbin 2321
TELEPHONE: (02) 4998 7766
FAX: (02) 4998 7475
E-MAIL: sobels@ozemail.com.au
WEB: www.ozemail.com.au/-sobels
ESTABLISHED: 1974
CELLAR DOOR: From 9am 'until the lights go off'
OWNERS: Private company, headed by Kevin and Margaret Sobels
VITICULTURIST: Jason Sobels
WINEMAKER: Kevin Sobels
1999 PRODUCTION: 7500 cases
MAILING LIST: Yes, and Sobels Family Wine Club
DISTRIBUTED: Red Rock Beverage, NSW
FEATURES: Drama and stage productions by the Travelling Troubadours, a Sydney
theatrical group. Picnic and barbecue facilities available.

You can't keep Kevin Sobels down. He's one of the Hunter's survivors and, as soon as trouble strikes here, he bobs up again there. Although I've found some of his wines technically questionable, he seems to have the knack of giving people what they want.

Kevin comes from a well-known South Australian winemaking family. His father, Larry, was the last member of Buring and Sobels, who owned the Quelltaler winery in the Clare Valley. Kevin worked for Seppelt in the Barossa Valley before moving to Denman Estate in the Upper Hunter in 1973 and then starting his own winery in Muswellbrook in 1974. Coincidentally, this was the year that Buring and Sobels sold Quelltaler to brandy makers Nathan and Wyeth.

In the late 1980s he was the winemaker at Parker Estate, now Bimbadgen, but he left there in 1991, buying and planting a block of land on Broke Road opposite The Rothbury Estate. A winery went up before the 1995 vintage.

Kevin and Margaret now have about eight of their 22 hectares under vine, with traminer the biggest area. From the early days, traminer has been their signature variety. Kevin tells me it's the biggest seller through the cellar door – and through Sydney restaurants. They also have an arrangement to take a substantial amount of fruit from a new vineyard at Martindale in the Upper Hunter.

The 1999 Verdelho didn't appeal to me, as I found some sulphide lurking. But, true to form, the two traminer wines were good.

1999 Traminer ($13)

Fragrant nose showing very good varietal fruit. The palate is soft and well balanced, with plenty of flavour and a little sweetness. A very attractive wine from an unfairly unfashionable variety. Good value.

1997 Traminer Sticky 375 ml ($25)

Golden colour. Caramel and toffee characters give the nose great richness. The palate is full-flavoured, the development overtaking the varietal fruit, and with plenty of sweetness. A bit pricey, but should go brilliantly with crème caramel.

1998 Shiraz ($18)

Subtlety is not the word here. The nose shows very rich, ripe fruit with a distinct portiness. There's a big, rich palate, with considerable flavour and plenty of soft tannin. Those porty overtones show through again. The wine makes up in flavour and impact what it lacks in delicacy and will please the lovers of 'big reds'.

Krinklewood Vineyard

ADDRESS: 712 Wollombi Road, Broke 2330
TELEPHONE: (02) 6579 1322
FAX: (02) 9968 3435
E-MAIL: krinklewood@bigpond.com
ESTABLISHED: 1998
OWNER: Rod Windrim
VITICULTURIST: Steve Gell
WINEMAKER: Simon Gilbert (contract)

Rod Windrim previously owned a vineyard and cottage on Palmers Lane, Pokolbin, which was also called Krinklewood, but he sold up and moved his operations to a new property south of Broke. He now has 16.4 hectares planted to semillon, chardonnay, shiraz and verdelho. He had a small amount of wine made in 2000, but this was not yet ready as this book went to print.

ADDRESS: Cnr Broke & Hermitage roads, Pokolbin 2320
PO Box 6265 Silverwater DC NSW 1811
TELEPHONE: (02) 9848 2103
FAX: (02) 9898 0200
E-MAIL: gavin@kulkunbulla.com.au
WEB: www.kulkunbulla.com.au
ESTABLISHED: 1996, as Kulkunbulla
CELLAR DOOR: Planned for late 2000
OWNERS: 11 private shareholders headed by Gavin Lennard
VITICULTURIST: Ken Bray and David Lowe
WINEMAKER: David Lowe and Jane Wilson (contract)
1999 PRODUCTION: 2600 cases
MAILING LIST: Yes
DISTRIBUTED: World Wine Estates (NSW)

This vineyard has had an excellent reputation in two previous incarnations and appears to be developing a third. As Glandore, owned by Jack Phillips, it was well known for its white wines, some of which were bought by Leo Buring and sold through his cellars in George Street, Sydney and later through his national brand. I tasted several of these from the 1950s only a few years ago and most were in great shape. For a while Leo Buring Rinegolde was made from semillon off Glandore. Unfortunately, the Hunter's nadir of fifty years ago was too much for the Phillips family, who pulled up their vines in 1960.

The land was replanted by The Rothbury Estate in 1969 and named the Brokenback Vineyard. Parts were planted with semillon and these vines produced some of the most spectacular whites in the Valley throughout the 1970s. (See The Rothbury Estate.) After Mildara Blass had bought Rothbury, some blocks of the Brokenback Vineyard were sold to Tyrrell's and the one that was to become Kulkunbulla to a group of shareholders led by Gavin Lennard. Gavin was previously managing director of two companies in Sydney, but had been a keen wine man for many years, so left the

corporate world to become managing director of their new vineyard.

The Kulkunbulla, according to a dreaming story, are the dancers in a corroboree who are celebrating the deeds of Nirunja, the Hunter. Nirunja is more familiar to Europeans as the constellation Orion and the Kulkunbulla are the three stars of his belt. The three stars also form part of the Kulkunbulla logo.

Part of the Brokenback vineyard had already been removed, so the 24 hectares currently contain only 7 hectares of vines – 1 hectare of semillon and the rest chardonnay. David Lowe, who would have come to know the vineyard well over his many years at Rothbury, makes the wines. Success came quickly as, with its first vintage of Brokenback Chardonnay, Kulkunbulla won the Vinkem Trophy for the best 1997 chardonnay at the 1997 Hunter Wine Show. That year was a very difficult one for whites, so this was a great achievement.

Both of the '98 chardonnays are attractive wines – I preferred them to the unoaked Nullarbor '99, which has heaps of flavour but also a bit of hardness. The semillons are quite full, even broad in style. Some appeared to have been given skin contact, which certainly maximises flavour, but often at the expense of finesse and balance. The '98 was one of these. However, the 1997 was a cracker, a triumph from this very difficult vintage for whites.

1997 Semillon

The colour's becoming a deeper yellow with age. There's beautiful development on the nose, with some straw characters appearing. The palate has lovely developing vanilla flavour and finishes with quite crisp acidity. Developing well, but will be so much better with more age. Keep till 2007. You won't be sorry.

1998 Chardonnay ($22)

Pale–mid yellow colour, still quite undeveloped. Very fine, elegant nose with good fruit intensity. The palate has good depth of ripe flavour, medium weight and attractive balance. This is not in the big, opulent Hunter style, but is altogether finer, yet with all the flavour you could want. It will probably develop better, and longer, than The Brokenback.

1998 The Brokenback Chardonnay ($31)

A slightly deeper yellow colour. This is a bigger, riper wine with more oak and other complexities. The palate shows more fullness and softness than the 'standard' '98 and would probably be most people's preference. However, I'll take the first one.

ADDRESS: Broke Road, Pokolbin 2320
TELEPHONE: (02) 4998 7507
FAX: (02) 4998 7322
E-MAIL: folly@ozemail.com
WEB: www.lakesfolly.com.au
ESTABLISHED: 1963
CELLAR DOOR: 10am–4pm 6 days, closed Sun
OWNER: Peter Fogarty
VITICULTURIST: Bob Davies
WINEMAKER: Stephen Lake
1999 PRODUCTION: 6000 cases
MAILING LIST: Yes
DISTRIBUTED: De Bono Fine Wine & Brew (NSW); Flinders Wholesale (Vic.)

I have described Max Lake and his huge contribution to the Hunter elsewhere in this book. As far as the drinker is concerned, however, Lake's Folly is Max's most notable and concrete achievement.

Having been knocked out by the quality of a 1930s Penfolds Dalwood Cabernet/Petit Verdot, Max became determined to emulate it. After a search that lasted several years, he bought a wonderful bit of red dirt, opposite McWilliam's Rose Hill vineyard, from Andy Phillips. The land had been previously planted to vines when it was owned by the Kayser and Kime families, but the last vines had been pulled out in the 1930s. Max planted cabernet sauvignon and shiraz, and later added merlot, petit verdot and chardonnay. The shiraz has since gone. All the grapes are estate grown on the vineyards around the winery.

The Lake's Folly reds immediately made a huge impression, partly as the produce of the first new Hunter winery in living memory and also because cabernet sauvignon had all but disappeared from the Hunter. The early wines were marked by lovely fruit and a fine balance, although some showed a bit of traditional Hunter pong. Chardonnay made its first appearance in 1974 and the wines from the beginning were very good, made in a full-flavoured but quite taut style.

Max and Joy Lake's son Stephen took over the winemaking from the 1982 vintage and Stephen has made a serious impression on the wines. The reds are fresher and cleaner, although still complex. The 'Folly Red', a blend of shiraz and cabernet sauvignon, has disappeared and the other Bordeaux varieties now supplement the cabernet sauvignon in the original wine. But it is the chardonnay style that is particularly distinctive. Running counter to most winemakers, Stephen prevents malolactic fermentation, as he thinks the wines keep a better structure and acid balance that way.

Stephen appeared at times a reluctant helmsman at Lake's Folly, so the locals were not entirely surprised when it became clear in early 2000 that the business was to be sold. In early May, three weeks before the scheduled auction date, the Lakes accepted a substantial offer from Peter Fogarty, a Perth businessman, who also has an interest in a winery in the Perth Hills. Stephen will remain as a consultant in the foreseeable future.

Lake's Folly

1998 Chardonnay ($36)

This vintage is absolutely typical of the Lake style. It combines peachy fruit with beautiful, lemony oak in a reasonably tight and beautifully balanced palate; it tempers intensity with elegance. Some complexity from bottle age is already beginning to appear, but the wine will continue to develop well for several years. A full-flavoured yet stylish wine contrasting the big, more opulent style of chardonnay that's more prevalent in the Hunter.

1998 Folly ($36)

This red, now a combination of cabernet sauvignon, merlot and cabernet franc, is more strongly built than Follys of the past. The nose shows concentrated fruit and hints of the tannins to come. There's also quite strong new oak, with a resiny overtone. On the palate, the wine is firm, with big cabernet fruit, some gum-leaf overtones and that resiny oak again. It finishes with firm astringency. This wine's not for current drinking, but demands at least five years in bottle to soften and develop. There's a long life ahead of it.

ADDRESS: McDonalds Road, Pokolbin 2320
TELEPHONE: (02) 4998 7684
FAX: (02) 4998 7324
WEB: www.lindemans.com.au
ESTABLISHED: 1843
CELLAR DOOR: 9am–4.30pm Mon–Fri, 10am–4.30pm weekends & public holidays
OWNERS: Southcorp Wines Pty Ltd
VITICULTURIST: Jerome Scarborough
WINEMAKER: Patrick Auld
MAILING LIST: Yes
DISTRIBUTED: Southcorp Wines, Australia and internationally
FEATURES: Wine Museum. Steven Room, featuring gourmandise wine and food matches.

Lindeman is the name that has by far the longest and most important history in the Hunter. Dr Henry Lindeman planted grapes at his property near Gresford in 1843. He was active in the early Hunter River Vineyard Association and travelled widely, learning about wine and seeking markets. Under his stewardship, and even more so under his son Charles, the company expanded very rapidly, buying several famous early vineyards and wineries. Most important of these was the Ben Ean winery, bought from John McDonald in 1912.

Lindemans survived the bank crash and recession in the 1890s and even the flood of cheaper wine from interstate after Federation. During the early part of the twentieth century it was trading actively in the Queen Victoria Building in Sydney and acquiring other Hunter vineyards that were having trouble in those perilous times. Kelman's Kirkton vineyard was one of these, bought in 1914, although Lindemans was virtually picking over the bones. They pulled up the vines in 1924. Unfortunately, the company itself eventually succumbed, going into receivership in 1930 and remaining there until the 1950s.

Through the 1950s and 60s, there's no doubt whatsoever that Lindemans was the outstanding maker of Hunter semillon. The

wine was made in three styles. The 'White Burgundy' was the fullest in body (occasionally containing some verdelho) and was the earliest to mature; the 'Chablis' was the most crisp and delicate wine, often from the first fruit picked, and was generally the most long-lived of the three; and the 'Riesling', that is Hunter River Riesling or semillon, was in between. All were simply brilliant wines that completely dominated the wine shows of the time. Their quality was reinforced by the parcels of mature wines reserved under the Lindemans 'Classic Release' programme for sale when mature – a programme which continues to this day. Some of these old semillons still open well. A bottle of the 1968 'Riesling' I opened in March 2000 was still drinking beautifully.

The reds from this period were also exceptional. Bin 1590 from 1959 still stands as the greatest Hunter red I have drunk and bottles of the two wines from 1965, Bins 3100 and 3110, which still crop up here and there, are also still magnificent. They will live comfortably for another twenty years. For a period, some Lindeman bottlings in 375 ml were in champagne bottles – I'm told because of wartime shortage. A half bottle of Bin 2579 from 1948 was in a mixed auction lot I bought in about 1980. The wine was in great condition – rich, soft and

Lindemans

complex – and an outstanding mature Hunter. I have already spoken, in my introduction, of the 1926 St Cora Burgundy. Many wines from the 1968, 1970 and 1980 vintages also still open well.

However, after the outstanding whites from 1970, the semillons lost their way and the mantle of top semillon maker moved to The Rothbury Estate. There were wines from 1975, 1979, 1984 and 1987 that developed well, but somehow the intensity and style were no longer there. Local speculation invoked several causes – the sale of the Sunshine Vineyard, which had provided much of the fruit for the earlier wines, the succession of winemakers at Ben Ean and even more obscure reasons. The widespread public clamouring for big, oaky chardonnays also diverted attention from finer Hunter semillon.

The reds lost some of their consistency, too. The 1983s, for instance, while excellent in their own right, have little style continuity with earlier Lindemans vintages.

Furthermore, there's no doubt that Lindemans' Hunter wines lost focus after the company was taken over by Penfolds and in the earlier Southcorp days. The wines sold slowly in the large, new portfolio and, rather than solve the problem, decreasing prices reinforced perceptions that the wines were not what they had been. To add further difficulties, Lindemans had decided to confront early on the inevitable changes to generic labelling – chablis, white burgundy, and so on – that were on the way. The traditional buyers of the Hunter semillons saw the Chablis become an unoaked chardonnay – and an ordinary one at that – and the disappearance of the White Burgundy.

Nevertheless, the company has now recognised the importance of the Hunter tradition and changes have been underway for several years. The addition of the Hunter to James Halliday's responsibilities at Southcorp and the refurbishment of the old Ben Ean winery confirm that new direction.

Lindemans draws fruit from 71 hectares of vineyard – 50 hectares of these shiraz, with the balance semillon and chardonnay. There is also a small block of pinot noir that usually goes into the Hunter sparkling red you can buy at the cellar door.

Ben Ean has now re-opened after an extensive refurbishment, which has mostly preserved the original features. The front wall is still there, made of bricks from the original Cawarra cellar at Gresford, dragged there in a bullock dray. However, the old open fermenters have gone, bulldozed aside. I'd have been sitting on the top of them, yelling 'Stop!' Also, I can't get used to the terra cotta exterior. Ben Ean has always been such a white building.

The Lindemans revival in the Hunter is well underway and goes beyond the more obvious changes at Ben Ean. The young semillons show the delicacy and intensity that they once did, and there are some very good reserve semillons from the mid-1990s still being held. The reds are also showing distinct improvement and a return to the soft, elegant Lindemans style, although some aren't quite there yet.

For instance, the '97 Ben Ean Vineyard Bin 9410 Shiraz has wonderful colour and nicely handled oak but looks a bit lean, without the silky richness I remember of their reds of long ago. It will clearly develop for many years, but will it ever get that suppleness that was the Lindemans hallmark?

The Reserve Chardonnays, on the other hand, deserve more attention than they usually get. Several of these from the 90s have had beautifully complex characters and the current '96 is typical. It has mature, nutty flavour, with lovely oak, lees complexity and excellent balance.

1998 Bin 9255 Semillon ($19.70)

It's a real pleasure to see that Lindemans is back on track with semillon. This one has a really fine, delicate nose, with lovely lemony fruit. The palate is fresh and crisp, even a touch lean, but that's absolutely right for the

style. The wine's quite undeveloped, suggesting that it's going down that bottle-age
path slowly. It shows great potential and is
strongly recommended. A long-term wine.

1996 Reserve Bin Semillon ($23)

This seems to be fuller and rounder in style
than the '98, but it's clearly handling age
with ease. The fruit is quite ripe, even with
some tropical notes, and there is a lovely
softness and balance. It may not be as long
lived as some, but it will be simply delicious
at around ten years of age.

1995 Bin 9003 Shiraz ($21.70)

A lovely, complex wine that's developing
well. It has ripe fruit that is building earthy
characters on the nose and a soft, elegant
palate with good flavour. It's enjoyable now,
but will continue to age well for many years.

Littles Winery

ADDRESS: Lot 3 Palmers Lane, Pokolbin 2320
TELEPHONE: (02) 4998 7626
FAX: (02) 49987867
E-MAIL: littleswinery@bigpond.com
WEB: www.littleswinery.com
ESTABLISHED: 1984
CELLAR DOOR: 10am–4.30pm 7 days
OWNERS: Suzanne Little and Ian Little
VITICULTURIST: Ian Little
WINEMAKERS: Suzanne Little and Ian Little
1999 PRODUCTION: 13,000 cases
MAILING LIST: Yes
DISTRIBUTED: Direct from vineyard (NSW); Wine 2000 Holdings (Qld)

The vineyard and winery now known as Littles started with Dr Quentin Taperell's second foray into winemaking. (The first, Quentin Vineyard, had by now been sold to Peter Marsh, becoming Marsh Estate.) However, Taperell this time got no further than planting 4 hectares of vineyard and putting up a shed before he decided to sell, and the Little family were the buyers. Ian Little had been a brewer in Sydney before working for Chateau Reynella in McLaren Vale. To guarantee the additional grapes they needed, they also bought the Honeytree Vineyard from Maurice Schlesinger in 1985 but they sold it just five years later. Suzanne Little shares the winemaking duties with husband Ian and until recently was a winemaker at Rosemount, commuting from Pokolbin to Denman. She is now back at Littles full-time, after the birth of their second child.

In 1997 the Littles bought a new vineyard towards the eastern end of Palmers Lane, which they called Daisy Hill. This is the name for part of the newly gazetted sub-region of Pokolbin, after the historic Daisy Hill winery across the Branxton Road. They also currently have a joint-venture agreement with Ed and Ian Kindred, which gives them access to grapes from the Kindred's Lochleven vineyard. This brought the vineyards owned by, or contracted to, Littles to 50 hectares.

The Daisy Hill vineyard has red–brown clay loams with weathered ironstone, a soil type quite common in the Lower Hunter. While not actually certified organic, the vineyard is managed using several organic techniques.

There are three ranges at Littles. The Reserve Series comes entirely from their own vineyards, while the Premium Hunter Valley label includes fruit from other Hunter vineyards. The New South Wales label, which inherited its design from the original Littles label, supplements Hunter grapes with others from Canberra, Cowra, Yenda and Orange.

I found the quality of the Littles wines good right from the beginning. I particularly remember some very good vintage ports, not a wine style the Hunter does well, but which obviously benefited from Ian's experience at Reynella.

The current crop of wines has also had good show success.

The '99 Gewürztraminer is rich and full-bodied, with plenty of ripe fruit. The Semillon Chardonnay has been a very successful wine for them – particularly the 1995 vintage, which has won several golds. There's a fair bit of new American oak in the 1998, which is soft and round and drinks very well. I preferred the oak balance in the '98 Reserve Chardonnay – a very complex wine, with plenty of full, ripe flavour.

1998 Reserve Semillon ($18)

Some smoky complexity from development is beginning to show here. The palate is round and soft, but quite fine in character, and the wine should continue to age well for several years. Great potential.

1998 Reserve Shiraz ($22)

This is a beautiful young red with a big future. That typical Hunter earthiness is beginning to show in the wine's development, giving it good complexity. The fruit is rich and ripe with a touch of chocolate and, while this wine is soft enough to drink now, it will be so much better in a few years' time.

London Lodge Estate

ADDRESS: Golden Highway, Gungal 2333
TELEPHONE: (02) 6547 6122
FAX: (02) 6547 6122
ESTABLISHED: 1988
CELLAR DOOR: '8–9 daily'
CHIEF EXECUTIVE: James Lloyd
VITICULTURIST: Barry Ghersi
WINEMAKER: Gary Reed (contract)
MAILING LIST: Yes
FEATURES: Old machinery, arts and crafts, restaurant, picnic area, river walks.

Stephen Horner seemed a bit suspicious when I spoke to him. No, he hadn't seen my fax and Joanne Horner couldn't remember speaking to me on the phone. Could I re-send the fax, please? No, sorry, we don't give away wine. You'll have to come up here or go to Newcastle if you want to taste it.

After I re-sent the fax I had an instant reply by phone, to the effect that information would be on its way and perhaps a bottle or two 'after I've spoken to my business partner'.

However, neither has materialised, so I can only report on what the *Australian and New Zealand Wine Industry Directory* tells me. (I don't know what to make of their cellar door times, though. Perhaps it's a breakfast event.)

The London Lodge vineyard was planted in 1988 and now has 20 hectares – across semillon, chardonnay, pinot noir, shiraz and cabernet sauvignon.

I thought the 1998 Cabernet Sauvignon was quite weedy and under-ripe when I tried it in the Hunter Wine Show that year, but the '98 Chardonnay was a good wine. The '97 Shiraz was pleasant, too, if lacking weight.

ADDRESS: 160 Cobcroft Road, Broke 2330
TELEPHONE: (02) 6579 1105
FAX: (02) 6579 1105
ESTABLISHED: 1987
CELLAR DOOR: No
OWNERS: Roy Meyer and Ian McAlpine
VITICULTURIST: Ian McAlpine
WINEMAKER: Roy Meyer
MAILING LIST: Yes
DISTRIBUTED: Direct from the vineyard

This vineyard is planted on land that was once part of Saxonvale, although there were no vines planted when the land was sold. It lies on a wonderful bank of red soil above the (now) Hope Estate winery. Industry records tell me the varieties include chardonnay, merlot, shiraz, cabernet franc and cabernet sauvignon, and that the 7 hectare vineyard is managed organically – a real challenge in a climate like the Hunter's.

The whole venture seems very hands-on: the name of the business is the maiden name of Roy's Meyer's mother and Roy designed the highly individual labels himself.

Roy's clearly a great enthusiast, but seemed reluctant to provide me with any information. He was also out when I called round.

'Oh! I hate writing about myself,' he told me over the phone.

Well, that makes it pretty difficult for anyone else to.

(Editor's note: From the brief experience I've had of Roy's wines, I can tell you he tends to release them very young – a year or less after vintage – and they are usually very bold, dark and fairly intense, if occasionally quite rustic and earthy.)

ADDRESS: Peppers Creek winery, Cnr Broke Road & Ekerts Lane, Pokolbin 2320
TELEPHONE: (02) 4998 7121
FAX: (02) 4998 7393
E-MAIL: sales@lowewine.com.au
WEB: www.lowewine.com.au
ESTABLISHED: 1994
CELLAR DOOR: 10am–5pm Wed–Sun, 7 days during school holidays
OWNERS: David Lowe and Jane Wilson
VITICULTURIST: David Lowe
WINEMAKERS: Jane Wilson (red) and David Lowe (white)
1999 PRODUCTION: About 9000 cases
MAILING LIST: Yes
DISTRIBUTED: The Main Domaine (NSW) and export

David Lowe was the winemaker at Rothbury Estate when Jane Wilson, a veterinary scientist, arrived in the Hunter from Scotland trying to satisfy her wanderlust. She got no further. David, a Roseworthy graduate, had been at Rothbury since 1979, and was to complete twelve vintages there before leaving to do his own thing. During that time he rose from Assistant to Chief Winemaker and eventually added the title of Group Vineyard Manager, with responsibilities for the Rothbury group's vineyard operations in other regions.

Initially, Jane ran a cheese distribution business – for the first time locals could buy something other than plastic cheddar – but it was not long before the two teamed up.

In 1994 they formed the Lowe Family Wine Company, leasing space in other wineries and making wine for their own brand and other companies on contract. Amongst these are Kulkunbulla and wines for the Neil Perry restaurant group, which includes Sydney's Rockpool. Their grapes now come from David's family vineyard in Mudgee, from local Hunter vineyards and, more recently, from Orange. After several years in the Oakvale winery, the Lowes now work down the road at Pepper's Creek. Currently they are building a new winery at

Mudgee, designed by Pokolbin architect Susie Lochhead, which should end their suitcase winemaking. Their main cellar door outlet will remain at Pepper's Creek.

Amongst the Lowes' early successes were the Vinkem Trophy for best chardonnay at the 1997 Hunter Valley Wine Show and two trophies for semillon with their 1998 the following year. This is a brilliant wine, with intense, lemony fruit and great length of flavour.

The Fordwich Vineyard '99 is a fairly broad style of semillon, with some straw characters to the fruit. It should age well in the short term.

1999 Fordwich Vineyard Botrytis Semillon ($25)

This dessert wine has concentrated botrytis characters over peachy fruit and a little new oak. The palate is soft, well-balanced and quite sweet. Try it with a fresh mango or fruit tart.

1998 Shiraz ($23)

This shows very ripe fruit with moderate depth of flavour. It's well balanced and soft and is worth keeping for a few years to gain complexity.

1999 Hunter Valley Merlot Rosé ($15)

Rosés come in many styles and sizes; this is quite a full one, with a deepish pink colour and plenty of flavour. It's soft and well balanced, without noticeable sweetness. With such a lack of good rosés, it's a relief to find an attractive one to recommend. Drink it while it's young.

1999 Hunter Valley Merlot ($25)

Young, berry fruit on the nose with some well-handled new oak. The palate is supple and well balanced, with good flavour and fine tannin. It's good to see this 'correct' style of merlot, a variety that's so often made as a cabernet look-alike. It should gain complexity over three years or so.

McGuigan Wines

ADDRESS: McDonalds Road, Pokolbin 2320
TELEPHONE: (02) 4998 7400
FAX: (02) 4998 7401
E-MAIL: mcguiganwines@bigpond.com.au
WEB: www.mcguiganwines.com.au
ESTABLISHED: 1992
CELLAR DOOR: 7 days
OWNERS: Listed public company
VITICULTURIST: Rodney McNamara
WINEMAKER: Peter Hall
MAILING LIST: Yes
DISTRIBUTED: McGuigan Wines (NSW); Hill International (Qld, Vic., ACT, SA); and export
FEATURES: Cellar door is accompanied by the Hunter Valley Cheese Company, Pokolbin;
Woodfired Bakehouse and Wine Country Souvenirs.

It became the cliche of the 1990s decade that a company's most valuable asset is its personnel. McGuigan Wines has one very major asset indeed – Brian McGuigan. I know of no person who understands the average wine consumer better than Brian. He demonstrated this brilliantly at Wyndham Estate, building Wyndham into a major international brand and successfully floating the company, before it was bought by Pernod Ricard.

There have been McGuigans in the Hunter for a long time. Brian's father Perc was the winemaker and manager for Penfolds at Dalwood Estate when Penfolds moved to the Upper Hunter in 1963. Perc and Brian bought the cellars and land Penfolds had vacated, which they renamed Wyndham Estate after founder George Wyndham. Now, with McGuigan Wines, Brian is at it again, and in just eight years he has built another major brand and another extremely profitable company.

There is no real secret to the success. It's built on soft, very palatable wines, often with the help of a skilfully judged touch of sweetness, and packaging that has wine appeal. The trouble is, other companies that try to emulate this success rarely achieve it. That's Brian's genius.

Another key to the McGuigan achievements, particularly in international markets, is Fay McGuigan, who is an export dynamo who easily matches her husband's energy.

McGuigan Wines has grown very rapidly and that growth has needed fuel. In 1995 the company bought the Richmond Grove Winery from Orlando Wyndham and followed this with the Richmond Grove Vineyard in the Upper Hunter the following year. Only a year later, the company found it still lacked winemaking capacity, so it bought the Hunter Estate winery (originally built as Hermitage Estate) in 1997. All of these were, of course, familiar to Brian during his time at Wyndham Estate. With the huge Hunter Estate firmly in McGuigan's grasp, the Richmond Grove Winery, just down the road, was no longer needed and this was leased to BRL Hardy to become Hunter Ridge. (Still with me?)

The McGuigan brand operates at several levels. The standard, high-volume lines are of similar style to the wines from Wyndham during Brian's time there: soft, fruity, easy drinking. Then there is the Bin Range, several of them declaring Hunter Valley. Further up the scale are the Personal Reserve and Shareholders wines.

2000 Bin 9000 Semillon ($14)

Very fresh, intense nose with tropical fruits and a hint of grass, almost sauvignon blanc-like. The palate is light, crisp and lively, with very attractive flavour and soft acidity. Delicious immediate drinking.

1999 Bin 7000 Chardonnay ($14)

An attractive wine with melon fruit and good balance. It's a little short and not especially complex but is a good chardonnay at the price.

1999 Personal Reserve Chardonnay ($26)

This is altogether a more complex wine, with well-handled oak and malolactic giving complexity. There's nice melon fruit and good overall balance. Good drinking.

1999 Shareholders Hunter Reserve Shiraz ($18.40)

The nose is quite closed at present but has very good depth of berry fruit and some attractive new oak. In the mouth, the wine has good flavour, with rich berry notes and a soft tannin balance. It needs a few years to develop more complexity and has a long life ahead of it.

1998 Personal Reserve Hunter Valley Cabernet Sauvignon ($32.90)

This has really concentrated, ripe, black-currant fruit on the nose, with sweet vanilla character from new oak. The palate's of medium body, perhaps a bit lighter than I had expected, but with very good depth of flavour and firm tannin to finish. You can drink it now, if it's not too firm for you, but it will be better still with two or three years more in bottle.

Macquariedale Estate

ADDRESS: 170 Sweetwater Estate, Rothbury 2335
TELEPHONE: (02) 4938 1408
FAX: (02) 4938 1408
E-MAIL: macqdale@turboweb.net.au
ESTABLISHED: 1993
CELLAR DOOR: By appointment. Also at Boutique Wine Centre, Broke Road.
OWNER: Ross McDonald
VITICULTURIST: Ross McDonald
WINEMAKER: Gary Reed (contract)
1999 PRODUCTION: 4000 cases
MAILING LIST: Yes, and Wine Tasting Club
DISTRIBUTED: Adderley Hammond (NSW)

Ross McDonald retired to the Hunter, settling on a small property near Branxton, but seems to have maintained a higher level of activity than most retirees do. Not long after, he extended his domain by adding a vineyard on Wilderness Road, bought from Tulloch's. This is planted with mature 25-year-old vines and has raised his holdings to 15 hectares, across semillon, chardonnay, merlot and shiraz. He has also been a project manager of the new pipeline, bringing water from the Upper Hunter to the Pokolbin area.

I greatly enjoyed both wines of his that I tried.

1999 Old Vine Semillon ($18.50)

Fresh, lemony fruit on the nose with a very attractive fragrance. The palate is crisp and lively with good depth of semillon fruit and clean acidity. It drinks well now as a light, crisp wine, but has very good potential for development in bottle, if you want a fuller, toasty style.

1998 Thomas Shiraz ($23.50)

Good berry fruit on the nose with hints of spice and quite noticeable American oak. The palate is medium bodied, with lovely flavour and balance, and finishes with fine soft tannin. The wine's balance and flavour mean that it's drinking well now, but it would be better left for a couple of years for the oak to marry in and for the flavour to become more complex. It may well turn out to be one of those elegantly styled, soft Hunter reds that ages gracefully for many years.

ADDRESS: Lot 1 Wilderness Road, Rothbury 2320
TELEPHONE: (02) 4998 7815
FAX: (02) 4998 7815
ESTABLISHED: 1996
CELLAR DOOR: Yes
OWNERS: Bob and Ann Rich
VITICULTURIST: Keith Holder (contract)
WINEMAKER: Gary Reed (contract)
DISTRIBUTED: Direct from vineyard
FEATURES: Accommodation in three two-bedroom cottages.

Bob and Ann Rich bought their 40 hectare property on the corner of the Wilderness and Branxton roads in 1996 as a place to retire to. Bob had worked in far-off places for Burns Philp and more recently had managed a courier business in Sydney. 'Instead of a couple of acres we bought a hundred, so we had to do something with it,' Bob said. They planted about 3 hectares of vines in 1997 – chardonnay, verdelho and shiraz – and built three two-bedroom cabins, which are fully self-contained. And the name? 'We've got five daughters, but we had twenty girls' names we liked. Ann always liked the name Madigan, but we never had a sixth daughter. So the vineyard's the daughter we didn't have.'

Their cellar door cottage opened in April and the Riches have some good wines for their first vintage, all made in a 'friendly' style for immediate drinking.

1999 Chardonnay ($14)

This is quite a delicate, straightforward style of chardonnay, without strong oak or other winemaking intervention. It has very attractive melon fruit and a medium-bodied palate with good flavour and a soft balance. It's probably best drunk in the next year, although it will gain some complex, toasty flavours with up to three years in bottle.

1999 Verdelho ($14)

The nose has plenty of ripe fruit, with typical pineapple character, and the palate is relatively dry, with a hint of tannin and good overall balance. Enjoy it while it's young and fresh.

1999 Shiraz ($16)

Here's a shiraz that is not made for bottle age and it doesn't matter, as it's a delicious glass of wine now. It has very attractive, sweet fruit on the nose and a smooth, well-balanced palate with plenty of soft berry flavour. It will become a little more complex with time – but not too much time.

ADDRESS: Palmers Lane, Pokolbin 2320
TELEPHONE: (02) 4998 7953
FAX: (02) 4998 7952
ESTABLISHED: 1989
CELLAR DOOR: 10am–5pm 7 days
OWNER: Terry John Maling
VITICULTURIST: Graham Doran
WINEMAKER: Gary Reed (contract)
1999 PRODUCTION: 4500 cases
MAILING LIST: Yes, with Wine 'Adoptions'
DISTRIBUTED: Direct from the vineyard
FEATURES: Accommodation available in two rooms: The Rob Roy Room and
The Lady of the Lake Room. Themed wine dinners in the banqueting room.

When the Maling family bought this property, it already had some vineyard that had been planted in 1971 by Ron Hansen of Wollundry. The Malings gradually extended this to the current 16 hectares and it now contains semillon, chardonnay, shiraz and cabernet sauvignon. Nothing unusual in that, you say. But what's amazing is that the wines since that first 1989 vintage, made next door at Calais by Gary Reed, weren't sold, but were cellared away until the main building and cellar door had been built. The main house was constructed using materials taken from heritage buildings damaged by the 1989 Newcastle earthquake.

On 20 March 1999, the wines were released for the first time. (Accountants would have conniptions.) No wonder they refer to themselves as 'the aged wine specialists'.

Terry Maling has a love of Sir Walter Scott, and the cellar door building has been named 'Waverley – Honour', after Scott's Waverley novels. It contains a complete 1871 centenary edition of them, flanked by the Waverley Collection of wines. The two guest rooms have been named after the novels, too.

The wine club operates a 'wine adoption scheme', and the adoption papers that applicants sign for a case of wine a year were drafted from the Family Court documents.

Choosing wine to adopt sounds like a peaceful alternative.

1990 Semillon ($50)

This is a magnificent example of aged semillon. The colour is now a medium–deep gold and the nose has taken on wonderful richness and buttered toast complexity. The palate has become richer, too, with beautiful vanilla and toasty flavours and a full, round body. With almost every semillon entry in this book, I refer to bottle age and what this can bring. If you're in any doubt, buy a bottle of this wine. It's a great example of mature semillon at its peak.

1991 Shiraz ($42)

This must have been a huge, porty red when it was young. The colour is a deepish brick red with an almost black density. The nose is very rich and mature, with caramel overtones, and shows signs that the wine was made from very, very ripe fruit. Those same characters show on the palate, which is full bodied and soft, with a sweet chocolatey flavour. This isn't an elegant Hunter red, but for sheer richness and flavour you have to be impressed. I estimate that it was at its best in 2000, and will probably stay much the same for several years.

ADDRESS: 1238 Milbrodale Road, Broke 2330
TELEPHONE: (02) 6579 1317
FAX: (02) 6579 1317
E-MAIL: marganfw@hunterlink.net.au
ESTABLISHED: 1989
CELLAR DOOR: Small Winemakers Centre, Pokolbin; Broke Village Store
OWNERS: Andrew Margan
VITICULTURIST: Andrew Margan
WINEMAKER: Andrew Margan
1999 PRODUCTION: 15,000 cases
DISTRIBUTED: Fesq & Co. (NSW, ACT); Nelson Wine Co. (Vic.); Wine Source (Qld);
Jonathon Tolley Wine Merchant (SA); and export.

Andrew Margan's dad Frank worked with Len Evans at the Wine Bureau in the 1960s and planted a vineyard in the Hunter in 1965. (He also ran The Cottage restaurant, which was the only place you could eat well in Cessnock in the early 1970s). All this obviously rubbed off on Andrew, who spent many years with Tyrrell's in both marketing and winemaking roles, before he started his own venture with wife Lisa.

They now have over 20 hectares of vines which stretch from the red clay slopes down to the creek flats of the Wollombi Brook, just outside Broke. Varieties include semillon, verdelho, chardonnay, shiraz, merlot, cabernet sauvignon and barbera. Andrew looks after the production side and Lisa the marketing. They also have a very substantial contract winemaking business, making wines for many vineyards in the Broke Fordwich area and far afield. Tasting from the tank with Andrew during the 2000 vintage, we tried wines from Orange, Coonabarabran and Ayers Rock – well, almost!

Their early wines were made in the Hill of Hope winery the other side of the brook, but the Margans now have their own new winery on Milbrovale Road. The first wines released were from the 1997 vintage, not a great vintage to start with as far as whites are concerned, but one of the first wines they made, the '97 Beyond Broke Semillon, won a trophy at that year's Hunter show – great going for that year. I really liked their '98 Semillon, too, which had lovely, lifted sweet fruit and excellent balance. They must be doing something right, as they also won the trophy as most successful exhibitor in the varietal classes at the 2000 Sydney Wine Show, something only the big players usually do.

The quality really shows in Andrew's wines and those that he's making for others. Andrew Margan is a name to watch.

All the current wines I've tried have really attractive fruit characters and are impeccably made. The '99 Verdelho is typical, with ripe, tropical fruit, rich flavour and a hint of sweetness. The '99 Chardonnay is also quite a big wine, with heaps of peachy flavour, but with really good balance and style.

1999 Semillon ($16.50)

Full fruit on the nose with overtones of hay and vanilla. Perhaps a hint of botrytis, too, like some of the Rothbury wines in the 70s. The palate is quite full and round, with good depth. This has the flavour to drink well immediately, and the fullness makes me think that it will develop fairly quickly in bottle. Try about four years.

1999 Botrytis Semillon ($185 per case)

Beautifully intense fruit, with pear and grapefruit characters. The palate is rich and luscious and has a lovely freshness and zing. Delicious. Best drunk while it's young and fresh.

Margan 1999 Shiraz ($19.70)

This is a beautiful young wine that's a good each-way bet. It has lovely, sweet berry fruit and is balanced and soft enough to drink quite soon, but I've no doubt it will cellar well for at least six years. During that time, it should develop lovely earthy complexity.

ADDRESS: Deasys Road, Pokolbin 2320
TELEPHONE: (02) 4998 7587
FAX: (02) 4998 7884
E-MAIL: marshest@aljan.com.au
ESTABLISHED: 1971
CELLAR DOOR: 10am–4.30pm Mon–Fri, 10am–5pm weekends
OWNERS: The Marsh family
VITICULTURIST: Andrew Marsh
WINEMAKERS: Andrew Marsh and Peter Marsh
1999 PRODUCTION: 7500 cases
MAILING LIST: Yes
DISTRIBUTED: Cellar door only
FEATURES: Private tasting room available.

Local doctor Quentin Taperell planted vines on this property on Deasys Road in 1971. The early wines were rather erratic in quality, but you could see enough to know that the vineyard had the potential to grow very good fruit. That potential didn't go unnoticed by Peter Marsh, a pharmacist who had been one of the early partners in Terrace Vale, next door. When Taperell decided to move to a new site in Palmers Lane and start a sparkling wine venture, Marsh took over, making his first vintage in 1978.

The vineyards have expanded to 40 hectares, planted to semillon, chardonnay, merlot, shiraz and cabernet sauvignon. Peter's son Andrew has gradually been taking over more of the responsibility and together they have built a solid reputation for Marsh Estate as one of the best small producers in the Hunter.

Not many Marsh Estate wines have come my way recently – they're sold only through the cellar door – but, as far as I can remember, I don't think I've ever had a poor one. I now know what I've been missing. The current range is one of the best I've come across. They're simply brilliant wines and the best are of breathtaking quality.

1999 Private Bin Semillon ($19.50)

This is one of the best semillons I have tried from the vintage. It has very good depth of fruit on the nose – ripe, with lovely vanilla and lemon characters. The palate is quite full bodied and round, with really excellent flavour and a lovely soft balance. If you're after a semillon with the flavour to drink young, look no further. Usually such wines develop fairly quickly, but I get the impression this could be a real keeper, too. Strongly recommended.

1999 Private Bin Shiraz ($25)

Deep purple–red. Incredibly rich berry fruit on the nose, with distinct, sweet vanilla oak, and showing great concentration. The palate is very rich and shows extraordinary depth and power, with really succulent, blackberry fruit. The wine has a lot of tannin, but this is so soft and balanced you barely notice it. A spectacular young shiraz that will develop brilliantly and gain great complexity. Don't be tempted to drink it now. Please give it ten years or so.

1998 Cabernet Sauvignon Vat N ($21)

Deepish colour with some brick beginning to appear. The nose is still a bit closed, but with

good depth and some cedary notes
beginning to appear. On the palate, there
is very good depth and concentration – real
sweet berry cabernet – and firm tannin
to finish. The wine needs a couple of years
for the bouquet to build and for complexity
to develop, and it will age much longer. It'll
be worth the wait.

ADDRESS: Lot 3 De Beyers Road, Pokolbin 2320
TELEPHONE: (02) 4998 7754
FAX: (02) 4998 7754
WEB: www.skybusiness.com/mcleishhunterwines
ESTABLISHED: 1985
CELLAR DOOR: 10am–5pm Fri–Mon or by appointment
OWNERS: Bob and Maryanne McLeish
VITICULTURIST: Graham Doran (contract)
WINEMAKER: Iain Riggs (contract)
1999 PRODUCTION: About 2200 cases
MAILING LIST: Yes
DISTRIBUTED: Direct from vineyard
FEATURES: Participation in Hunter Harvest Festival and Budburst Festival.

Bob McLeish is a heavy construction engineer whose business has frequently taken him overseas. At home, a more restful existence called, so in 1985 Bob and his wife Maryanne bought a block behind Tulloch on De Beyers Road and planted vines. For the first few years they lived in a caravan on weekends, but they now have a home-from-home and cellar door. 'We want it to be as relaxing as possible for visitors,' Bob told me, in such a laid-back way that it was pretty convincing.

Bob and Maryanne's first vintage was made in their garage in Sydney but they've now opted for a more relaxed method and pass the grapes to Iain Riggs at Brokenwood.

The McLeishes now have 6.3 hectares of vineyard planted with semillon, chardonnay, shiraz, cabernet sauvignon and verdelho.

Of the two whites I tasted, I preferred the semillon. The 1999 Chardonnay is very individual, with strong, buttery malolactic flavours and a full-bodied, slightly oily palate. I found those flavours a bit too much but they're exactly what the McLeishes want. Besides, my taste clearly isn't representative, as apparently the wine's simply walking out the door.

1999 Semillon ($15)

The nose has really beautiful depth of semillon fruit, with a touch of vanilla, in the classic Pokolbin mould. The palate's delicate, with very good flavour and balance, yet has lovely, intense flavour. A brilliant young semillon that I'd strongly recommend for those who want some superb drinking in five to ten years' time.

ADDRESS: Broke Road, Pokolbin 2321
TELEPHONE: (02) 4930 7332
FAX: (02) 4930 7100
E-MAIL: meereapark@hunterlink.net.au
WEB: www.meereapark.com.au
ESTABLISHED: 1991
CELLAR DOOR: Boutique Wine Centre, Broke Road
OWNERS: The Eather family
WINEMAKER: Rhys Eather
1999 PRODUCTION: 12,000 cases
MAILING LIST: Yes
DISTRIBUTED: The Main Domain Wine Company (NSW); The National Wine Merchant (SA); Liquor 2000 (Qld); and export.

Thomas Eather and family arrived in the Hunter Valley in 1826 when they settled on a large property near Bulga, which they called Meerea, meaning 'beautiful mountain'. As was common at the time, the Eathers had many crops, one of which was a vineyard planted along Cockfighter Creek.

At about the same time, a relative of the Eathers, Alexander Munro, planted the Bebeah vineyard between Singleton and Branxton, not far from the Kelman vineyard, Kirkton. The growth of his enterprise was so rapid that Munro had to buy grapes from other local vineyards and, at one time, had such large stocks that he could have supplied each person in New South Wales with half a bottle. He also exported to several countries. One of those grape growers was Thomas Eather, although when Eather's wife discovered that her husband was supporting Munro's 'immoral liquor trade' he was forced to replant his vineyard with table grapes. The Temperance Movement has a long history.

Munro's greatest international success was at the 1882 Bordeaux International Exhibition of Wines where he was one of five Hunter winemakers to receive gold medals; the others were William Kelman at Kirkton, Carl Brecht at Rosemount,

John Wyndham at Dalwood and Philobert Terrier at St Helena. As a result of these and other international successes, particularly against the French, the New South Wales Legislative Assembly commissioned a report, which said of Bebeah, 'Of all the New South Wales exhibitors, Mr Munro, owner of vineyards at Bebeah, in the Hunter Valley, has sent the most remarkable collection; he is certainly an able grower; all his wines have been very properly treated; not one sample found faulty'.

Those same table grapes were grafted over to chardonnay in the 1970s and more chardonnay was planted in 1989 and 1994. In 1995, the Eather family sold Meerea Park to Newcastle businessman John Peschar but retained the name. By this time, Rhys Eather had caught the wine bug and the family had planned its return to the wine industry. With two ancestors like that, he probably didn't have much choice.

Their first wines were released in 1991. There are basically two ranges. At the top is the 'fountain' label, which shows and commemorates the fountain in Burdekin Park, Singleton, which Munro gave to the town after retiring as its first mayor. These wines are entirely from the Hunter. Within this are three 'Alexander Munro' wines – semillon, chardonnay and shiraz – which are 'the best Meerea Park can offer each year'. The 'art style' label offers wines from various regions where vineyard, grape variety and year combine to produce good quality.

The '99 Semillon has moderate depth of fruit and a nice fresh balance, more a keeper – say, six years – than a drink-now wine. The '98 Alexander Munro Chardonnay is the opposite: a big, tropical-flavoured wine that's absolutely ready and should be drunk soon.

1998 Alexander Munro Shiraz ($45)

This is a very closed-up, tight wine at present – a typical 1998. However, there's great, latent fruit there and, given time, this should open out magnificently. Give it ten years and you'll have a wonderful, mature Hunter with considerable flavour. It shouldn't tire till well past twenty. Great quality.

ADDRESS: 341 Mount View Road, Millfield 2325
TELEPHONE: (02) 4998 1571
FAX: (02) 4998 0172
E-MAIL: millfieldwines@bigpond.com.au
ESTABLISHED: 1997
CELLAR DOOR: 10am–4pm Fri & Sat
OWNERS: David and Sue Lowes
WINEMAKER: David Fatches
2000 PRODUCTION: 4000 cases
MAILING LIST: Yes
DISTRIBUTED: Direct from vineyard

I can't remember a Hunter winery bursting on to the scene in quite the way Millfield has. A gold medal and two trophies at the 1998 Hunter Valley Show for its first semillon, the '98; a gold for the first chardonnay the following year; rave reviews from the UK wine press; similar enthusiasm from the Australian press. And the wines deserve it all.

David and Sue Lowes built their winery barely in time for the 1998 vintage. (Note the 's' in their name; this is not David Lowe of Lowe Family and (previously) Rothbury. However, to add to potential confusion, David 'singular' was consulting to David 'plural' in the early stages.) David's in commercial banking, previously with Schroeder's and now with Chase Manhattan.

At present the Loweses have just a small, bush-pruned vineyard around the winery but more vines will follow later. They currently buy grapes on contract from other growers – and pretty good grapes they must be, too. You can't make wines like these from ordinary fruit. David Fatches, who has made all their wines to date, has behind him experience at Wyndham Estate and Sutherland and a few vintages in Bordeaux. His brief was to concentrate on the Hunter classics and that's exactly what he's done,

with semillon, shiraz and chardonnay. To reinforce the transformation that Hunter semillon and shiraz show with age, Millfield has already started laying down wines for a museum release programme.

The wines all have a really fine touch. There's no skin contact in the whites, no botrytis influence, and the oak, when used, is subtle. They are all elegant, stylish wines, but certainly don't lack flavour. Good though the chardonnays are, David F knows that this is where his biggest challenge lies. 'To make great chardonnay, you've got to have layers on layers of complexity,' he told me. He's using a multiplicity of fermentation and maturation techniques to achieve this. The shiraz lacks a bit of weight at present, something David acknowledges, although he showed me some '00 wines in wood which have much greater strength.

The very stylish, understated labels perfectly match the wines.

1998 Semillon ($19.50)

This is a simply brilliant wine – the double trophy winner. The nose is quite full, with intense vanilla fruit and some straw appearing with bottle age. On the palate, there are very complex hay and straw characters, sweet fruit and a lovely soft balance. The wine has terrific length. It will develop beautifully until at least 2005.

1999 Semillon ($19.50)

Another very good wine, without the great length of the '98, but still with intense lemon and hay character. It will age as well as the '98, possibly longer.

1998 Chardonnay ($22)

Beautiful, ripe peachy fruit on the nose, with subtle oak and a little development. The palate is filling out well, with rich flavour, softness and complexity, although it's still quite fine, for all that character. Drink it immediately or within a year or so.

The '99 ($22) has fresh melon fruit and nice butterscotch complexity from malolactic and lees aging. It should go the same way as the '98, perhaps staying a bit finer.

1999 Shiraz ($20) and *1998* Shiraz ($18)

I greatly preferred the '99, which has very traditional Hunter characters, with some leather and earth already showing over the red berry fruit. It has a good balance and soft tannins and will develop well over three or four years. The '98 has similar characters, but is lighter in weight and should only need another couple of years to reach its best.

Mistletoe Wines

ADDRESS: Hermitage Road, Pokolbin 2335
TELEPHONE: (02) 4998 7770
FAX: (02) 4998 7792
E-MAIL: mistletoe@hunterlink.net.au
WEB: mistletoe.com.au
ESTABLISHED: 1989
CELLAR door: 11am–4pm Mon–Fri, 11am–6pm weekends & public holidays
OWNERS: Ken and Gwen Sloan
VITICULTURISTS: Ken Sloan and Ken Bray
WINEMAKER: John Reynolds (contract)
1999 PRODUCTION: 2700 cases
MAILING LIST: Yes, and wine club
DISTRIBUTED: Direct from the vineyard and export.
FEATURES: Two private guest rooms in Mistletoe Guesthouse, overlooking the vineyard.
Picnic and barbecue facilities. Pokolbin Gallery, featuring fine art.

Many years back, this block was owned by Johnnie 'JK' Walker, the Sydney restaurateur and wine merchant who did so much to introduce his customers to wine and the Hunter Valley. The Sloans bought the property from JK's son John in 1989. They had had a long love affair with wine and had been frequent visitors to the Hunter from the New South Wales Central Coast, where Ken had been a manufacturer of souvenirs – soft toys, chocolate-coated macadamias, and so on. You'll have seen his stuff in duty free shops. After managing a hundred staff, you'd think Ken would be taking it easy, but he still seems to have his hands full.

Mistletoe was one of the early estates in the Hunter, giving its name to this area around Hermitage Road. The Sloans' land had also been part of Hermitage Estate and when this company fell on hard times in the 1970s it removed the vines and the posts ... but not the wires. Ken says the local tractor garage has been kept in business solely on mending his punctures.

The Sloans planted shiraz, semillon and chardonnay over 1990 and 1991 and they now have 4.5 hectares under vine. Their cellar door building has a gallery next to the tasting area, with displays of art and crafts from several artists in the Lower Hunter and Lake Macquarie area. The Sloans have an arrangement with Cooks Hill Fine Art Galleries in Newcastle.

All the wines I tried were very good. Mistletoe is clearly a maker that deserves to be better known.

'It's a shame you weren't here yesterday,' Ken told me. 'We had a vertical of all our semillons for the Wine Club'. Hmm. It sounds like it's worth being a member. I can at least give you a mini-vertical below.

The 1998 Chardonnay has fresh, melon fruit, a nice touch of oak and a soft, round, well-balanced palate. The Shiraz from the same vintage has rich berry fruit, with some earthy complexity beginning to show, and a lovely, rich, soft palate. It's a good each-way bet: drink it now or cellar it for at least six years. There is also a Rosé from the 2000 vintage that is absolutely delicious. It's packed with fresh, juicy fruit and the sweetness is balanced by a light touch of tannin. Drink it straightaway.

1999 Semillon ($16)

Light, lemon-grass character on the nose with a trace of cheese, possibly from fermentation. The palate is crisp and fresh, with good flavour. Good aging potential.

1998 Semillon ($16)

This is a real contrast with the traditional Hunter semillon. It has been picked much riper yet still fermented dry, so it has a very soft, round palate with a fullness approaching a chardonnay. The flavour is still fresh, with lovely vanilla overtones. The wine has great development prospects over five years or so. Strongly recommended.

1997 Semillon ($17)

Good, developing, toasty characters appearing on the nose over lemony fruit. Fresh, lightly structured palate, with good fruit and balance. A good wine from a difficult year. It will age further.

1996 Semillon ($17)

The nose is showing very attractive, developed semillon character, yet the palate remains quite tight and fresh, which says there's still potential there. This is more the classic Hunter style than the '98. Drink it by 2001 or keep for a few more years.

ADDRESS: Talga Road, Lovedale 2321
TELEPHONE: (02) 9816 4088
FAX: (02) 9816 2680
ESTABLISHED: 1984
CELLAR DOOR: No
OWNERS: Andrew and Hady Simon and John Baker
VITICULTURIST: Ken Bray
WINEMAKER: Rhys Eather
1999 PRODUCTION: 3600 cases
MAILING LIST: Yes
DISTRIBUTED: Red+White Wine (NSW)
FEATURES: Accommodation in fully equipped, four-bedroom house in the vineyard.

Molly Morgan must have been an extraordinary woman. She was a Second Fleet convict, transported for stealing £4 worth of yarn, but escaped back to England after five years and lived bigamously with a second husband until he accused her of setting fire to his house. Within a few years she was back in New South Wales, again for petty theft, but this time she was eventually settled in the Hunter Valley, where she took a land grant on the site of today's Maitland CBD. She was widely praised for her charitable work with the sick and for building a school and a church. She also bought land on the ridge near Allandale, which now bears her name.

Molly Morgan Vineyard was planted on this same ridge by Sydney barrister Geoff Petty in 1984. In 1997, three partners – Andrew and Hady Simon and John Baker – bought the vineyard, to which had already been added part of the original Belbourie vineyard, which gives Molly Morgan fruit from nearly forty-year-old vines. The Simons were for many years the owners of Camperdown Cellars, which they developed into Sydney's biggest wine retailer, with a great reputation for service. They had also been partners in the Simon Whitlam vineyard and Arrowfield, with Nick Whitlam. Baker had also been

in the retail wine trade, at various times owning Quaffers in Double Bay, The Newport Bottler and Grapefellas at Epping.

Between the two vineyards, Molly Morgan now has nearly 12 hectares, nearly 6 of these being old semillon on the Belbourie block, plus chardonnay, shiraz and some additional semillon. Until recently, the wines were made by Geoff Broadfield, but now Rhys Eather has the job.

Old Vines Semillon *1999* and *Joe's Block* Semillon *1999* (both $18.90)

These are two quite similar wines in the classic 'keeping' style of Hunter semillon. Joe's Block is showing just a touch of development, with some honey notes appearing on the nose, while the OV is fresh and lemony. Both wines are fine and delicate on the palate, and both will clearly develop well, but the OV has more fruit intensity, making it the better long-term proposition. They'll both blossom in time, but the OV will be that much more rewarding.

1999 Chardonnay ($19.75)

Attractive bacony overtones give this wine some complexity, complementing the full, melon fruit. The palate is quite full bodied, with plenty of fresh flavour and a suggestion of sweetness. Good drinking while very young.

1998 Shiraz ($19.75)

The nose shows very attractive fruit, with some raspberry overtones and a little sweet, sappy new oak. There's good, quite complex flavour on the palate, a nice balance and plenty of soft tannin. You could enjoy this before 2001, but it will be so much better with another five years or so in bottle.

Moorebank

ADDRESS: Palmers Lane, Pokolbin 2321
TELEPHONE: (02) 4998 7610
FAX: (02) 4998 7367
E-MAIL: moorebank@ozemail.com.au
WEB: www.moorebank.com.au
ESTABLISHED: 1977
CELLAR DOOR: 10am–4pm Fri–Mon & public holidays. Other days by appointment.
OWNERS: Debra Moore and Ian Burgess
VITICULTURIST: Ian Burgess
WINEMAKER: Iain Riggs and Gary Reed (contract)
1999 PRODUCTION: 2000 cases
MAILING LIST: Yes and wine club
DISTRIBUTED: Direct from the vineyard

This property started as the Kerguelen Vineyard, which Debra Moore and Ian Burgess bought in 1977. 'Burgo' was managing the cellar door sales area at Wyndham Estate at the time. They now have 6 hectares of vineyard, planted to chardonnay, semillon, merlot and gewürztraminer. Their shed on the property houses aged winemaking equipment from an old winery that belonged to Debra's forebears.

Their business card cum leaflet reads 'Moorebank's intention is to stay small to maintain attention to detail with quality control of fruit, pruning and ever increasing research into reduced pesticide usage. The pre-requisite being to enhance and encourage the laws and rhythms of nature, as fine wine begins long before it goes to the winery.' This may sound rather 'high muesli', but the wines are down to earth. They also sell a range of unfermented grape products, like jams, coulis and pickled grapes.

1999 Summar Semillon ($21.50)

The nose is quite floral, with intense grassy notes. Lightness and crispness are the main features on the palate, with that grassiness again showing, and there's reasonable length. As the name (sort of) suggests, this

is a refreshing glass of wine now. It should also improve over a few years. And yes, it is summar!

1999 Gewürztraminer *Dry Style* ($21.50)

This is a white for people who want to know they have something in their mouth. It's big, ripe and full bodied – almost viscous – with rich lychee flavour, distinct tannin and a dry finish. Some traminer's not for wimps, and this wine proves it. In Alsace they'd drink this with roast goose and pickled cabbage. We might have to settle for Thai.

1999 Charlton Chardonnay ($25.50)

A very individual style of chardonnay, as it relies for much of its character on strong, coconutty American oak. All the same, the nose is fresh and the palate has plenty of fruit. The wine's of medium body and the finish is soft and balanced, without much impact from oak tannin. It will develop in the short term, but will be best as an early drinker.

1999 Merlot ($25.50)

This is a deliciously attractive young merlot. In the mouth, you'll find the supple fleshiness that merlot should bring, and good berry and leafy flavour. A distinct tannin grip on the finish doesn't destroy the balance. That same sweet fruit gives the nose a fragrant lift, assisted by a little new oak. The wine will clearly develop well for several years, but most people will enjoy it now for its seductive flavours.

Spicy Grape Sauce ($18.50)

This is simply great stuff! It's a sweet/ savoury grape sauce, flavoured with allspice and other exotic flavours, that would go brilliantly with cold meats or sausages. I had it with beef and rocket patties – yum!

Mount Broke Wines

ADDRESS: Adams Peak Road, Broke 2330
TELEPHONE: (02) 6579 1313
FAX: (02) 6579 1313
E-MAIL: mt.broke.wines@hunterlink.net.au
ESTABLISHED: 1997
CELLAR DOOR: 10am–5pm weekends & public holidays, or by appointment
OWNERS: Phil and Jo McNamara
VITICULTURIST: Phil McNamara
WINEMAKER: Contract – Monarch Winemaking Services
1999 PRODUCTION: About 300 cases
MAILING LIST: Yes
DISTRIBUTED: Direct from vineyard
FEATURES: Cafe and wine tasting facilities opening in mid-2000.

This vineyard is one of the most recent additions to the Broke area. It lies on the west side of the Wollombi Brook, to the south of the village, an area that's largely unexploited for vineyards to date, and it should have good potential. The McNamaras have planted 8 hectares of vineyard comprising merlot, shiraz, cabernet sauvignon, verdelho and barbera. The vineyard is difficult to find, although this will presumably change once the new facilities are open. The McNamaras sent scant information and no wines have come my way. There was no one at home when I called, so I can't tell you anything more about them.

ADDRESS: 1325 Broke Road, Broke 2330
MAIL: 59 Cassilis Street, Coonabarabran NSW 2357
TELEPHONE: (02) 6842 3271
FAX: (02) 6842 3330
E-MAIL: mounteyre@email.com
ESTABLISHED: 1970
CELLAR DOOR: No. Broke Village Store & the Hunter Valley Wine Society
OWNERS: Eve & Aniello Iannuzzi, Theo & Soula Tsironis
VITICULTURIST: Neil Grosser (contract)
WINEMAKER: Dan Crane (contract)
MAILING LIST: Yes

Mount Eyre was recently bought by a small partnership headed by Dr Aniello Iannuzzi from Coonabarabran. The 20 hectares of vineyard are planted to semillon, chardonnay, shiraz, cabernet franc and cabernet sauvignon.

I liked the 1998 Semillon as a young wine; it had delicate, lemony flavour and the acid balance to ensure a good life. Their other wines have not come my way, as Dr Iannuzzi preferred to wait until the 2000 vintage was available, from their new winemaker.

Mount Pleasant

ADDRESS: Marrowbone Road, Pokolbin 2320
TELEPHONE: (02) 4998 7505
FAX: (02) 4998 7761
E-MAIL: mcwines@mcwilliam's.com.au
WEB: www.mcwilliam's.com.au
ESTABLISHED: 1921
CELLAR DOOR: 10am–4.30pm 7 days. Coaches by appointment.
OWNERS: McWilliam's Wines
VITICULTURIST: Graham Doran
WINEMAKERS: Philip Ryan and Scott Stevens
MAILING LIST: Yes
DISTRIBUTED: McWilliam's Wines, nationally
FEATURES: Winery tours at 11am each day for a small charge. Elizabeth's Cafe.

This vineyard was planted in the 1880s by Charles King, but for much of its history its name has been inextricably linked with that of Maurice O'Shea. O'Shea was by all accounts an interesting character, born of a French mother and Irish father, and sent to study winemaking in France. On his return in 1921, the family bought the King property, which O'Shea renamed Mount Pleasant. O'Shea rapidly gained a reputation as a skilled winemaker and gifted blender of wine. He sourced wines from several other regions of Australia, including north-east Victoria and McLaren Vale, as well as from other Hunter winemakers. Often he used code names for his wines, so that 'Richard' or 'TY' indicated the wines had been bought from Dan Tyrrell, 'Charles' from Elliotts and so on. I'm not sure if 'Stephen' was one of these, but the '52 was a stunner. The codes extended to wines from his own vineyards: the Old Hill vineyard became 'OH', the Old Paddock 'OP' and the Rosehill Vineyard 'RH', and some of these abbreviations continue to this day.

The O'Shea style was often one of subtlety, more than power (although, thanks to the hot, dry vintage, '57 Charles was a simply immense wine). I have tried several O'Sheas labelled 'Light Dry Red', possibly never

intended for even short-term aging, which have lasted gracefully for fifty years. His series of 'Mountain' wines in the late 1930s was extraordinary and 1954 Richard Hermitage was one of the greatest reds of its time. In only the last few years, I have drunk reds from 1945 and 1947 which have opened magnificently. Other greats are too numerous to mention.

It has been said that O'Shea was a poor business manager. To be fair, he had bought into the wine industry at an appalling time. Vineyards were being pulled up; Lindemans, the most successful Hunter company of the previous sixty years, had gone into receivership; and sales of table wine were falling with the rise of fortifieds. Whatever the reason, a distant company from the Riverina, McWilliam's, bought a share of the winery in 1932 and acquired full ownership in 1941. With McWilliam's' support, O'Shea was able to expand his vineyards, although what sort of business sense this made at the time, I am not sure. They bought the Lovedale Vineyard, next to the airstrip on the Branxton Road, from the Love family in 1938. (Alas, the war intervened: the vineyard was acquired and the vines were pulled up to extend the airstrip. It was replanted after the war.) Then they bought land from the Dunn family in the early 1940s, which became the Rosehill Vineyard. This is on Broke Road opposite Lake's Folly and the Draytons' Lambkin Estate and it shares with those vineyards a rich red clay loam.

O'Shea died in 1956 and the baton passed to Brian Walsh, who had shared the winemaking duties with O'Shea for a short period before his death. In some sort of record, Mount Pleasant has only ever had three winemakers in its seventy-nine years: O'Shea, Walsh and the current winemaker Philip Ryan, who took over in 1978.

The vineyards now total 150 hectares and are planted with riesling, semillon, chardonnay, pinot noir, merlot, shiraz, cabernet franc, cabernet sauvignon and verdelho. Some of those vineyards are amongst the best in the valley. Lovedale, on sandy soil, is superb semillon country and provides the fruit for the reserve semillon 'Lovedale', previously known as 'Anne'. Rosehill and the vineyards on the slopes of Mount Bright near the winery are on wonderful red clay loams, the best land for reds. However, attempts to find new sites weren't always successful; the 'Hundred Acre', along McDonalds Rd next to Rothbury, lasted barely ten vintages. Mount Pleasant also buys a substantial amount of fruit from contract growers.

The Mount Pleasant style of white and red has evolved for the better under Phil Ryan's stewardship. In the 1960s and 70s, the whites were quite lean, with a rather appley hardness, but they are now softer and have more middle palate. The reds have always been of a softer, more delicate style than those from other companies, and Phil hasn't lost that softness. What he has done is increase the flesh and the flavour. He's also got rid of the tarry character that marked – or marred, depending on your attitude – the wines for many years. The source of this character, which was present in the McWilliam's Riverina reds as well, was the subject of much speculation in the industry and the company was very

sensitive to comment. It was probably mercaptan derived but, anyway, it's gone.

My notes below concentrate on semillon and shiraz. It's not that the other varieties don't warrant attention. The current '98 and '97 chardonnays are very good indeed and are much more complex than in previous years. The '98 O'Shea Chardonnay is similar, with either solids fermentation or skin contact giving a light tannin texture to the wine. Also there's a tremendous '98 Merlot, with rich berry fruit, complex earthy characters and plenty of firm tannin. It's just that the semillons and shirazes are even better and have a greater pedigree.

The '95 and '96 Elizabeths are looking very good at present, with a little more fullness and softness than some other recent vintages. As always, they are great value in aged semillon, even if the price is beginning to creep up. (And so it should.) However, the '95 Lovedale, below, is a stunner.

1995 Lovedale Semillon ($38.50)

Mid-yellow colour. The nose is simply beautiful, with very intense developing vanilla character. The palate is even more startling, the wonderful softness, balance and roundness in the mouth being the main features. The flavour is very complex, with lovely bottle-aged characters, yet it is still fresh. It's intriguing to find that this wine has skipped from the '86 to the '95 vintage. (I don't know whether there's a wine in between waiting for a later release). Compared with the '84 and '86 Lovedales, this wine seems to be developing more quickly, although I don't really mind, as it is so simply delicious and clearly has a few years ahead of it yet. A great example of developing Hunter semillon. Buy it.

Mount Henry Pinot Shiraz *1997* ($25.50)

This is quite an intriguing wine. It's not obviously a pinot blend, but it does have attractive, sweet fruit character. The nose has good depth, with some red berries, and the palate starts the same way.

Quite quickly, however, it becomes firm and tight, more typical of the vintage than the varieties. The wine has good flavour and will clearly age very well, to become complex, aged wine. It will be fascinating to see how much it softens in the process.

Rosehill Shiraz *1997* ($24.70)

Rather closed nose, with very good depth of fruit and some spicy overtones. The palate has wonderfully rich flavour, yet it's still quite latent and doesn't seem to be giving as much as it wants to. It's also quite firm and undeveloped. There's no great point in drinking this yet, but have faith. The wine has great potential, so just leave it alone for at least six years.

Old Paddock and *Old Hill* Shiraz *1996* ($24.70)

If ever there was a red to speak of the change in Mount Pleasant, this is it. It is a huge contrast to the weak OPs and OHs of recent memory. The nose is very undeveloped, with excellent depth of rich fruit and some cloves and cedar characters from new oak. The palate is also quite backward, with wonderful flavour and plenty of soft tannin. This is a tremendous Hunter red in the making. The flavour will fill out further and the bouquet will build a lovely fragrance and complexity. Just give it time. Ten years should do.

Maurice O'Shea Shiraz *1996* ($31.75)

I compared this with the OP and OH above for some time. There are strong similarities, but this wine seems to have greater richness, a fuller body and an even greater future than the earlier wine. It has layers of soft, ripe tannins and a wonderful, fleshy balance. A great Hunter red.

ADDRESS: Mount View Road, Mount View 2325
TELEPHONE: (02) 4990 3307
FAX: (02) 4991 1289
E-MAIL: mountviewestate@bigpond.com
ESTABLISHED: 1971
CELLAR DOOR: Yes
OWNERS: Polly and John Burgess
VITICULTURIST: Harry Tulloch
WINEMAKER: Harry Tulloch
1999 PRODUCTION: 4500 cases
MAILING LIST: Yes, and wine club
DISTRIBUTED: Direct from the vineyard
FEATURES: Two wine releases a year to coincide with the two Mount View Region festivals:
Harvest Festival in April; and Vines, Wines and Music in October.

When the Tulloch family sold their winery to Reed Paper Mills in 1969, Harry Tulloch was a reluctant vendor but didn't have the wherewithal to buy out the rest of the family. Instead, he started Mount View. At this stage, Harry was already an accomplished viticulturist. He had managed the establishment of the Hollydeen vineyard near Denman in the 1960s and also served as a research viticulturist with the Department of Agriculture in South Australia.

Harry's son Keith graduated from Roseworthy in 1984 and shared the winemaking duties at Mount View, in later years working also at Lindemans and, from 1993 to 1996, The Rothbury Estate. Since leaving Rothbury, Keith has worked as a winemaking consultant.

At the start, Mount View specialised in verdelho, but the vineyard has since grown to 7 hectares with the addition of semillon, chardonnay, pinot noir, merlot, shiraz and cabernet sauvignon. Like his dad before him, Keith didn't have the readies, nor perhaps the inclination, to take over Mount View when Harry decided to sell. So, in April 2000, the property was bought by Polly and John Burgess. John is the manager of the Sydney Aquarium and now commutes weekly to his day job. Polly manages Mount View, so she's the one you're likely to see during the week. Harry Tulloch will still be around to give them advice in the early stages.

If you like big-flavoured whites, the '98 Reserve Chardonnay is for you. It has complex flavour, with heaps of ripe peachy fruit, oak and malolactic, but you'll need to drink it soon. The '96 Liqueur Verdelho ($18, 375 ml), which has a bit of a cult following, is delicious, with toffee and nectarine characters and lovely softness and balanced sweetness. I bet it's great with soft cheeses.

1999 Verdelho ($16)

Fresh, youthful pineapple fruit on the nose leads to a richer than expected flavour, with very good depth. There's a bit of tannin, which dries the finish but leaves the wine with good overall balance. An attractive verdelho that won't get any better.

1998 Reserve Verdelho ($17)

This is quite a contrast to the '99. There's very ripe tropical fruit on the nose, with some toastiness from bottle age giving complexity. The palate is full bodied and very full flavoured yet is not blowing out, and the finish is still quite tight. All the same, it's not

Mount View

a wine I'd be keeping, so enjoy it as soon as you can with richly flavoured food.

1998 Reserve Shiraz ($24)

Raspberry and spice characters are to the fore on the nose, and a little earthiness is appearing with bottle age. There's a hint of liquorice, too. The wine is rich and full flavoured, soft and round in the mouth, with complex characters and plenty of balanced tannin. This could be drunk right away, but will be so much better with time in the bottle.

1998 Reserve Merlot ($22)

It's good to see merlot performing so well in the Hunter. This one has quite a complex nose, with rich, fleshy fruit and lovely berry character. The palate is plump and round, with a beautifully soft balance and plenty of fine tannin. It probably won't continue to show distinctive varietal character, but it should develop into a beautifully mellow, soft wine over many years.

ADDRESS: 1239 Milbrodale Road, Broke 2330
TELEPHONE: (02) 4965 8777 or 6579 1499
FAX: (02) 4965 8666 or 6579 1477
E-MAIL: gail@nightingalewines.com.au
ESTABLISHED: 1997
CELLAR DOOR: 10am–4pm Fri–Sun; Wed, Thurs by appointment
OWNERS: Paul and Gail Nightingale
VITICULTURISTS: Paul Nightingale and Andrew Margan
WINEMAKER: Andrew Margan (contract)
1999 PRODUCTION: 3000 cases
MAILING LIST: Yes, and boutique wine club
DISTRIBUTED: To restaurants by own sales team
FEATURES: A variety of events through the year – Annual Grape Stomp, March;
Christmas in July; Nightingale Wines Anniversary, September; Carols by Candlelight;
and New Year's Eve.

Wine labels are an integral part of selling wine. Sometimes they can get you to buy a vineyard. Paul and Gail Nightingale have a publishing business in Warners Bay, near Newcastle, producing educational books and CD ROMs. They had been disagreeing over one of the new McGuigan labels and eventually could only settle the argument with a bet. Gail won, and Paul paid out with shares in McGuigan Wines. As they became involved in the company through shareholders' meetings and so on, one thing led to another, and eventually they bought land just outside Broke and planted a 12 hectare vineyard of semillon, chardonnay, verdelho, shiraz and cabernet sauvignon.

They have since started a mail order Club Boutique and added a winery and Tasting House for cellar door sales. You can't miss the flags after you drive out of Broke. Presiding over all is the Nightingale emblem, which to me looks more like an owl than a nightingale. (But, then, the owl is a much more distinguished looking bird.)

If you enjoy a soft, sweeter style of verdelho, Nightingale's '99 should appeal to you. It has plenty of flavour, too. The '99 Semillon is a fuller, broader wine than most from the year, giving it enough flavour for early drinking, and there's a little honey from bottle age there already. It should develop well in the short term into a big 'Hunter White Burgundy' style. The '99 Botrytis Semillon has intense, fresh, lemony fruit and well balanced sweetness. It's not especially complex but the freshness and flavour make it delicious. Their Gail Force Port didn't blow me away, though.

1999 Unwooded Chardonnay ($17)

Unwooded chardonnay is a surprisingly difficult wine to get right. This one works because of its fruit quality. There's lovely fruit on the nose, with melon and white peach characters, and the palate is full-bodied, soft and round. There's a suggestion of sweetness that fits the overall balance. Drink it now for its fruit and freshness.

1999 Cabernet Sauvignon ($19)

Softness, flavour and drinkability are the words here. The wine has very attractive, sweet, berry fruit, very good balance and fine, soft tannins. It's not especially complex, nor constructed for long bottle aging, but is a simply delicious drink now.

Oakvale

ADDRESS: Broke Road, Pokolbin 2320
TELEPHONE: (02) 4998 7520
FAX: (02) 4998 7747
E-MAIL: info@oakvalewines.com.au
WEB: www.oakvalewines.com.au
ESTABLISHED: 1893
CELLAR DOOR: 10am–5pm 7 days
OWNERS: Richard Owens
VITICULTURIST: Stuart Davies
WINEMAKER: Michael Glover
1999 PRODUCTION: about 15,000 cases
MAILING LIST: Yes, with wine club
DISTRIBUTED: Direct from the vineyard
FEATURES: The Oakvale Wine and Food World – winery, cellar door, delicatessen, espresso coffee shop, 'the largest wine and food bookshop in NSW', Australian and overseas wine shop, 1890s Old General Store museum, children's playground and picnic tables. (Enough for you?)

The logo says 'Oakvale – family owned since 1893'. Not quite true, but forgivable. And the families have changed along the way.

The property had originally been a dairy farm, but coalminer William Elliott, who bought it in 1893, planted vines and built a winery. Over the years, the vineyards expanded as the Elliotts bought land at Belford, Broke/Fordwich and Pokolbin. The family was one of the few Hunter survivors from the early years, in part thanks to the Elliotts Wine Saloon on the Wollombi Road, Cessnock, which provided ready sales of fortified wines to the local public in the old 'fourpenny dark' days. (The saloon later became the headquarters for the Hunter Valley Wine Society and is now Corky's Restaurant.)

The Elliott table wines built a solid reputation. The reds came from the Oakvale Vineyard itself and from Tallawanta, between Broke and Thompsons roads. The whites were semillons from Fordwich and, particularly, the Belford Vineyard, which developed lovely honeyed flavours with age. In the 1950s and 60s, Elliott shiraz was a component of the Mildara Yellow Label Cabernet Shiraz, at the time one of the

greatest reds in the country and which still drinks magnificently today.

In 1974 Doug Elliott accepted an offer from Hermitage Estate (not a family, surely) and sold the business, with the exception of Belford, which is still owned by his son John. Hermitage went into receivership not long after and the Elliotts found themselves back at Oakvale. In 1985 they sold again, this time to a Sydney solicitor, Barry Shields, and his wife Jan. The Fordwich and Tallawanta vineyards went their separate ways; Fordwich is now owned by the Bainton family and Tallawanta by the new Hunter Village Gardens which is re-developing the area from McDonalds Road through to the Tallawanta Hotel.

Unfortunately, the Oakvale name suffered during these changes and a new generation of visitors was now coming to the Hunter unaware of the great Elliott reds. Also, the vineyards around the winery had been badly affected by the elephant and longicorn beetles, which can eventually destroy vines, so the Shieldses found they had little with which to re-build.

In 1999, they sold to businessman Richard Owens and his wife Mary. Owens was a successful retailer, starting the Shoeys supermarket chain, which later became Bi-Lo. He had already planted a section of vineyard in Milbrodale Road, Broke, which he called Milbrovale. Geographically speaking, he has therefore come close to re-uniting part of the original Elliott holdings, although the new Broke vineyard was planted more recently, in 1995, and is a short distance from the original Elliott vineyard.

Milbrovale totals 34 hectares and is planted to verdelho, semillon, chardonnay and shiraz. Oakvale is now barely 2 hectares. The Milbrovale wines, before the purchase of Oakvale and the 2000 vintage, were made on contract at The Rothbury Estate, and it is an ex-Rothbury winemaker, Michael Glover, who now makes the wines. There are a few wines labelled Milbrovale to work their way through the system but from now on all will appear under the Oakvale label. There are two ranges: Classic, on the one hand; and the slightly more expensive Peach Tree (whites) and Peppercorn (reds).

Both the semillons are truly classic Hunters, neither of them hugely user-friendly at present (in a typical Hunter semillon way) but which have extraordinary potential to age in bottle. Like many winemakers, Michael has some tremendous wines from 2000. I tasted several semillons with wonderfully rich fruit and a simply stunning shiraz from the old Oakvale vines, a very deeply coloured wine with powerful, sumptuous flavour and masses of soft tannin. It reminded me strongly of the old Elliott wines. They don't have much of it, so I pray it's kept separate.

1999 Classic Semillon ($16.95)

The two semillons were made using different methods, this one with highly protective winemaking – that is, using inert gas cover to prevent juice oxidation, keeping the juice cold and fermenting cold. It has a fragrant lift of fruit on the nose and delicate fruit on the palate, which has very crisp acidity and is even a touch lean.

1999 Peach Tree Semillon ($19.95)

This wine was made with more oxidative handling, so there's less fragrance on the nose and the fruit is not so obvious, but there's a fuller middle palate and better overall balance. You pays yer money … Both have at least ten years' development in them, during which they'll get much richer, toasty flavour. They're both recommended.

1999 Peach Tree Chardonnay ($22.95)

Full, peachy fruit on the nose with well-handled new oak. The palate is quite fine, with delicate yet intense fruit, and is fresh and well balanced overall. It's worth keeping till about 2001 if you want more fullness and some toasty complexity.

1998 Classic Shiraz ($18.95)

This was the first vintage off Milbrovale and it's turned out very well. It has lovely sweet and spicy fruit, with suggestions of raspberry and a touch of oak. The palate's of medium weight, with good flavour and a hint of chocolate, finishing with fine tannin. The wine will develop beautifully into a soft, stylish Hunter red. I actually preferred it to the more expensive 1999 Peppercorn Shiraz ($24.95), which shows a bit more new oak. In addition to the difference in flavour, the palate doesn't quite have the roundness of the Peach Tree.

Peacock Hill Vineyard

ADDRESS: Palmers Lane, Pokolbin 2320
TELEPHONE: (02) 4998 7661
FAX: (02) 4998 7661
ESTABLISHED: 1968
CELLAR DOOR: 10am–5pm Fri–Mon plus school & public holidays
OWNERS: George Tsiros and Sylvia Laumets
VITICULTURIST: George Tsiros
WINEMAKERS: David Lowe and Jane Wilson
1999 PRODUCTION: about 1500 cases
MAILING LIST: Yes
DISTRIBUTED: Direct from the vineyard
FEATURES: Peacock Hill Lodge, a two-bedroom guesthouse with many facilities including fully equipped kitchen and tennis court.

John Jenkins Peacock must have been one of the first settlers in the Pokolbin area when he took up a land grant here in 1841. I'm not sure whether he planted vines or whether it remained for The Rothbury Estate to do so in 1968, when it planted shiraz and cabernet sauvignon and, in 1984, chardonnay. Peacock Hill was managed as part of Rothbury's Herlstone Vineyard. Since Rothbury, the land has had several owners, including former Rothbury employees David Lowe and Dennis Power.

The current owners, George Tsiros and Sylvia Laumets, bought Peacock Hill in 1995 and have since been replacing the trellising and generally rejuvenating the vineyard. Where possible they have been using environmentally conscious methods of vineyard management. Nearly one hectare of merlot will be planted soon and a small area of cabernet franc reworked.

The vineyard and lodge have sweeping views over many parts of the Lower Hunter.

1998 Jaan Shiraz ($28)

This is an attractive, lighter bodied shiraz that has the softness and balance to drink well early. It's good drinking as a young wine and will gain some nice earthy complexity by 2003.

ADDRESS: 110 Old North Road, Belford 2335
TELEPHONE: (02) 9913 1088
FAX: (02) 9970 6152
WINERY TEL: (02) 6574 7222
E-MAIL: winedoc@sneaker.net.au
WEB: www.pendarves.com.au
ESTABLISHED: 1986
CELLAR DOOR: 11am–5pm weekends
OWNERS: Dr Philip and Mrs Belinda Norrie
VITICULTURIST: Ray Dibley
WINEMAKER: Greg Silkman (contract)
1999 PRODUCTION: 10,000 cases
MAILING LIST: No. 'Haven't time, yet.'
DISTRIBUTED: Haviland Wine Merchants, Broken Bay Beverages (NSW); and export.
FEATURES: Three-bedroom cottage with full facilities for rent (bookings, 02 4991 4000).
Pétanque and barbecues at the cellar door. Tasting room in French provincial style.

There may be people around with more energy and frankness than Philip Norrie, but I haven't met them. While others pursue their passions separately, Philip has combined his – medicine, history and wine – in several ways. As well as being a medical practitioner at Elanora Heights, on Sydney's upper North Shore, he has written books on doctors who have founded wine companies – Lindeman and Penfold – plus another on Leo Buring. His book *Vineyards of Sydney* is essential reading for anyone interested in the history of wine in Australia. He founded The Australian Medical Friends of Wine Society, published a booklet (with McWilliam's Wines) on wine and health and has written several other books. He has also rewritten the Wine and Health sections of the *Oxford Companion to Wine* (ed. Jancis Robinson)

Philip sees himself as 'the world's wine-industry wine doctor' and is writing a PhD thesis on the history of wine as medicine. This will provide him with more grit to abrade the anti-alcohol lobby. Grind, Philip, grind!

Somewhere he found the time to establish Pendarves Estate, near Belford, which now has 20 hectares of vines across a wide range of varieties. Philip's wife Belinda designed the Pendarves label, which commemorates

Australia's first vineyard on the shores of Sydney Cove.

Pendarves has won Most Successful Exhibitor awards at the Hunter Valley Small Winemakers Show plus several trophies and gold medals.

1999 Chambourcin ($17.75)

This shows how attractive chambourcin can be at an early age. It has a brilliant, deep-purple colour. The nose has beautiful, ripe, sweet berry fruit and shows very good depth. The softness, rich flavour and great balance make the wine delicious drinking and the tannins are really fine and soft. Enjoy this while it's fresh and lively. Many chambourcins don't age well and, besides, when this one's gone, there'll be the next vintage.

1998 Verdelho ($18.10)

Pendarves seems to have good success with this grape. There's good fruit on the nose, which is holding its freshness yet showing some toasty complexity. The palate has plenty of flavour, with a touch of sweetness you barely notice and a nice soft finish. It was probably at its best in 2000. The 1997 Verdelho is holding up surprisingly well, showing more toastiness than the '98, but is otherwise quite similar.

Pepper Tree Wines

ADDRESS: Halls Road, Pokolbin 2321
TELEPHONE: (02) 4998 7539
FAX: (02) 4998 7746
E-MAIL: ptwinery@peppertreewines.com.au
WEB: www.peppertreewines.com.au
ESTABLISHED: 1993
CELLAR DOOR: 9am–5pm weekdays, 9.30am–5pm weekends & public holidays
OWNER: James Fairfax
VITICULTURIST: Carl Davies
WINEMAKER: Chris Cameron
1999 PRODUCTION: 38,000 cases
MAILING LIST: Yes, and Premium Wine Club
DISTRIBUTED: Young and Rashleigh (NSW); Maxxium (Vic., Qld, SA, WA); and export
FEATURES: Merlot tasting and ball, November.

Pepper Tree started as Murray Robson Wines in a venture between Murray and James Fairfax. (See also under Briar Ridge.) The company became Pepper Tree after Murray's departure in 1993. Fairfax had acquired the Oakdale Vineyard, planted on the site of the original Audrey Wilkinson Vineyard, from the consortium of Sydney businessmen that had re-developed it in 1969, and this is the source of most of the company's Hunter fruit. Pepper Tree also owns 10 hectares of vineyard in Coonawarra and has planted in Western Australia.

Winemaker Chris Cameron has had extensive experience in sales and marketing; this shows in some innovative wine styles and packaging, which probably won't appeal to the traditionalists. He's also a very energetic promoter.

The Pepper Tree wines are flavoursome and very accessible. The Merlot has become a specialty, after the company picked up a major international award, although I found some of the early wines very oaky.

The brilliant Robert's Restaurant and The Convent Guesthouse are in the same 'village' complex, so what more do you need for a visit?

Pepper Tree has quite a range of wines from various regions and has made some interesting wines from malbec, a variety that doesn't often perform well in Australia. There's very little of it in the Hunter, but Pepper Tree seems to have done well with it. The '98 Reserve has good flavour and balance, with smoky oak giving complexity. I have seen inconsistency with some of the wines. The 1996 Shiraz was outstanding when I had it on release, but I recently found two bottles of it dull and rather oxidised. The 1997 was also a tremendous wine – full, soft and balanced, and with rich earthy character – and I hope it stays that way.

1998 Reserve Semillon ($19)

This wine says a lot about Hunter semillon. The nose is quite fine and delicate, with fresh lemon and hay characters. The palate is crisp and tight – really quite light in weight, but with good balance. And the label declares only 9.8 per cent alcohol. At that level, almost any other variety from any other region would be unbalanced and herbaceous – that is, under-ripe. But for Hunter semillon it's nothing unusual. Nevertheless, this wine is a keeper, unless you like very light, crisp young wines. Have faith; after a few years you'll see a transformation.

ADDRESS: Cnr Broke Road & Ekerts Lane, Pokolbin 2320
TELEPHONE: (02) 4998 7121
FAX: (02) 4998 7121
ESTABLISHED: 1987
CELLAR DOOR: 10am–5pm Wed–Sun
OWNER: Peter Ireland
VITICULTURIST: David Lowe
WINEMAKER: Peter Ireland and David Lowe
MAILING LIST: Yes
DISTRIBUTED: Direct from vineyard
FEATURES: Restaurant – Cafe Enzo. Antique shop. Peppers Creek Yacht Club accommodation.

The main focus when you arrive at Peppers Creek is on the antique shop. It's where you're most likely to park, and the winery and tasting area are next door. Here the emphasis is on the Lowe Family wines, as David and Jane Lowe base their cellar door sales here, although there are usually a few Peppers Creek wines available to try.

I wasn't all that fond of the '97 Chardonnay, which has strong orange peel characters from botrytis and is developing quickly. The '98 Semillon was much more enjoyable and more varietally typical.

1998 Semillon

The fruit on the nose is quite fine and just beginning to develop some complex, nutty characters. The wine's crisp and dry in the mouth, with lemony fruit and straw from development mingling. It should fill out and gain more flavour and complexity over several years.

Peschar Vineyards

ADDRESS: Milbrovale Road, Broke 2330
TELEPHONE: (02) 4952 2068
FAX: (02) 4952 2377
E-MAIL: john.peschar@peschar.com.au
WEB: www.peschar.com.au
ESTABLISHED: 1978
CELLAR DOOR: At Hunter Valley Wine Society, Broke Road, Pokolbin;
and the Broke Village Store
CHIEF EXECUTIVE: John Peschar
VITICULTURIST: Tim Lesnik
WINEMAKER: Tyrrell's (contract)
MAILING LIST: They don't say.

'No', John Peschar's secretary said, 'Mr Peschar is not interested in being in your book.'

'But isn't he interested in selling his wine?' I asked.

'Yes, but if you can't get the information off the website, then that's all.'

The website, in fact, told me very little. (The contact information above is from the *Australian and New Zealand Wine Industry Directory*.) One page of the website tells me the vineyard is at Broke, while another tells me it's in the Upper Hunter. I hope no one gets lost trying to find it.

It does tell me the Peschar family's 12 hectare vineyard is at Bulga and was originally planted 50 years ago. (This is approximately true for 2 hectares of the current twelve, which were originally planted to table grapes in the early 1950s and then grafted to chardonnay in the late 70s. More chardonnay was added in 1989 and 1994, making those vines 11 and 6 years old. The property and vineyard were bought from the Eather family (see the entry under Meerea Park). The grapes are apparently sold to Tyrrell's and a small proportion of the wine is bottled under the Peschar label.

The 1998 Chardonnay was awarded a silver in the Hunter Valley Wine Show in 1998 (I didn't judge that class) and again in 1999, so it should be a pretty good wine. The '99 appears not to have been entered in the 1999 show. The wines were not available for tasting when I called at the Broke Village Store and the Hunter Valley Wine Society, but you may have better luck.

Peterson House

ADDRESS: Cnr Broke & Branxton roads, Pokolbin 2320
TELEPHONE: (02) 4998 7881
FAX: (02) 4998 7882
WEB: www.petersonhouse.com.au
ESTABLISHED: 1994
CELLAR DOOR: 9am–5pm
OWNERS: The Peterson Family
VITICULTURIST: Ross Drayton
WINEMAKER: Gary Reed (contract)
MAILING LIST: Yes
DISTRIBUTED: Direct from the vineyard
FEATURES: Restaurant – Magnum Cafe, lunches 7 days, dinner Fri and Sat.

Even with Petersons and Calais operating successfully, Ian and Colin Peterson must have needed another challenge. In 1994 they bought land opposite Joe Lesnik on the Branxton Road and started Petersons' Champagne House. The 'Champagne' has gradually assumed less emphasis, probably because of the impending banning of the name for Australian wine.

The main building houses their sales area and a restaurant, Magnum Cafe. The méthode champenoise production takes place in a separate building and store behind. The base wines are fermented at Calais and returned to Peterson House for the second fermentation. The 12 hectare chardonnay vineyard that surrounds the complex provides part of the fruit required, the balance coming from Calais and Petersons.

The tasting area is very smartly set out and there you can taste a wide range of sparkling wines, including reds. I thought they had all been very well produced and there was only one – the '99 Sparkling Merlot – that I didn't take to because it had a very jammy fruit character.

1996 Semillon Pinot Noir ($22)

If you like big flavours in your sparklingwines, this is for you. The nose has developed toasty and candy characters and the palate concurs, with big flavour, quite a thick balance and persistent Vegemitey character on the finish. It's fully mature and lacks some elegance, but you certainly know you have it in your mouth.

1997 Chardonnay Pinot Noir ($22)

This is quite a contrast to the Semillon Pinot and altogether much finer. The nose is fresh and complex, with quite delicate fruit and a little breadiness. In the mouth, it's crisp, fine and fresh and quite in the mainstream style for these varieties. Very attractive.

1997 Pinot Chardonnay Pinot Meunier ($36)

The nose is altogether bigger than the Chardonnay Pinot, a lot of the difference coming from the mushroomy, fungal characters of the pinot meunier. This grape also fills out and broadens the palate and adds some very attractive, meaty complexity. It's adistinctive, flavoursome wine, but whether you think it's worth the difference in price is up to you.

ADDRESS: Mount View Road, Mount View 2320
TELEPHONE: (02) 4990 1704
FAX: (02) 4991 1344
ESTABLISHED: 1981
CELLAR DOOR: 9am–5pm Mon–Sat, 10am–5pm Sun
OWNERS: The Peterson family
VITICULTURIST: Ross Drayton
WINEMAKER: Gary Reed
1999 PRODUCTION: 15,000 cases
MAILING LIST: Yes and wine club
DISTRIBUTED: Classical Wines (NSW)

Petersons became one of the first new vineyards in the Hunter when local pharmacist Ian Peterson and his family established it in 1971. They had bought the land back in 1964, but hadn't thought of planting vines until most of their neighbours did. There must be something in this, they thought. At the start, they sold their grapes but in 1980 they built a winery and the following year employed Gary Reed as winemaker. They rapidly made a great name for themselves, particularly with chardonnay and semillon, although I remember some good shiraz, too. An unusual feature of one chardonnay was that it was a blend of three vintages, a treatment that worked surprisingly well, as it had the complexity and richness of an older wine with the freshness of youth. This continues today with their Cuvée, which is now a two-vintage blend.

They now have 20 hectares of vineyard across semillon, chardonnay, pinot noir, merlot, malbec, shiraz and cabernet sauvignon.

For many years the Peterson wines were made at the Calais winery, owned by Colin Peterson, but now that this has been sold

they'll be made in a new Peterson winery to be built near Mount View Road. Gary Reed is returning from Monarch as winemaker.

The '97 Semillon ($19.50) has some of the leanness of the year, but it does have good lemony fruit and is fresh. It will age for many years.

1998 'Shirley' Chardonnay ($28)

(I preferred this to the Cuvée ($19.50), which has attractive tropical fruit and good balance but lacks real complexity.) This has a very complex nose, with toasty oak and malolactic characters. The palate has really great flavour – melon fruit, oak, the works – and lovely balance and length, although you are paying for it.

1998 Back Block Shiraz ($42.80)

Here again, I preferred this to the cheaper '98 Shiraz which is a bit on the plain side. The Back Block has sweet, rich fruit with a slightly tarry overtone and distinct French oak. It's a typical '98 in the mouth – excellent depth of flavour and plenty of fine tannin and will develop well for many years.

Petersons

It actually needs some time for that oak to integrate.

1998 Cabernet Sauvignon ($27.10)

Here, I go the other way. The 1998 Back Block Cabernet is certainly the bigger wine, but it's a bit chewy and closed up, so it may not completely soften. I preferred the cheaper wine for its berry and leafy fragrance. It's balanced, flavoursome and easy to drink, with fine tannins, so you can enjoy it young, over a couple of years.

ADDRESS: 82 Elderslie Road, Branxton 2335
TELEPHONE: (02) 4938 1146
FAX: (02) 4938 1146
CELLAR DOOR: 10am–4pm weekends & public holidays
OWNERS: Peter and Anne Went
VITICULTURIST: Peter Went
WINEMAKER: David Hook (contract)
1999 PRODUCTION: 350 cases
MAILING LIST: Yes
DISTRIBUTED: Direct from the vineyard
FEATURES: Pierrot's Villa, a cottage overlooking the vineyard, available for overnight and longer accommodation.

Wine features strongly in the Went family. Anne's family comes from the Burgundy region of France and her father, Jean-Charles Renaud, worked in both the vineyards and winery at Dalwood Estate when they were owned by Penfolds. Time spent with his wife's family in Burgundy fired Peter's enthusiasm, to the extent that he studied viticulture and wine science at Charles Sturt University and now lectures in the same subjects at the Hunter Institute of Technology at Kurri Kurri.

They have combined the 'heart' of Burgundy with the 'head' of the Hunter by planting chardonnay and pinot noir alongside semillon and shiraz.

I tried their chardonnay and pinot noir and thought the pinot was the pick of the two, the chardonnay showing some hardness.

1999 Pinot Noir

Soft, sweet fruit on the nose, with good varietal character. The palate is soft and well balanced, the fruit nicely matched with a touch of oak. It's varietally true and attractive for early drinking.

Piggs Peake

ADDRESS: 697 Hermitage Road, Pokolbin 2335
TELEPHONE: (02) 6574 7000
FAX: (02) 6574 7070
E-MAIL: piggspeake@cn-newc.com.au
WEB: www.131shop.com.au
ESTABLISHED: 1997
CELLAR DOOR: 10am–4pm 7 days. Groups by appointment.
OWNERS: Bruce Willan, Steve Dodd and Tony Miller
WINEMAKERS: Steve Dodd and Lesley Minter
1999 PRODUCTION: 9000 cases
MAILING LIST: Yes
DISTRIBUTED: Direct from vineyard and export
FEATURES: Display of local artists, including Janine Matthews. Espresso coffee.

Naming wineries can be as difficult as naming children. The partners here were having trouble finding a name that clicked and were casting around for possibilities. Assistant winemaker Lesley Minter was reading a novel set in Swaziland, which has a mountain called Pig's Peak, and she threw this up as a half-serious suggestion. You can guess the rest. And, yes, they get people calling in just because they like the name. And, yes, one or two of these have been pig farmers.

Piggs Peake has only a small vineyard near the winery, so almost all the fruit is bought from growers. Hunter grapes predominate, but some red and a botrytis semillon come from Mudgee. Steve Dodd also does some contract winemaking for other small vineyards.

A particularly exciting wine is the 1998 Mudgee Tempranillo Cabernet. Tempranillo is a wonderful Spanish grape that has only recently been planted in Australia and this wine has the supple, fleshy palate and rich fruit that I'd expect from the variety. The 1999 Semillon ($18) is fresh and light, with a touch of vanilla from new oak and attractive flavour.

1999 Mount View Verdelho ($14)

Fine, pineapple fruit on the nose with beautiful freshness. The palate is medium bodied with good depth of flavour and a fine, soft finish. Good drinking.

1998 Lovedale Chardonnay ($20)

This wine has quite a full, buttery nose with a little development appearing and lending further complexity. The fruit and new oak are well married on the palate, which has medium weight and good depth of flavour. It's approaching its best.

1998 Lovedale Shiraz ($20)

The nose is very complex, with ripe, spicy fruit and distinct tarriness from highly toasted new oak. There's rich fruit on the palate, although I found that burnt oak character dominates at present. Otherwise, the palate's in good shape, with balance and fine tannins. Give it a few years and that oak should marry in better.

ADDRESS: McDonalds Road, Pokolbin 2320
TELEPHONE: (02) 4998 7524
FAX: (02) 4998 7765
E-MAIL: pokolbin@aljan.com.au
ESTABLISHED: 1980
CELLAR DOOR: 10am–6pm 7 days
OWNERS: John Hindman and Richard Friend
VITICULTURISTS: John Hindman and Phil Swanell
WINEMAKER: Neil McGuigan (white, contract), Monarch (red, contract)
MAILING LIST: Yes, starting
DISTRIBUTED: Direct from the vineyard
FEATURES: Taylor's Restaurant.

One of the owners has a company called Efficiency Displays Marketing, which I thought quite ironic, given Pokolbin Estate's complete lack of response to my several requests for information. Luckily the cellar door staff were very helpful.

Pokolbin Estate is currently in its most stable period for a while. In 1987 it was bought from the MacDougall family after Stanlee and Saxonvale folded. There are currently 11 hectares of vines, including semillon, shiraz, and riesling – one of the few remaining blocks of this variety in the Hunter. Many of the vines are quite old and this shows in the depth of fruit in the wines.

Of the chardonnays, I preferred the standard '98 ($19), which has good melon fruit and a nice touch of oak on the nose and a beautifully balanced, soft palate. The '98 Reserve ($24) is rather dominated by vanilla characters from new American oak.

1998 Semillon ($23)

Pokolbin Estate has turned out some top quality semillons. I remember a '96 or '95 that was outstanding. This '98 is looking very good, too, with a full nose showing plenty of varietal vanilla (but not from oak). The palate is soft and round, with lovely

flavour and balance. It's just beginning to come out of that 'in-between' phase and from here on will develop beautifully. Strongly recommended. The '97 Semillon ($18) is being re-released. It has some tropical fruit salad overtones from botrytis, yet is soft and balanced. It's fully ready as a young wine – delicious.

1998 Riesling ($18)

The nose is developing some very characteristic kerosene overtones, typical of the variety. The palate is quite full and broad – it couldn't be confused with a Clare or Eden Valley wine – but is surprisingly varietal for the Hunter. I'd say it's close to its best now. (The 'Hunter Riesling' on the label is confusing; it may make people think this is a semillon under its old name.)

1998 Shiraz ($30)

This shows lovely, rich, spicy fruit on the nose with earthy and leathery characters beginning to develop. The wine's soft and round in the mouth, with rich flavour – a little oak assisting – and fine tannins. It should develop over many years into a beautifully mellow, soft 'Hunter burgundy' with very complex flavour.

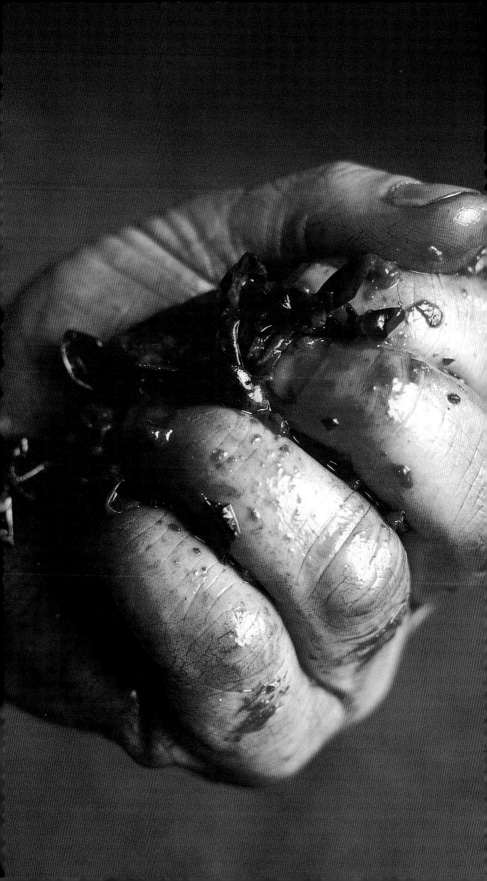

Tawny Port *Small Barrel* ($40)

There are few examples of top quality tawnies still made in the Hunter and this one is worth seeking out. It has excellent depth and rancio on the nose from long wood age and a very rich, complex flavour. It's on the sweet side, but is well balanced and finishes dry, all the same. Wonderful.

ADDRESS: 229 Wollombi Road, Broke 2330
TELEPHONE: (02) 9667 1622
FAX: (02) 9667 1442
E-MAIL: info@harbridgewines.com.au
ESTABLISHED: 1988
CELLAR DOOR: By appointment only. Tastings also at Hunter Cellars, Broke Road, Pokolbin, and Broke Village Store (weekends only).
OWNER: David Clarke
VITICULTURIST: Evan Powell
WINEMAKERS: Phillip Ryan and Neil McGuigan (contract)
1999 PRODUCTION: 24,000 cases
MAILING LIST: Yes
DISTRIBUTED: Harbridge Fine Wines (NSW); Prime Wines (Vic.); Pacific Liquor (Qld); Fine Wine Wholesalers (WA)
FEATURES: Accommodation in two-bedroom cottage in Cockfighter's Ghost Vineyard. Australian Opera Gourmet Weekend at Poole's Rock each October.

'Australia's other outstanding rock' says the brochure. You certainly can't miss it. And you wouldn't want to be around when the next one rolled down the hill. The original Poole lived about 100 years ago and was apparently a 'character', widely known to the locals of the time. The current Poole was founded by David Clarke – both with an 'e' – a Sydney businessman and chairman of Macquarie Bank. Amongst David's other hats are: president of the National Council of Opera Australia, and chairman of Goodman Fielder Ltd and Brian McGuigan Wines. ('With this bread and wine ...'). He's also Chairman of the Royal Sydney Wine Show and has been a partner in Smithbrook in Pemberton, WA, and the burgundy producer Domaine de la Pousse d'Or.

Somewhere amongst all of this activity David found time to buy land to the south of the Broke township and plant chardonnay. A few years later he bought the Cockfighter's Ghost Vineyard at 331 Milbrodale Road, which also has a two-bedroom cottage available for rent. Make sure you have a strong nightcap before you go to bed. The story goes that six explorers sent by Governor Macquarie to open the inland route from Windsor to Wallace Plains in the Hunter were crossing a branch of the Wollombi Brook when one of the horses, Cockfighter,

foundered. The party couldn't save it and the convict gangs that drove the road through the area called the creek Cockfighter. It's said that the horse's ghost haunts the creek to this day.

1999 Cockfighter's Ghost Unwooded Chardonnay ($16)

Fresh, melony fruit on the nose, combining ripe fruit characters with a hint of grassiness. That ripeness gives plenty of flavour and softness to the palate, which is rich and well balanced. Very attractive indeed. Drink it now, while it's fresh.

1998 Cockfighter's Ghost Semillon ($16)

This wine is just beginning to come out of that 'in-between' period that semillon goes through, when it's no longer fresh and lemony but not yet developed and toasty. The nose has some attractive nutty characters appearing and the palate is filling out and becoming rounder with age. You can enjoy this immediately or keep it for several more years so that it fills out further.

1998 Cockfighter's Ghost Chardonnay ($17)

The nose has very good depth, with rich, peachy fruit and very well married oak. Suppleness and balance are the main features of the palate, which is beautifully soft and polished and shows that same ripe flavour as the nose. Lovely drinking young and unlikely to get any better. I preferred this to the Poole's Rock Chardonnay, which is now quite developed and should be drunk up. It won a gold medal at the 1998 Hunter Wine Show, but has clearly developed considerably since then.

1997 Cockfighter's Ghost Shiraz ($21)

I was enormously impressed with this wine. Sure, there are bigger reds about, but what I loved was the beautifully fragrant bouquet that has developed, showing a complex earthiness, and the superbly balanced, supple palate, with its intense flavour. The brick colour and the development tell me the wine is approaching its best in 2000, but it may well hang on gracefully for several years after. Delicious.

ADDRESS: Cnr McDonalds & Pokolbin Mountain roads, Pokolbin 2321
TELEPHONE: (02) 4998 7523
FAX: (02) 4998 7523
E-MAIL: mail@regdraytonwines.com.au
WEB: www.regdraytonwines.com.au
ESTABLISHED: 1989
CELLAR DOOR: 10am–5pm 7 days
OWNERS: Robyn Drayton, Craig Armstrong and family
VITICULTURIST: Craig Armstrong
WINEMAKER: Andrew Spinaze (contract)
MAILING LIST: Yes
DISTRIBUTED: Direct from vineyard
FEATURES: Museum of five generations of family memorabilia. Gift gallery and shop. Barbecue and picnic area. Bi-annual 'Brunch and Munch Amongst the Vines', March and October. Sunset barbecue and stroll amongst the vines, Saturdays (and weekdays by appointment). Giant chess and draughts board.

The sign outside the entrance says 'Beware Feral Children'. I'm not sure how feral they've been, but children have been a major part of the Drayton family since Joseph Drayton arrived in Australia in 1853. There are Draytons all over Pokolbin and the sixth generation is now upon us. They're probably the ferals. (See also the entry under Drayton Family Wines.)

Reg Drayton had been the winemaker up the hill at Drayton Family Wines for many years but split with the company in 1989, taking with him the Lambkin Estate, Pokolbin Hills Estate and Ivanhoe Vineyard. Reg and wife Pam set up Reg Drayton Wines on the Pokolbin Mountain Road behind their home, putting up a slab-sided building as their cellar door. Reg was widely known as one of the gentlemen of the Hunter, quietly going about his business in a thorough but relaxed country way. I never heard him speak a single ill word of others.

Tragically, Reg and Pam were killed in the Seaview air disaster on 2 October 1994, while flying to Lord Howe Island on holiday. Their children Robyn and Stephen immediately stepped into the breach, although not long after, in 1996, they decided to go their separate ways. Stephen and wife Tracey took

Ivanhoe Vineyard, while Robyn and husband Craig Armstrong kept the Lambkin and Pokolbin Hills Estates. Lambkin, from the maiden name of William Drayton's wife, is next to Lake's Folly and opposite Mount Pleasant's Rosehill Vineyard, on a wonderful crown of red soil. Curiously it's planted largely with white varieties, not reds. Pokolbin Hills Estate is the property around their cellar door on Pokolbin Mountain Road. The two vineyards total 43 hectares across semillon, chardonnay, shiraz, cabernet sauvignon and verdelho.

Largely, I'd guess, from Robyn's considerable drive, Reg Drayton Wines won the Small Business Award for the Hunter Valley in 1999.

The wines are attractive and 'correct' Hunter styles, although a few lack a bit of excitement. Here are the highlights.

The 1999 Pokolbin Hills Verdelho is quite a lean, tight interpretation of the variety, with good acidity and as clean and dry a finish as you'll find in verdelho. The wine has a good track record, as previous wines have won gold in the Hunter Valley Show and I think this one has won a silver. Try it if the bigger, sweeter styles of verdelho are a bit much for you.

Reg Drayton Wines

1999 Lambkin Semillon ($19)

Delicate semillon fruit on the nose, with some pleasant hay-like overtones. The palate is crisp and dry, in the classic 'Hunter chablis' style, with a light grassiness and a balanced, soft finish. You can enjoy this now as a lighter style of refreshing semillon, but it is much better kept for many years to develop greater richness and toastiness. Great potential. The '98 vintage of this wine is simply brilliant.

1999 Pokolbin Hills Chardonnay ($17)

Ripe varietal fruit on the nose with some peach characters and only a small oak influence. The palate has medium weight, attractive flavour and good overall balance. This style of Hunter chardonnay takes some bottle age with ease. After two years you'll have a lovely, complex, toasty chardonnay.

1997 Pokolbin Hills Shiraz ($20)

This wine seems to be developing quite slowly. The colour still has some purple and the ripe, spicy fruit on the nose is not yet showing that Hunter earthiness. The palate has good depth of flavour and is relatively soft for a '97. (Most are quite firm.) The wine has the softness to drink well young, but should age for some years into a mellow, soft Hunter red.

ADDRESS: Yarraman Road, Wybong 2333
TELEPHONE: (02) 6547 8127
FAX: (02) 6547 8013
E-MAIL: contact@reynoldswine.com.au
WEB: www.reynoldswine.com.au
ESTABLISHED: 1967, 1989 as Reynolds
CELLAR DOOR: 10am–4pm Mon–Sat, 11am–4pm Sun & public holidays
OWNERS: The Reynolds family and private shareholders
VITICULTURIST: Mark Vella
WINEMAKERS: Jon Reynolds and Nic Millichip
1999 PRODUCTION: 15,000 cases
MAILING LIST: Yes, with The Top 500 Club
DISTRIBUTED: Negociants Australia (nationally) plus export
FEATURES: Cafe open on weekends.

The story of Reynolds Yarraman converges from three directions to the point when Jon and Jane Reynolds arrived in the Upper Hunter. Jon had worked for The Rothbury Estate in its early years before studying winemaking at Roseworthy. After graduating in 1975, he spent three years with Chateau Reynella before joining their neighbours Thomas Hardy. Hardys had bought Western Australian winemaker Houghtons in 1976 and the company moved Jon to the Swan Valley, where he played a pivotal role in Hardys' rapid rise in fortunes. This included the establishment of Houghtons White Burgundy as Australia's biggest selling white wine and the company's first steps with grapes from Margaret River and Mount Barker. He also did his own reputation no harm in the process.

However, both Jon and Jane were keen to return to the Hunter so, in a move that surprised many in the industry, Jon joined Wyndham Estate as senior winemaker in 1985. During his four years with Wyndham, Jon developed several new wines, including the Hunter Chardonnay and Bin 888 Cabernet Merlot. In his last year there, 1989, wines made by him won 10 trophies and 35 gold medals.

In 1967, and before Jon's arrival at Rothbury, Sydney surgeon Dr Bob Smith joined with grazier David Hordern to establish Wybong Estate, near Muswellbrook in the Upper Hunter. They planted 18 hectares, mostly semillon and shiraz and, two years later, were in need of a winery, and here's where the third thread to the story comes in. The solution to their need was not one that many would have found: they bought a prison. This was the old jail building at nearby Bengala, which they dissembled and rebuilt at Wybong. The result is a simply beautiful building that also features other natural materials such as ironbark beams and pine shingles.

The vineyards were clearly very good and a few excellent wines were made from them. But the quality reaching the bottle was somewhat inconsistent and the property clearly needed re-vitalising. That happened in 1989 when Jon and Jane arrived and Wybong Estate became Reynolds Yarraman.

Since then there have been many excellent wines. I particularly remember the 1992 Hunter Semillon in the 1999 New South Wales Wine Awards, when we chose it as Best Mature Dry White. It was a fabulous example of toasty, rich Hunter semillon. I really liked the '89 Cabernet Merlot when I last tried it,

too. It was rich and complex, with a nice minty overtone.

Since the 1991 vintage, Jon has been sourcing grapes from Orange and is now part of a joint-venture vineyard there. This brings the company vineyards to 60 hectares. And Orange will soon play a much bigger role, as Jon and Jane have now outgrown their winery and will be leaving their jail to build a new winery in the Orange region. (Did they pay $200?)

I liked all the Orange wines from the 1998 vintage – Chardonnay, Merlot and particularly the Cabernet Sauvignon.

1999 Semillon ($15)

This is quite a full-bodied style of semillon, the type that the Upper Hunter can do reasonably often, rather more so than Broke or Pokolbin. It has full fruit on the nose, with hints of straw – even a little hessian – from bottle development appearing. It's been made as a fuller style, as there's a light touch of tannin that fills out and broadens the palate further. It has the flavour to match, too. The bigger impact makes this pretty enjoyable now and the wine will clearly age into a full-flavoured, toasty white quite soon. (I greatly preferred this to the '98, which seemed to be somewhat botrytis affected.)

1999 Shiraz ($18)

The nose shows heaps of character, with big, even slightly stalky, extracted fruit and new oak. That stalky character shows a bit on the palate, too, but the flavour is very big and rich, so it's unlikely to bother most people. This isn't a wine for early drinking, so give it a few years – it will live for at least ten – and you'll have a very richly flavoured, complex wine.

Murray Robson Wines

ADDRESS: Bellona, Old North Road, Rothbury 2335
TELEPHONE: (02) 4938 3577
FAX: (02) 4938 3411
ESTABLISHED: 1970
CELLAR DOOR: All day, 7 days
OWNERS: Lynley and Murray Robson
VITICULTURIST: Murray Robson
WINEMAKER: Murray Robson
1999 PRODUCTION: 4000 cases
MAILING LIST: Yes
DISTRIBUTED: Cellar door only

I have already written of Murray's two previous winemaking ventures under the Briar Ridge and Pepper Tree entries. (Murray would probably argue that they are simply previous sites for the one venture, Murray Robson Wines.) After leaving the Fairfax winery in Broke Road, Murray spent some time in hotel management in Newcastle. However, I didn't think it would be long before Hunter wine called him back, and so it proved. In 1996 Murray and Lynley bought a property at the Rothbury end of the Old North Road, which they planted with a mix of varieties that will be familiar to their customers in the old Mount View days: semillon, shiraz, chardonnay, traminer, pinot noir, merlot and cabernet sauvignon. The vineyard is currently only 4 hectares, set in 8 hectares of landscaped park.

The main building shows Murray's typical flair and has been built in part from timber taken from an old farmhouse which was on the property. The ancient mulberry and pepper tree at the front hint at the age of this original home. The winery building contains a tasting cottage above and an underground winery floor beneath. The building has won two awards for design and workmanship.

Also familiar is the label: still the starkly elegant design that graced his early wines

and still with every label hand-signed by Murray. You'll recognise, too, the signs that identify each variety planted in the vineyard, although at first I thought the stakes along the path to the winery, each with a single vine, were marking the graves of loved and long-lost pets.

Murray's commitment is summed up in his brochure: 'I am here every day to personally show and discuss our wines with visitors.'

Sadly, most wines were unavailable when I called, but I did taste two.

1997 Chardonnay

This is outside the mainstream style. It has a very complex nose with nutty developed characters not unlike a bottle-aged meursault. The palate shows similar complexity and has quite an elegant weight, finishing with fairly tight acidity. Lovers of the soft, peachy Hunter style won't go for this, but those who want more funky character will enjoy it, particularly with food.

1996 Bushman's Red Cabernet Shiraz Merlot

This is a one-off – well, it's actually the second Murray has made, but still a rarity. For a four year old, it has unbelievably youthful colour and flavour. (It has only recently been bottled and, I'd guess, spent much of its life cold and in a small tank). The nose has very young berry fruit and an almond overtone. That freshness and youth is there on the palate, too, with a supple balance and fine tannin. Think of this as one year old and you'll get the idea. It was drinking well in 2000 and should fill out a little further over a couple of years.

Rosemount Estate

ADDRESS: Rosemount Road, Denman 2328
TELEPHONE: (02) 6549 6400
FAX: (02) 6547 6499
E-MAIL: mail@rosemountestates.com.au
WEB: www.rosemountestates.com.au
ESTABLISHED: 1969
CELLAR DOOR: 10am–4pm Mon–Sat, 10.30am–4pm Sun
OWNERS: The Oatley family
VITICULTURIST: Peter Hayes
WINEMAKER: Philip Shaw
MAILING LIST: No, but planning to soon.
DISTRIBUTED: Rosemount Estate nationally and export
FEATURES: Vineyard Brasserie: Morning tea Tuesday–Sunday 10am–12 noon;
Lunch Tuesday–Sunday 12 noon–2pm. Barbecue facilities at weekends.

You have to admire Rosemount. From a standing start, when it released its first wine in 1975, it has grown to be about the thirteenth-largest wine producer in the country and the fifth-biggest exporter by value. In the process, it has not put a single foot wrong, at least as far as an outsider can see.

Rosemount burst on to the scene with two wines you'd hardly expect from the Hunter – a gewürztraminer and a riesling. (While riesling rarely succeeds in the Hunter, gewürztraminer does more frequently than you'd think.) Both had major wine show successes and paved the way for Rosemount's first big seller, a blend of the two: Traminer Riesling. Rosemount had timed its arrival perfectly; it had high quality white wines at the beginning of the white wine boom. The winemaker was John Ellis, recently graduated as Dux from Roseworthy, who became strongly identified with the company in the time he was there and presided over the establishment of a very consistent quality. Ellis moved on in 1981, first to Tisdall, to which he also gave a flying start, and then to start his own company, Hanging Rock at Macedon. Mark Turnbull spent a short while at Rosemount, before being replaced by a winemaker from

Lindemans, Philip Shaw, who has been the chief winemaker ever since and who is, to a considerable extent, the public face of Rosemount, both in Australia and overseas.

This rapid start was all the more remarkable when you consider that the Oatleys had no wine industry experience. Bob Oatley had been a coffee trader, selling coffee from Papua New Guinea to the main markets of the northern hemisphere. When he bought Rosemount, he was hoping to combine three of his great interests – Charolais cattle, thoroughbred horses and wine. What he hadn't realised was that Rosemount had previously had a vineyard on its land, established by German migrant Carl Brecht in 1864. The underground fermenters were still there to prove it.

In addition to the skills of John Ellis and the early advice of consultant John Stanford, Rosemount was lucky to appoint Chris Hancock, previously a winemaker with Penfolds, who applied his flair and knowledge of the industry as general manager to guide Rosemount's development over the next 20 years. While the winemaking team was important, it's no exaggeration to say that Hancock is largely responsible for where the company is today.

Rosemount had timed its entry with Traminer Riesling to perfection. It then did the same thing with chardonnay. They had some unexpected assistance from a chance remark from the (then) New South Wales premier Neville Wran, who declared he had decided not to go into federal politics after mulling it over with a bottle of Rosemount chardonnay.

Some plantings of chardonnay had come Rosemount's way when it bought the Roxburgh Vineyard from Denman Estate in the late 1970s. Grapes from this vineyard provided the backbone of a new wine, the 1980 Show Reserve Chardonnay. It went on to win a double gold medal at the International Wine and Spirit Competition in England, which made the UK market sit up and take notice. In 1983 the first Roxburgh Chardonnay was made, and the rest is history.

A few years before, Rosemount had also bought Wybong Estate from Penfolds, which had provided the vineyards and a winery to support its rapid growth, and then the Mount Dangar Vineyard. It also planted more vineyard still and had rapidly become the major player in the Upper Hunter. It still is.

Almost all of this vineyard was bought or planted to support Rosemount's white wines. For reds, it looked further afield, firstly buying land in Coonawarra and later buying grapes from elsewhere in South Australia, particularly McLaren Vale. The generosity of McLaren Vale's reds was exactly what Rosemount needed for the Diamond Label range and the link was further cemented when it bought Ryecroft. McLaren Vale now supplies the fruit for one of Rosemount's flagship reds, Balmoral Syrah, named after the Oatleys' family home in the Hunter, while Coonawarra supplies the Show Reserve Cabernet. Further purchases closer to home included the Mountain Blue and Hill of Gold vineyards in Mudgee, which have, almost overnight, lifted the image of this very uneven region. Philip Shaw's own vineyard in Orange supplies grapes

for the Rosemount Orange Chardonnay and Cabernet Sauvignon.

With the exception of the Hill of Gold wines and the very pedestrian Ryecroft range, all the wines in this empire appear under the Rosemount brand, which makes for a very strong and consistent personality. Rosemount had opened offices in the UK in 1983 and the USA in 1985, so this same message now consistently appears across international markets, something few exporters have achieved.

Rosemount wines are full flavoured and approachable in style, the reds sometimes assisted by a deft touch of residual sweetness that generally goes without notice. The flagship reds are absolutely typical of their various regions and, while having considerable potential to develop in bottle, are always very drinkable on release. I think the Orange Vineyard wines are particularly exciting, as they show Rosemount's consistently intense flavours, but with the additional finesse typical of this cool region. I didn't really enjoy the style of the early Roxburgh Chardonnays, which I found too broad and dominated by malolactic flavours; I always preferred the Show Chardonnay. However, Roxburgh's style has become finer through the 1990s, with a much better balance of fruit flavours and winemaking complexity.

Rosemount has recently been taking grapes from the Adelaide Hills – its Sauvignon Blanc contains some of this fruit – so one feels an Adelaide Hills range may not be far away. Its flagship wines now cover many of Australia's classic regional styles. My only quibble would be, where's the Lower Hunter Shiraz?

Even after all this activity, I can't see Rosemount standing still. There's clearly more to come.

You no longer have to travel past Denman to visit Rosemount. The company has installed a cellar door area in the Hunters Lodge restaurant, near the corner of Ingles Lane and Oakey Creek Road.

Rosemount Estate

1998 Show Reserve Semillon ($22.50)

In the traditional Rosemount style, this is a full-bodied, full-flavoured semillon, but they appear to have dropped the oak that the wine had in earlier vintages. There's very attractive lemony fruit on the nose, with a little development beginning to appear. The palate is quite full in style, with big flavour and a little tannin adding texture. Short-term bottle age is all this needs if you want to add toasty complexity.

1997 Roxburgh Chardonnay ($52.60)

This is a reasonably restrained Roxburgh, following the trend of recent years, but also, probably, because of the vintage. The nose is very complex, with fruit, oak, malolactic and lees characters all in there. The palate is full and richly flavoured, with oak quite noticeable but all the characters combining in a very complex way. For all its size, the wine is reasonably tight and not blowing out as many other Hunter chardonnays would be at three years of age. Knowing earlier Roxburghs, it will probably hang in there for a few additional years. (The Giant's Creek Chardonnay, by contrast, seemed to be developing more quickly and was dominated by malolactic characters.)

ADDRESS: Broke Road, Pokolbin 2320
TELEPHONE: (02) 4998 7363
FAX: (02) 4993 3559
WEB: www.mildarablass.com
ESTABLISHED: 1968
CELLAR DOOR: 9.30am–4.30pm 7 days
OWNERS: The Mildara Blass Wine Group
VITICULTURIST: Roger Dixon
WINEMAKER: Rob Guadagnini
1999 PRODUCTION: about 330,000 cases
MAILING LIST: Yes, via the Rothbury Wine Society
DISTRIBUTED: Southern Cross Wines and Benchmark Wines
FEATURES: 'The Grape to the Glass' tour and taste at 10.30am daily, featuring a vineyard tour, visit to the winery and tasting. The Rothbury Cafe, open for lunch daily, featuring regional produce. Picnic days in April and spring.

Rothbury was an important part of my own wine upbringing and I had been a frequent visitor there until it lost its independence to Mildara Blass. So it was with some trepidation that I visited The Estate for the first time in several years.

Rothbury had started as one of the (many) visions splendid of Len Evans. It was initially a single vineyard – Rothbury – on land bought from Murray Tyrrell, who was also one of the shareholders. (The Tyrrell family home became Rothbury's office.) But very shortly afterwards, three other syndicates joined in – Brokenback, Herlstone and Homestead Hill.

The concept was simple: make wine from the classic Hunter varieties, all from estate vineyards with quality one can control, and sell it direct to the public, largely via a society, which would also hold educational – and hedonistic – dinners and tastings. The concept seemed to work brilliantly at first. The main building won the Blackett Award for Industrial Architecture. The semillons, under ex-Lindemans winemaker Gerry Sissingh, rapidly and deservedly gained a reputation as the best in the Hunter. The ribbon dinners were a huge success, greatly enlivened by Evans' flair and enthusiasm,

and their fame spread rapidly all over the country.

Members held different levels of membership, depending on the tasting skill they had shown. Candidates would submit to a tasting test and, if successful, were awarded a higher grade of ceremonial ribbon, which the members wore at the dinners. The tests themselves were a great opportunity to learn. A shareholders scheme, which allowed members of the society to own a share of Rothbury, proved successful and cemented the members' emotional ties. Rothbury prospered.

Then the tide turned. Rothbury's vineyards were originally about 80 per cent red, as were most of the new ones in the Hunter, and the quality of the Rothbury's early reds rarely matched that of the whites. And in the 1970s, everyone wanted white. Not every member was prepared to buy the case each of red and white that the budget had required. As all vineyards came on stream, it became clear that not all delivered the quality required for the estate wines; and some gave very low yields, not uncommon in the Hunter. Gerry Sissingh's return to Lindemans and a short run of indifferent vintages seemed bad omens. Interest rates rose to 20 per cent.

Rothbury struggled through, losing some of its high ideals along the way, but without compromising its quality. It was one of the few large ventures from around 1970 to survive intact. One of its huge successes was Cowra Chardonnay; it was Rothbury that virtually single-handedly put Cowra on the wine map. It also, at last, started to do well in retail distribution and soon it had taken over several interstate companies, including Baileys at Glenrowan and Saltram in the Barossa.

Rothbury then listed on the stock exchange – a perfectly logical thing to do, but the timing proved unfortunate. With the success of Australian wine overseas and a national shortage of grapes, Rothbury's vineyards and export franchise looked attractive to the predators and, after a brief skirmish with BRL Hardy, Rothbury fell to the Mildara Blass Group. There seemed nothing left of the original ideals. The vision had evaporated. Hence my trepidation as I approached the steps.

I was pleasantly surprised to find that little had changed. The Cask Hall looks just the same as when those grand dinners were held there (and they still are). I was pleased to see Gerry Sissingh's name back on some of the Rothbury wines. (Gerry and David Lowe are retained as consultants to give direction in wine style.) The look of the members' mailings remains familiar. And I was to find that there are still some very good Hunter wines under the Rothbury label. The source of those wines may have changed, as the vineyards in the Lower Hunter have contracted to a relatively small 35 hectares, but Rothbury is clearly getting some good fruit.

The wines I tasted fall into two groups: the 'retail' wines, which you'll find widely distributed; and the Society wines, which you can buy only through the Rothbury Society.

Retail Wines

The '98 Hunter Valley Shiraz has some vegetative, tomato-like characters that I didn't enjoy, but the Brokenback Shiraz of the same year is a cracker.

1998 Hunter Valley Semillon ($15.80) and *Brokenback* Semillon ($21.40)

It was a great pleasure to see these wines; they gave me faith that all is still well with Rothbury semillon. At present the HV wine is the better drink – it's fuller and rounder in the mouth, with some straw-like development appearing and an attractive softness. Drink it straight away or within a few years. The Brokenback is the sleeper. It's altogether tighter and crisper on the palate, although the nose is already filling out with some complexity. This is a ten-year wine if you have the patience.

1998 Brokenback Shiraz ($27.80)

This wine combines concentrated shiraz fruit with plenty of new oak. The oak flavour's quite strong at present, but it's been well handled and time will help. Give it, say, four years of life and you'll find complex, cigar-box characters and a richly flavoured wine. It will live much longer still.

The Rothbury Wine Society

1999 Gerry Sissingh Selection Semillon ($20)

This is a top young semillon that reminds me of the great wines from the 1970s. It has fine, lemony fruit on the nose with an aromatic lift. The palate is crisp and fresh, even a bit lean at the start, but has lovely flavour and soft acidity. A classic semillon that will age gracefully for at least ten years. Strongly recommended. (I didn't like the '97 as much. It's developing quite quickly, too.)

1999 and *1998 Black Label* Semillons ($19)

These are rather fuller, broader wines than the '99 Sissingh and don't have the same delicacy. They will certainly develop in bottle, but over a shorter period, becoming full-flavoured wines in the traditional 'white burgundy' style.

Black Label Shiraz

These are three beautiful Hunter reds at different stages of development, but showing very similar style. All three have considerable potential to develop in bottle, to make lovely, soft, complex reds of traditional Hunter flavour.

1998 ($24)

A cracker of a young wine, with very rich, blackberry fruit on the nose, subtle oak and a little earthiness beginning to develop. The palate is full bodied, round and soft, with great depth of flavour. It won two trophies at the 1999 Hunter Wine Show and clearly deserved them.

1997 ($24)

Rich berry fruit and hints of tar, earth and chocolate combine in a very complex way on the nose. The palate has plenty of rich flavour and slightly firm tannins but avoids the toughness of some '97s. (The '97 Sissingh Selection *was* on the tough side, however, although it has heaps of flavour.)

1996

A return to the style of the '98. This has softened further and the bouquet is developing beautiful, earthy complexity. It's smooth enough to drink young, but is better left for a few years yet.

Rothbury Ridge

ADDRESS: Talga Road, Old Rothbury 2320
TELEPHONE: (02) 4930 7122
FAX: (02) 4930 7198
E-MAIL: rothburyridge@telstra.easymail.com.au
WEB: www.rothburyridgewines.com.au
ESTABLISHED: 1998
CELLAR DOOR: Yes
OWNERS: Public company
VITICULTURISTS: Greg Moore and Rod Harris.
WINEMAKER: Monarch Winemaking Services (contract) with Peter Jorgensen
1999 PRODUCTION: 5200 cases
MAILING LIST: Yes
DISTRIBUTED: Direct from vineyard and website
FEATURES: Rothbury House, with accommodation for fourteen adults on the vineyard.

Peter Jorgensen seems to be a man of many parts. He got to know the Hunter as a flying instructor at Cessnock Airport and has also been involved in a business exporting fruit wines. He had previously established Bluebush Estate on Wilderness Road, but sold this and started a vineyard resort on Talga Road in 1988. The vines gave their first crop in 1992.

In 1998, Rothbury Ridge was floated as a public company and part of Jorgensen's land and vineyard were sold into it in 1999. Jorgensen retained some vineyard and buildings, including Rothbury House, which is available for hire. The company has also bought the Stanleigh Park vineyard on Wilderness Road.

In addition to the Hunter stalwarts semillon, chardonnay, verdelho, cabernet sauvignon and shiraz, Rothbury Ridge has planted chambourcin and durif. The latter is one of the first plantings of the variety in the Hunter – I think Tamburlaine was the first – and will be watched with great interest.

The wines are named for people associated with the company and, I'm pleased to say, don't quite follow the 'red for the men and white for the ladies' rule. ('Steven', mercifully, is a chardonnay, avoiding confusion with Steven Vineyard

Shiraz from Lindemans and Stevens Vineyard Shiraz from Tyrrell's.) They also carry initials to indicate the style of the wine – FBW for Full Bodied White, and so on – in the manner of Huntington Estate.

I tasted many wines at Rothbury Ridge – twelve, in fact, leaving a few more untasted. I'll simply say that most were good and will describe the highlights here.

The Durif will be worth watching in the future as the 1999 Mount Royal Reserve ($27) is true to the variety. It has intense, sweet berry fruit and quite chewy tannins. 'Big red' lovers, take note.

Stanleigh Park Reserve Semillon *1999* ($24)

This was my pick of the wines. It has really fine lemon and vanilla characters on the nose, intense but delicate. The palate has that same depth and delicacy, with very good balance and soft acidity. This has really great aging potential and should be a stunner in five to ten years. Unlike some 'keepers', it has the flavour to drink well now, too. Recommended, although it's more expensive than most.

1999 Early Release Chambourcin ($17)

This wine shows the attraction of chambourcin for early drinking, provided you like some vanilla from new oak and a hint of volatility. It has sweet berry fruit on the nose, the new oak, and a soft, supple palate with mild tannin. I believe it was at its best when I tasted it in 2000. (If you want more strength in your chambourcin, 1998 Edgar ($20) has greater depth of flavour, smoky oak, and firmer tannins to match. There's also a 1999 Mount Royal Reserve Chambourcin ($27), which has very ripe, plum-jam fruit and heaps of oak.)

1999 James Shiraz ($19)

The nose has beautiful red berries, with sweet new oak. Soft, well balanced palate with lovely flavour and soft tannins. The wine is not full bodied, but could be one of those elegantly structured, soft Hunters that ages gracefully for many years. It's soft enough to be drunk quite young.

Rothvale Wines

ADDRESS: Deasys Road, Pokolbin 2320
TELEPHONE: (02) 4998 7290
FAX: (02) 4998 7290
E-MAIL: rothvalehunterhabit@bigpond.com.au
WEB: www.users.bigpond.com/rothvalehunterhabit
ESTABLISHED: 1974
CELLAR DOOR: 10am–5pm 7 days
OWNERS: The Patton Family
VITICULTURISTS: Max Patton and Luke Patton
WINEMAKERS: Max Patton and Luke Patton
1999 PRODUCTION: about 3500 cases
MAILING LIST: Yes, and Vintage Club
DISTRIBUTED: Direct from the winery
FEATURES: The Hunter Habit, a group of cottages offering accommodation, with one, two or three bedrooms. All cottages are fully self-contained.

This vineyard was originally planted by three partners – Peter Meier, who was then the secretary of the Rothbury Estate Society, Sydney friend and businessman Lang Walker and QC Russell Bainton. They planted largely semillon and chardonnay, selling the grapes to Tyrrell's, as well as building the Rothvale holiday cottages. Tyrrell's also managed the vineyard for several years, eventually buying it in 1984. They ran it until they sold to the current owner, Max Patton, in 1997.

Max had practised as a vet, initially in Forbes and Parkes (NSW), and later in Sydney, interspersed with periods of study at Cambridge and London Universities where he became 'an over-educated clod'.

The Pattons built a winery in 1998, barely in time for that vintage. Rothvale now has 20 hectares under vine – half of these the original vines, and half new plantings of shiraz and cabernet sauvignon which yielded their first crop in the 2000 vintage.

Max's fiancée Ann Wilson is the sales and marketing manager and his son Luke is general manager and helps run the vineyard.

Some of the wines show a lot of oak and will appeal to people who like its vanilla and toasted flavours to the fore. The '98 Reserve Chardonnay is a good example. Perhaps oak-matured wines come more naturally to Rothvale, as I found the 1998 Unwooded Chardonnay a bit big and coarse for my liking.

1999 Semillon Chardonnay ($20)

This shows plenty of ripe fruit, with tropical characters – probably from the chardonnay – and a little semillon grassiness. The palate is fresh, crisp and lively. It drinks very well young and should fill out further over a couple of years.

1998 Tilda's Shiraz ($35)

Vanilla from new American oak is what you first notice on the nose, but the oak has been well handled. There's also good depth of fruit. The palate is soft enough for the wine to be drunk immediately and it will get some nice cedary complexity over two or three years. If you like oakier reds, then give this a try.

ADDRESS: Marrowbone Road, Pokolbin 2320
TELEPHONE: (02) 4991 1770
FAX: (02) 4991 2482
E-MAIL: saddlerscreek@ozemail.com.au
WEB: www.saddlerscreekwines.com.au
ESTABLISHED: 1991
CELLAR DOOR: 10am–5pm 7 days
CHIEF EXECUTIVE: John Johnstone
WINEMAKER: Philip Ryan (contract) with John Johnstone
1999 PRODUCTION: 15,000 cases
MAILING LIST: Yes, and Club Equus
DISTRIBUTED: Fesq & Co. (Qld); Alepat Taylor (Vic.)
FEATURES: Club Equus gives members access to the Bluegrass Tasting Room, limited release wines and Museum stock, with a discount on normal cellar door price.

The story goes that John Johnstone and his partners in Classic Packaging, which supplies oak and wine packaging materials to the industry, wanted to build a warehouse near Pokolbin but were denied planning approval by the local council. But they could get one for a winery, so Saddlers Creek was born. (And the packaging materials lived in a shed at the back.)

At the beginning, they had no vineyards of their own, but purchased fruit from local growers. They have since planted 15 hectares of vines (chardonnay, merlot, cabernet sauvignon, shiraz, sauvignon blanc, semillon) and also take grapes from other premium regions, including McLaren Vale, Langhorne Creek and Mudgee.

The winemaking is shared between their own winery and Mount Pleasant. As you'd expect, the presentation of the wines is quite startling, making use of innovative bottle shapes and beautiful design. (And lest the cynics say that the more that is spent on packaging, the less that's spent on the wine,

just remember: a pretty label won't get you a repeat sale if the wine's no good.)

Saddlers Creek has developed a good reputation and now supplies a number of top Sydney restaurants. Nevertheless, I've found the Saddlers Creek reds are better than the whites.

1998 Equus Hunter Shiraz ($23)

Softness, rich flavour and balanced tannins are the features here. But don't let the 'easiness' of this wine deceive you; it has the potential to develop for many years. A rich, flavoursome Hunter red from a top year.

1998 Bluegrass Cabernet Sauvignon ($23)

Ripe, concentrated fruit on the nose with lashings of sweet American oak. The palate has lovely rich flavour and good balance, and finishes with fine but firm tannin. There's great potential here and the wine should develop cigar-box complexity over several years.

Sandalyn Wilderness Estate

ADDRESS: Wilderness Road, Lovedale 2320
TELEPHONE: (02) 4930 7611
FAX: (02) 4930 7611
E-MAIL: sandalyn@hunterlink.net.au
WEB: www.huntervalleyboutiques.com.au
ESTABLISHED: 1988
CELLAR DOOR: 10am–5pm 7 days. Groups by appointment.
OWNERS: Sandra and Lindsay Whaling
VITICULTURIST: Keith Holder (contract)
WINEMAKER: Adrian Sheridan (contract)
1999 PRODUCTION: 4000 cases
MAILING LIST: Yes
DISTRIBUTED: Direct from vineyard
FEATURES: Lovedale Long Lunch May 2000; Opera Pops, held in cellar door March & September; Christmas fund for Sydney's Children's Hospital Luncheon. Disabled facilities and picnic area. One hole golf course.

Many wineries feature sculpture in their grounds, but it's rare that you meet anything with quite the same presence as when you enter Sandalyn. The split personality of Henry Moore is a very striking, and I'm told very valuable, piece by Drago Marin Cherina, but there's no worry about overnight theft. It's six metres tall and weighs six tonnes.

The Whaling family – Sandra, Lindsay and daughter Sally – started planting in 1987 and now have 8 hectares of semillon, verdelho, chardonnay, pinot noir and shiraz. 'We like drinking it!' was Lindsay's main reason. He is currently manager for the Steel River Project in Newcastle, which is seeking to develop broader employment opportunities during the phase-out of BHP's operations.

The Whalings have made a specialty of méthode champenoise, unusually a chardonnay–verdelho blend, which matures in the cellars under their cellar door building. 'Tuscan-styled' buildings seem as common as olive trees in the Hunter nowadays, but the Italian decorations in the interior of the cellar door area are beautifully and very individually done. A friendly cat farewells you as you leave, but can you spot the mouse? Bacchus, the golden retriever, is rather livelier in his attention.

1997 Sparkling Chardonnay Verdelho ($22)
This blend works surprisingly well and you can try it at many Hunter restaurants. It has a fresh, lively nose, with good complexity and a touch of toastiness. The palate is crisp and balanced, with attractive flavour.

1998 Chardonnay ($18)
This is right in the mainstream of Hunter chardonnay style, with ripe, peachy fruit and plenty of new oak. A generously flavoured chardonnay for drinking over the next year or two.

1998 Conservatory Shiraz ($20)
Fragrant berry fruit on the nose, with some sweet oak. The palate has good flavour and is on the firm side, needing a couple of years in bottle to settle down. Good potential over four to five years. This vintage appealed to me much more than the '97.

196

ADDRESS: Gillards Road, Pokolbin 2321
TELEPHONE: (02) 4998 7563
FAX: (02) 4998 7786
E-MAIL: sales@scarboroughwine.com.au
WEB: www.scarboroughwine.com.au
ESTABLISHED: 1987
CELLAR DOOR: 9am–5pm 7 days
OWNERS: Ian and Merralea Scarborough
VITICULTURIST: Ian Scarborough
WINEMAKER: Ian Scarborough
1999 PRODUCTION: 10,000 cases
MAILING LIST: Yes
DISTRIBUTED: NSW, direct from the winery; Prime Wines (Vic.)

'Scarbie' started in the Hunter as the winemaker for Tulloch in the early 1970s and during his years there was responsible for some brilliant whites. The '74 Semillon and Semillon Chardonnay were outstanding and still drink well. He left to work as a consultant in various parts of Australia and California, but eventually returned to the Hunter, where he (Ian) and Merralea bought a block of superb red soil from Hungerford Hill on a knoll overlooking Broke Road and Gillards Lane. Ian looks after the vineyards and winemaking and Merralea applies her delightful, bubbly charm as marketer and promoter. They now have 10 hectares of vineyard planted to chardonnay and pinot noir.

Given his experience with semillon and shiraz at Tulloch, why has Ian chosen to specialise in these two? Isn't pinot unsuited to the Hunter? The ever-relaxed Scarbie drawls, 'I'd challenge that. When the vineyard's mature, you can make good pinot here.' And, I have to admit, the Scarborough pinot's a good one. As for semillon, the Scarboroughs recently bought 40 hectares of land on the Branxton Road that was once part of the Lindemans Sunshine Vineyard, and this should give them a supply of outstanding grapes. 'I'm still looking for the block to plant shiraz on,' Scarbie added.

Their son Jerome is the vineyard manager for Lindemans. Is this a dynasty forming?

Scarbie has always tried to create complex chardonnays and these two wines are good examples.

1998 Chardonnay ($18.50)

This has really fine fruit, with beautifully complex, nutty overtones on the nose. The palate has excellent complexity, too, with wonderful depth of rich flavour. Alcohol provides plenty of body, without the wine appearing 'hot'. It's drinking beautifully as a young wine, although previous Scarborough chardonnays, including the '96 below, suggest it will take on more complexity over a couple of years.

1996 Chardonnay ($22)

Bottle age has filled out this wine and created some really interesting flavours. It is now quite full and peachy – an opulent wine, with complex, bottle-aged flavours. I'll hazard a guess that it won't taste better than it was in 2000.

Pinot Noir *NV* ($20)

The wine I tasted combines 1997 with a little 1996. Rich, complex nose with good depth of fruit, which has overtones of black plums. The palate has plenty of ripe flavour and is

quite firm, although it avoids the bitterness
of some Hunter pinot. It still needs time to
develop and soften.

ADDRESS: Lot 300 Hermitage Road, Pokolbin 2320
TELEPHONE: (02) 4998 7996
FAX: (02) 4998 7996
E-MAIL: ilsorbo@bigpond.com
ESTABLISHED: 1999
CELLAR DOOR: No
OWNERS: Letitia Cecchini
VITICULTURIST: Letitia Cecchini
WINEMAKER: Letitia Cecchini
2000 PRODUCTION: Not yet producing
MAILING LIST: No
DISTRIBUTED: No
FEATURES: Trattoria Arlecchino.

When ill health forced the Cecchini family to sell Serenella Estate in the Upper Hunter (see James Estate) Tish Cecchini couldn't face leaving wine behind. In 1999 she bought from Murray Tyrrell a 46 hectare block near the corner of Hermitage and Broke roads, and Serenella was reborn.

Tish's passion is her new trattoria 'Arlecchino' (Harlequin), which is due to open before 2001. It will provide the famished cellar-door goer with simple, homemade Italian meals. 'This is not fine dining,' she assured me.

Tish has already built and equipped a new Serenella winery next to the trattoria where she plans to make the trattoria's wine. She has planted 3 hectares of sangiovese and one of shiraz. Maybe she'll sell some; maybe the trattoria will take it all. Whatever the outcome, that end of Hermitage Road won't be quite so quiet any more.

Smithleigh

ADDRESS: Cobcroft Road, Broke 2330
TELEPHONE: 0414 406 934
FAX: (02) 9681 1038
E-MAIL: smithleigh@yahoo.com
ESTABLISHED: 1997 (as Smithleigh)
CELLAR DOOR: No. Broke Village Store.
OWNERS: Roderic Smith and John Leigh
VITICULTURIST: Ken Bray
WINEMAKER: Andrew Margan (contract)
1999 PRODUCTION: 2500 cases
MAILING LIST: Yes
DISTRIBUTED: Direct from the vineyard

In 1997 Rod Smith and John Leigh bought one of the blocks that Lindemans was selling during a re-structuring. The 8 hectare vineyard lies on the gentle slopes below the old Saxonvale winery, now Hope Estate, on the east side of the Wollombi Brook. It had first been planted in 1974 and is now bearing semillon, shiraz, chardonnay and verdelho.

They had their first vintage in 1998, not a bad year to start, with immediate success. Their semillon won one of the top slots in the 1999 New South Wales Wine Awards, where I thought it looked really stunning. I thought it was also outstanding in the 1998 Hunter Wine Show and unlucky not to get a gold. (It got a very high silver.)

I haven't tasted the more recent wines but, with the vineyards and winemaking in good hands, we can expect some more great things from Smithleigh.

ADDRESS: 270 Old North Road, Belford 2335
TELEPHONE: (02) 9427 6812
ESTABLISHED: 1974
CELLAR DOOR: No
OWNERS: Frank Brady
VITICULTURIST: Frank Brady
WINEMAKER: Frank Brady
1999 PRODUCTION: 65 cases. (Frank says BIG DROUGHT)
MAILING LIST: Yes
DISTRIBUTED: Direct from the vineyard

I first tasted Taliondal cabernet masked, during an options game towards the end of a late Hunter dinner. 'Yes, definitely cabernet … Which state? Hmm, could be Western Australia, perhaps South Australia, not New South Wales.' And then, having discovered it *was* from New South Wales, was it from Young or Mudgee? Maybe there's more to Hunter cabernet than I think. All power to you, Frank Brady!

Power is something Frank Brady knows a bit about. He was chairman and then general manager of the New South Wales State Electricity Commission for eleven years. And power is nothing new to the Hunter Valley. Coal was discovered before wine in the Hunter and coal, together with the electricity that's made from it, is big business. It was that business that brought Frank Brady to the Hunter. He obviously liked what he saw, because in 1974 he bought a block of land near Belford and planted nearly 3 hectares of cabernet sauvignon and gewürztraminer. For a while he sold the fruit to other wineries but he started making his own wine in the late 1980s. He has recently returned to selling his traminer grapes so that he can concentrate on the cabernet.

And the name? It seems that four-year-old Katherine, the youngest of Frank's six children, often played with imaginary play-mates. One evening she refused to come in to dinner, as she was busy playing with 'Princess Taliondal'. Taliondal became a family joke and, later, the name of the vineyard.

I've since tried the 1996 Cabernet Sauvignon, which I thought far too oaky, but the '98 is in much better balance. Frank sent me a bottle of his 1997 Traminer, which I found absolutely typical of the variety, with plenty of flavour and good balance.

1998 Cabernet Sauvignon

Deepish purple–red colour. Rich blackberry fruit on the nose, with excellent freshness and depth, plus a nice touch of oak. The palate is full bodied, with plenty of ripe flavour and firm but balanced tannins. The berry fruit and tannin structure are quite un-Hunter-like, but the region will exert its influence as the wine ages. It has great potential – at least ten years.

ADDRESS: McDonalds Road, Pokolbin 2320
TELEPHONE: (02) 4998 7570
FAX: (02) 4998 7763
E-MAIL: sales@tamburlaine.com.au
WEB: www.tamburlaine.com.au
ESTABLISHED: 1966
CELLAR DOOR: 9.30am–5pm 7 days
OWNERS: Landos Pty Ltd
VITICULTURIST: Gary Jenner
WINEMAKER: Mark Davidson with Simon Thistlewood & Michael McManus
1999 production: 45,000 cases
MAILING LIST: Yes, and tasting club
DISTRIBUTED: Direct from vineyard

... Tamburlaine, the scourge of God ... (I doubt that this is Fred Nile's favourite wine.) Lance Allen, the local general practitioner who founded Tamburlaine in 1966, was a fan of Christopher Marlowe, and the Mongol warrior, whose plundering didn't quite make it to the Hunter, featured on the original label. But as the current owners say in their blurb 'The name Tamburlaine has been maintained, nothing else remains the same.'

Mark Davidson and colleagues – at the time including Greg Silkman, now at Monarch and Allandale – bought the vineyard from Lance Allen and rapidly gained a great reputation for red wines. The quality now stretches across all their wines. What's unusual is that virtually all their production is sold directly to the public, either through cellar door or through the mailing list, which has a staggering 10,000 members. The rest goes to local restaurants.

The vineyard now has 12.5 hectares across a wide sweep of varieties – sauvignon blanc, semillon, chardonnay, merlot, malbec, shiraz, cabernet sauvignon, verdelho, chambourcin and durif. Tamburlaine also makes wine on contract for a few smaller vineyards.

The '99 Pokolbin Semillon is light and fresh, with good lemony fruit. It will develop well over several years. The 1999 Verdelho is typically generous in flavour, with ripe, tropical fruit and a full-bodied palate that finishes with a light grip. Good immediate drinking.

'The Chapel' Reserve 1999 ($22)

This is Tamburlaine's top red of the year and the quality shows. There's really beautiful, soft berry fruit on the nose, which has very good depth and the beginnings of some lovely earthy complexity. In the mouth, the wine has very good flavour, the new oak nicely understated, and plenty of soft tannin. The overall soft structure of the wine and the excellent balance are strong features. There are bigger wines around, but they don't have the beautiful style of this one. It should develop in bottle for many years yet. Recommended.

ADDRESS: Hunter Cellars, Hunter Valley Gardens, Broke Road, Pokolbin 2320
TELEPHONE: (02) 4998 7521
FAX: (02) 4998 7796
E-MAIL: tempus.two@bigpond.com
WEB: www.tempustwo.com.au
ESTABLISHED: 1997
CELLAR DOOR: 10am–5pm at Hunter Cellars, Broke Road, Pokolbin.
Groups by appointment.
CHIEF EXECUTIVE: Lisa McGuigan
WINEMAKER: Peter Hall
DISTRIBUTED: Tempus Two

Tempus Two is yet another venture from the McGuigan family, who brought you Wyndham Estate and McGuigan Wines (after they had shed some Brothers). This one is headed by Lisa McGuigan and uses the production base of McGuigan Wines and winemaker Peter Hall to bring a range of wines with grapes sourced from the Hunter, Barossa, Cowra and Mudgee.

Tempus Two uses some very sexy packaging, with love hearts and exotic bottles, amongst other things. The Botrytis Semillon bottle looks stunning, like a crystal Roman amphora.

The Tempus Two wines have been made as middleweights. They have good flavour but achieve this with a delicate touch and without high levels of ripeness and alcohol. The '98 Broke Vineyard Chardonnay is a good example. It has good depth of fruit, with a fair measure of smoky oak, and the earlier picking has given the wine a lighter touch.

1999 Somerset Vineyard Verdelho ($11.50)

This is a finer style of verdelho, with quite delicate fruit, a medium bodied palate and good, crisp acidity. It's not a 'big' wine but is all the better for it, and has really attractive freshness and balance. It should develop some toasty complexity over a couple of years.

Terrace Vale Wines

ADDRESS: Deasys Road, Pokolbin 2321
TELEPHONE: (02) 4998 7517
FAX: (02) 4998 7814
E-MAIL: wines@terracevale.com.au
WEB: www.terracevale.com.au
ESTABLISHED: 1971
CELLAR DOOR: 10am–4pm 7 days
VITICULTURIST: Alain Leprince
WINEMAKER: Alain Leprince
1999 PRODUCTION: 8000 cases
MAILING LIST: Yes
FEATURES: Lunch first Sunday in May to celebrate end of vintage.

Is Alain Leprince the longest serving Hunter winemaker? I can't think of another. Terrace Vale was started by a large group of partners, including Bruce Tyrrell and PeterMarsh (now at Marsh Estate) and made a great impact early in its life, particularly for its whites. I well remember some early semillons and the trophy-winning 1979 Chardonnay was still amazingly fresh when I had my last bottle in the mid-1990s. More recently, the 1989 Bin 2 Chardonnay won the Graham Gregory Trophy for best museum white at the 1997 Hunter Wine Show. I thought it was a beautifully complex, soft and full-flavoured wine. Their semillons have also developed well, so clearly many of their wines have great potential to age. Nevertheless, there's been some inconsistency at Terrace Vale. True, the vagaries of vintage weather in the Hunter don't allow total consistency, but I've seen a few wines that were not as sound as they might have been.

Yet, when they're good, the Terrace Vale wines can be very good indeed and they have a very strong following. A wine that they've had great success with – and not an easy style in the Hunter – is Elizabeth, their sweet dessert white. I really liked the '96,

made from sauvignon blanc, which had lovely, luscious apricot flavours.

I didn't enjoy the 1998 Bin 1 Semillon, which seemed lean and backward, although it may come round, given time in bottle. However, the 1998 Chardonnay is a tremendous wine.

1998 Bin 2 Chardonnay ($198 per case)
Ripe fruit and sensitively handled new oak combine beautifully on the nose. Softness and balance are the best features of the palate, with very attractive fruit flavour and good, clean acidity on the finish. An elegant, flavoursome chardonnay that will age well if you're after more toasty complexity.

1998 Cabernet Merlot ($216 per case)
Come in lovers of big reds! This wine has simply huge concentration, with heaps of fruit extract and some tarry notes. There's also a lot of tannin, but the wine still retains balance. It will clearly develop for some years and build considerable complexity, but whether the fruit or the tannin will finally win I can't say. Whichever, it will have a very long life.

ADDRESS: De Beyers Road, Pokolbin 2320
TELEPHONE: (02) 4998 7717
FAX: (02) 4998 7774
ESTABLISHED: 1987
CELLAR DOOR: 10am–5pm 7 days
OWNERS: Steve and Sue Lamb
VITICULTURIST: Steve Lamb
WINEMAKER: Steve Lamb
MAILING LIST: Yes
DISTRIBUTED: Direct from the vineyard
FEATURES: Self-contained accommodation at the vineyard.

The folk at Thalgara weren't the least bit interested in speaking with me or supplying information. Were they trying to conceal something? (Apparently not, as I found the wines were fine when I called round.)

Steve Lamb bought the block from Jay Tulloch in 1987 with some vineyard already planted. There are now 6 hectares planted to semillon, chardonnay, shiraz and cabernet sauvignon. Thalgara reds have come my way more often than the whites, which seems just, as there have been some excellent reds made. The 1995 was exceptional.

Reserve Chardonnay ($20)

This is a blend of 1996 and 1997, presumably to overcome some of the problems in the latter vintage. I found it very complex and still quite fresh. It has a lovely soft, balanced palate, with complex lees overtones.

Very attractive current drinking. I didn't enjoy so much the '98 Show Reserve Chardonnay ($25). After the other chardonnay it seemed a bit hot and bland.

1998 Show Reserve Shiraz ($35)

This follows the example of the '95, with very rich fruit that shows excellent depth. The palate is quite big in structure, with wonderful flavour and strong but balanced tannin. It needs time, but will be wonderful by about 2005 and live for many more years. The '97 Shiraz ($30) is also very good.

ADDRESS: PO Box 606, Cessnock 2325
TELEPHONE: (02) 4998 7645, 0418 456 853
FAX: (02) 4998 7645
E-MAIL: athomas@hunterlink.net.au
ESTABLISHED: 1997
CELLAR DOOR: Small Winemakers Centre, McDonalds Road, Pokolbin
OWNER: Andrew Thomas
WINEMAKER: Andrew Thomas
1999 PRODUCTION: 1250 cases
DISTRIBUTED: Direct from the vineyard

As the son of McLaren Vale grape grower and winemaker Wayne Thomas, Andrew Thomas was 'weaned off the breast onto big, fleshy shiraz'. For many years he was a winemaker at Tyrrell's, with responsibility for their brilliant semillons and chardonnays. In 1997, restless feet urged him to make his own wine from purchased grapes, which he made at the Capercaillie winery in 'spare time' during vintage at Tyrrell's. (I didn't know winemakers had any of that.)

Thommo and his wife Jo have bought a 10 hectare block on the Hermitage Road, great wine grape country, where they'll be planting semillon and building a house and eventually a small winery.

He's set out to make two distinctive styles of wine. The semillon will be 'a traditional aging style' but with some immediate appeal, thanks to selecting the right yeast, and a trace of residual sweetness – nothing new to Lindemans, Brokenwood and others. His red will capitalise on the synergy between Hunter and McLaren Vale shiraz, which he thinks is 'quite outstanding'. Again,

he has history on his side, as in the 1950s and 60s Hardys and Mildara made many outstanding wines from this blend and later Penfolds and Brokenwood followed this line.

How's he faring? Read on!

1999 Semillon ($19)

Fairly full fruit on the nose, with a hint of straw, yet quite fresh. The palate has depth of flavour and some fullness, with good overall balance. This semillon has the flavour to be drunk young but it will develop very well, so aging would be my choice.

1998 Shiraz *(Hunter/McLaren Vale)* ($32)

Great potential here. Concentrated blackberry fruit and smoky oak create complexity, although the wine is still quite closed up. There's excellent depth of flavour and firm tannin, but the wine will need some time to come round. It needs at least three years, but will take ten and more. A tremendous young shiraz.

ADDRESS: Pokolbin Mountain Road, Pokolbin 2320
TELEPHONE: (02) 4998 7435
FAX: (02) 4998 7529
ESTABLISHED: 1970
CELLAR DOOR: 10.30am–4pm 7 days
OWNERS: The Tinkler families
VITICULTURISTS: Ian and Usher Tinkler
WINEMAKERS: Ian and Usher Tinkler, with Philip Ryan
1999 PRODUCTION: 900 cases
MAILING LIST: Yes
DISTRIBUTED: Direct from the vineyard
FEATURES: Vineyard tours each weekend. Grapes, figs, avocados, stone and citrus fruits in season, honey, jams and pickles. Display of paintings from local artists in cellar door.

I remember, on my early trips to the Hunter, the prominent sign at the end of McDonalds Road as you turned left into Oakey Creek Road – Tinks Table Grapes, written in white with a broad paintbrush on a piece of black tin. If you wanted fruit to take back to Sydney or if you were desperate for a dessert for that Saturday evening meal you were cooking (the only place open in Cessnock after 12pm on Saturday was the Ampol garage on Branxton Road), then Tinks was the place to go.

The Tinklers have been in the Hunter for five generations, which means before the Ampol garage, so I guess they've done a lot of business.

In 1970 they started planting vines on their land at the foothills of Mount Bright, not far from Mount Pleasant and Draytons, and they now have 35 hectares, across semillon, chardonnay, verdelho, shiraz, merlot, pinot noir, cabernet sauvignon and muscat. The vineyard is in two sections. One is around their cellar door, which was the Fleming vineyard and winery about 100 years ago and which in 1890 also housed the original Pokolbin school. The other is directly under Mount Bright, off Marrowbone Road. From the beginning they have been selling their fruit to Mount Pleasant, but since 1995 they have retained some for themselves. Both

brothers, Usher (Bill) and Ian, are involved in the business, Bill dividing his time between the vineyard and their Merriwa cattle property, while Ian, who is a wine science graduate from Charles Sturt University, moves between the vineyard and the winery.

The brothers, and their late father Gordon, have tried as far as possible to match grape variety with soil type. If you want to hear more, join their vineyard tour, which takes place each Saturday and Sunday at 11am. It sounds like a must for anyone interested in Hunter viticulture. Kathie and Leonie Tinkler look after the cellar door. Someone in the family must be a natural marketer, as the naming of their wines is clever and the information they sent me was better prepared than that from many other companies.

1997 School Block Semillon ($14)

The wine has lovely toast and vanilla characters on the nose, without the botrytis you'll find in some '97s. The palate is fresh and delicate, with very good depth of flavour and a soft balance. It's drinking beautifully and will age for several years.

1997 Mount Bright Chardonnay ($16)

Complex, peachy fruit on the nose with some bottle development, yet still fresh. The palate has rich, soft flavour, with toastiness adding to the varietal fruit. It was probably drinking at its best in 2000. The 1998 Lucerne Paddock Chardonnay is a rather leaner, tighter version of the above, which you'll enjoy more if you want fresher chardonnay fruit and less complexity.

1998 Mount Bright Merlot ($20)

Sweet berry and earthy characters mingle on the nose in quite a complex way. The palate has very good flavour, with mouth-filling tannin which, while firm, does have some overall balance. This is not a supple, fleshy merlot, but the flavour's 'correct' for the variety and the wine will undoubtedly soften over a few years.

1998 Côte d'Or Shiraz ($20)

What a pleasure to see a wine from this historic Wilkinson vineyard! The Tinklers manage the vineyard for Eric Roberts, the current owner. It's not a big wine, but relies on fruit delicacy and balance for its quality. The sweet fruit on the nose is beginning to gain earth and leather characters as it ages. In the mouth, there's lovely Hunter shiraz flavour, without noticeable oak, and soft balanced tannin to finish. This wine can be drunk right away but, if cellared, will develop into a graceful, mature wine.

And the figs are great!

ADDRESS: 1273 Milbrodale Road, Broke 2330
TELEPHONE: (02) 6579 1308
FAX: (02) 9719 1833
E-MAIL: tonyrmears@msn.com.au
ESTABLISHED: 1997
CELLAR DOOR: 10am–4pm weekends & public holidays
OWNERS: Robin and Tony Mears
VITICULTURIST: Trevor Tolson
WINEMAKER: Adrian Sheridan (contract). Andrew Margan from 2000.
MAILING LIST: Yes
DISTRIBUTED: National Liquor Company

Tinonee has a brief but interesting history, so I hope you're paying attention. (I needed to.) In the mid-1990s the land was owned by Michael Hope of Hope Estate, but he swapped it for another property with Ian Craig. Craig bought grapes from local vineyards and had several whites made by Adrian Sheridan at Calais Estate. He made the reds himself on the property, which he named Tinonee. He also planted 15 hectares of vines – chardonnay, verdelho, shiraz, merlot, chambourcin and (very innovatively) durif – but did not persevere until their first crop, selling the vineyard to Robin and Tony Mears.

The Mears have a medical practice at Drummoyne in Sydney and now, like many other doctors before them, leave tracks on the Wollombi Road each weekend. Their vineyard is the first as you leave Broke along the Milbrodale Road and adjoins light bushland that sweeps down to the Wollombi Brook, a picturesque spot. The soils should be very good for whites.

The Mears built the pretty cellar door cottage that now looks out over the vineyard and took the first grapes from their vines in the 2000 vintage. They also inherited the previous stock.

That stock is a bit of a mixed bag, but there are some wines worth trying. The two whites from 1997, a difficult vintage for whites, as you're probably bored from reading, are now quite developed. It you like big, toasty flavours and the fruit-salad complexity that botrytis brings, you should like them. But '98 was a much better vintage all round.

1998 Verdelho ($16.60)

The nose has plenty of ripe, pineapple fruit and a richly flavoured palate. There's a hint of sweetness and the overall balance is good. This will drink very nicely into 2001.

1998 Merlot ($21.40)

Ripe, berry fruit on the nose, with good depth of character. The palate is soft, round and plump, with good balance and mild tannin. The wine's beginning to drink well, but will develop over four years or so. (I did not enjoy the '97, however, which was under-ripe and dank.)

1998 Shiraz ($18.90)

This is a very attractive wine with good berry fruit on the nose, a well-balanced, soft palate and plenty of fine tannin. It is already quite enjoyable but may be deceptive; I suspect it will age gracefully into a soft, round 'Hunter burgundy' style with five or six years in bottle. It's a bargain, too.

ADDRESS: 725 Hermitage Road, Pokolbin 2335
TELEPHONE: (02) 0411 214 478
FAX: (02) 9498 5317
E-MAIL: thelusbys@bigpond.com
WEB (under construction): www.tintilla.com
ESTABLISHED: 1993
CELLAR DOOR: Weekends, by appointment
OWNERS: The Lusby family
VITICULTURIST: Bob Lusby
WINEMAKER: Jon Reynolds (contract)
1999 PRODUCTION: 2250 cases
MAILING LIST: Yes
DISTRIBUTED: Direct from the vineyard
FEATURES: Olive grove. Fruit to date has been pickled and oil will be made from 2001.

In Tintilla we see another example of the medical profession's love of wine. Lake's Folly started the medicine ball rolling in the Hunter and the exercise keeps growing. (At least doctors now admit that wine is good for your blood pressure, provided you don't overdo it, and are even prepared to recommend it.)

Blood pressure is something Bob Lusby knows a little about. He's a vascular surgeon, who studied medicine at the Bristol Royal Infirmary, the same place as my father did. (It's a small world.) He also has another link to wine. He's a distant relative, by marriage, of James Busby, regarded by many as the father of the Australian wine industry. What's more, his wife Mary is a descendant of Lieutenant Shortland, who discovered the Hunter River in 1797.

You might think that health was also the reason that Bob planted olive trees on his property as well as grapes. I'm sure he's aware of the benefits of olive oil to health, too, but the explanation is much simpler: 'I just love Italy,' he told me. Bob spent some time there on a NATO scholarship and fell in love with the country. It's therefore no surprise that sangiovese was amongst the varieties he planted on his vineyard.

The Lusbys now have 10 hectares of grapes – semillon, merlot, shiraz, cabernet sauvignon and sangiovese – which are almost entirely surrounded by bush. Bob studied viticulture at the Hunter TAFE and manages the vineyard himself. He was on the tractor when I arrived.

By the time you read this, the Tintilla cellar door should be open and you'll find a very distinctive range of wines. The most unusual is a rosé, Rosado di Jupiter, made from sangiovese and merlot. The '99 has quite full fruit, with a touch of sweetness when it first gets to your mouth, but rapidly dries to a very good, savoury flavour and finishes firm and dry. The '98 Saphira Sangiovese is varietally typical and correct, with cranberry fruit, some leathery complexity and quite drying tannins. On a more traditional Hunter note, the '99 Semillon is fresh and delicate, with lovely depth of hay-like fruit on the nose. It will age brilliantly.

1999 Catherine de Medici Sangiovese Merlot ($22.50)

Blending these two varieties is not unusual; it has a precedent in the 'super-Tuscans', the modern Chianti-style wines from the really serious producers in Tuscany. The two varieties work well in this wine, too, the

20 per cent fleshy merlot filling out the leaner sangiovese. The wine has quite a savoury nose, with hints of berries and leather, and quite a dry, lean middle palate that's typical of Chianti. The tannin astringency may seem too dry, but have the wine with food and it's a different story. Strongly recommended to those who understand.

1999 Show Reserve Shiraz ($22.50)

This vineyard obviously does well with the Hunter stalwarts, too. The fruit in this wine is sweet and intense, with blackberry characters and sweet, spicy French oak. Given the flavour concentration, the palate's quite soft and stylish and has very good balance. There's great potential here. The wine should age beautifully into a soft, complex Hunter red. The 1998 vintage had similar depth of fruit, but with some more savoury, tar and tobacco notes. I preferred the younger wine.

Tower Estate

ADDRESS: Cnr of Broke & Halls roads, Pokolbin 2320
TELEPHONE: (02) 4998 7989
FAX: (02) 4998 7919
E-MAIL: sales@tower-lodge.com.au
ESTABLISHED: 1998
CELLAR DOOR: 10am–5pm Sun–Fri, 10am–6pm Sat. Mini-buses
and coaches by appointment.
OWNERS: Fourteen private shareholders, including Len Evans AO, OBE,
Brian McGuigan AM, John David, Ken Cowley and Rick Stein.
WINEMAKER: Dan Dineen
1999 PRODUCTION: 8000 cases
MAILING LIST: Yes, and restricted-membership wine club, Tower 200
DISTRIBUTED: Direct from the vineyard

Tower Estate is the latest of many visions splendid to come from that extraordinary idea-generating machine, Len Evans' head. After The Rothbury Estate had been snatched from him by competing bids from first BRL Hardy and then Mildara Blass (during which Evans' comments did little to bring him a consultant's role) he found his hands uncharacteristically empty. Evans Family Wines was a fully developed concern and required only a little of his time. At such a juncture, most other people in their late sixties would be happy to relax a little, but not Evans, so he hatched the idea for Tower.

Len approached several friends and colleagues in the wine industry and elsewhere with something like 'I want some money. Don't expect a profit, but we're going to have some fun!'

There are two aspects to Tower. The first, and most obvious from Broke Road, is the winery. This was built – at some great expense with, for example, copper guttering and downpipes – in time for the 1999 vintage. The tower itself reminds me distinctly of an Inca temple, which the solid lintel and door and ceramic features (made by Evans himself to represent each partner) do nothing to dispel. Len tells me his tile is the one with the belligerent face.

The interior is sparsely but elegantly appointed. You can see the relationship to Evans Family and the early days of Rothbury – pale, stuccoed brick walls, stark lighting, cool features in iron and wood.

Tower's aim is to make classic regional wines by taking fruit '... from regions that best suit a particular grape variety ...'. Thus we can taste Adelaide Hills sauvignon blanc, Clare Valley riesling, Coonawarra cabernet sauvignon and others; also Hunter Valley semillon, verdelho, chardonnay and shiraz. Tower will make only 1000 cases of each wine.

First call on the wines will be from the Tower 200 club, just 200 subscribers who will take a case of each wine per year. There is also an unrestricted list for those who want to buy the occasional case and be kept in touch with what's going on. This will also form the waiting list for the Tower 200 Club.

The second part to Tower is The Lodge. This is accommodation on a grand and distinctive scale. Surrounding a central courtyard are twelve guest suites, each with its own small courtyard and complete en suite facilities. Each room is designed with an individual theme, along the lines of Evans' own home, Loggerheads (and copied by Casuarina). Thus there is a Roman room, a French

Provincial room, an Elizabethan room and others. The building cost $6 million to build and equip. There is a large, grand dining room and the kitchen is run by Robert Mollines from Robert's, next door.

Tower Lodge will target the corporate market in particular, but it also provides a place to stay if you want something lavish and quirky and where quality and style are paramount. Oh yes, you need to be able to afford it, too.

I tasted several wines in barrel with Dan Dineen, ex-Mount Pleasant and Brokenwood winemaker. There are excellent 1999 shiraz wines from the Tallawanta and Howard vineyards. The wines have lovely Hunter style – sweet fruit, softness, medium body and fine tannins. There are also some exceptional wines from 2000. The reds from other areas showed great regional style, too.

1999 Howard Semillon ($22)

The Howard vineyard on Oakey Creek Road has a great reputation amongst winemakers, so trust Evans to get some of the fruit. This is quite a tight, reserved wine with nice tropical overtones to the fruit. It may not be forward enough to appeal to some people immediately, but it's definitely a long-term keeper in the traditional Hunter 'Chablis' style. Great potential.

1999 Verdelho ($20)

This is the sort of interpretation of the variety I would have expected from Tower. It's quite a refined verdelho, with delicate, lifted fruit and a medium-bodied palate that finishes with crisp acidity. If you're after big ver-delhos, go to Wandin Valley or James Estate; but if you want your flavour in a more delicate framework, this is the one for you.

J Y Tulloch and Sons

ADDRESS: De Beyers Road, Pokolbin 2320
TELEPHONE: (02) 4998 7580
FAX: (02) 4998 7226
WEB: www.tulloch.australianwines.com.au
ESTABLISHED: 1895
CELLAR DOOR: 9am–4.30pm Mon–Fri, 10am–4.30pm weekends
OWNERS: Southcorp Wines
VITICULTURIST: Jerome Scarborough
WINEMAKER: Greg Jarrett
1999 PRODUCTION: 30,000 cases
MAILING LIST: Yes, and 1895 Club
DISTRIBUTED: Southcorp Wines nationally

Tulloch is one of the great names of the Hunter Valley that has faded in significance as far as classic Hunter wine styles are concerned. While Tulloch has two big sellers in its Verdelho and Brut Cuvée, it is no longer at the forefront of shiraz and semillon as it once was.

There are plenty of bad debts in the wine industry, but not many people start a wine business in settling them. John Younie Tulloch is one who did. In 1895, when a storekeeper in Branxton, he accepted a vineyard in payment of a bad debt. The vineyard was in poor condition, but Tulloch restored and expanded it, calling it Glen Elgin. Later the company bought 300 acres from soldier settlers at Fordwich to add to the original vineyard at Pokolbin.

Times were hard for Hunter wineries after 1900, and few sold their wines in bottle and under their own label until the latter half of the twentieth century. Tulloch, like others, sold wine in bulk to other winemakers or to merchants like Leo Buring and Rhinecastle. Rhinecastle's Johnnie Walker was a great promoter of wine, starting many enthusiasts on their way and introducing them to the Hunter. Walker suggested that Tulloch start its own label, which it did from about the 1954 vintage. This was

an outstanding one in the Hunter, and for Tulloch in particular, and the 1954 Private Bin Dry Red is still drinking magnificently. I am in no hurry to drink my one and only bottle.

Tulloch made a succession of wonderful red wines through the 1950s and 60s and many of those wines are still beautiful. However, even selling bottled wine, the returns were still not great. Tulloch's several family members were faced with the choice of trying to expand, which they could not afford, or parting with the company, and so the family sold to Reed Paper Mills in 1969. In the next few years, Tulloch passed to Gilbeys, the international wine and spirit group based in the UK.

The 1970s were not a great decade for Hunter reds, but there were many excellent whites, in particular a trio from Tulloch in 1974 – a semillon, a semillon chardonnay and a verdelho. The '74 Semillon won several golds and trophies and some bottles still open well. There was also a superb chardonnay from 1980. Gilbeys sold Tulloch to Allied Vintners, which itself eventually passed to Southcorp Wines, where it rests today.

Over time, the fortunes of the individual wines fluctuated; the semillon and chardonnay gradually departed, other than for cellar door sales, and the verdelho became Tulloch's most important wine. Most of the fruit for this comes from the Upper Hunter and the wine is made in a fresh, fruity, off-dry style.

The flagship red wine is now Hector, named after John Younie's son and the father of Jay Tulloch who, until recently, was the manager of Tulloch and Southcorp's Hunter operations. (Jay and wife Julie now have their JYT Wine Company down the road.) In some years Hector is a lovely Hunter red, showing some new oak maturation (which the old Tulloch reds never did) and it has snagged the odd gold and trophy at the Hunter Wine Show. It's on the firm side, as Hunter shiraz goes, and matures very well. The first vintage, 1987, will still age for a few years, but somehow Hector lacks the full, rich character of those brilliant wines under the old red and white Tulloch label.

Verdelho is Tulloch's biggest seller and it's easy to see why. It gives attractive flavour in a very 'easy' drinkable style. It often scoops a few medals in the shows. The '99 has attractive tropical fruit, just a suggestion of sweetness and a bit more grip on the finish than other recent years.

1995 John Younie Semillon ($18)

This is available at the cellar door only, so I'd make the trip. The nose has plenty of ripe, tropical fruit, and toasty, developed complexity. The palate is quite full and broad, with plenty of flavour and good balance. It's a bigger semillon than most, from a very good year, and now close to its best.

1996 Hector ($32.50)

The nose is quite complex, showing some earthy notes from development and a touch of camphor, probably from the oak. The palate's quite firm and tight, with very good flavour and plenty of tannin to dry the finish. It's developing slowly, so you can safely cellar it for several years yet.

JY Port ($17.50)

This is something of a rarity. Most of the ports you'll find in the Hunter come from far afield and are little different from what you can buy in your local bottle shop. JY is made largely from Hunter shiraz and has aged for many years in small wood at the Tulloch winery. It is quite rich and full in style, on the sweeter side, but with excellent rancio and a little wood tannin to dry the finish. It's a glimpse of the Hunter's history, when every winery would have made ports, sherries and muscats.

ADDRESS: Broke Road, Pokolbin 2320
TELEPHONE: (02) 4993 7000
FAX: (02) 4998 7723
E-MAIL: btyrrell@Tyrrell's.com.au
WEB: www.tyrrell's.com.au
ESTABLISHED: 1858
CELLAR DOOR: 8am–5pm Mon–Sat. Closed Sun.
OWNERS: The Tyrrell family
VITICULTURISTS: Cliff Currie, Rob Donaghue
WINEMAKERS: Andrew Spinaze and Mark Richardson
MAILING LIST: Yes
DISTRIBUTED: Tyrrell's (NSW & Qld); Rutherglen Wine & Spirit (Vic.); Porter & Co. (SA); West Coast Wine Cellars (WA)
FEATURES: Old, earth-floored winery, which is of great historic interest. The slab hut was once the Tyrrell family home.

It's difficult to know where to start with Tyrrell's – history, their ground-breaking wines or my own memories, which are many. Hmmm, the last one seems right. One of my friends, Harry Jitts, had been buying Tyrrell's wines for some years when I started getting interested in wine, so drinking eight-year-old shiraz and semillon with Harry was a real treat. As far as I was concerned, they were the best wines in the world. I described in the introduction my first trip to Tyrrell's. This was to taste the 1971 vintage in wood, a year described by Murray, when we got there, as the worst in living memory, hardly a great start. (Murray even went so far as to call 1971 a BAD VINTAGE on the front label. I suppose this provides a balance to 'the best vintage since 1965'!)

As chance would have it, I met Anne Tyrrell not long after. She was managing the cellar at Bulletin Place in Sydney for Len Evans, so trips to the Hunter became more frequent. (I could mention a dinner with the Tyrrells at The Cottage restaurant when Len, on arrival, planted a juicy big kiss on the cheek of James Halliday's long-haired nephew, whose back was turned to him, but Len might rap my knuckles, so I won't.) During one of those visits, I was given a treat, a taste of a rare new grape variety that Tyrrell's was experimenting with – chardonnay. I'd like to say that the wine was a stunning revelation and that the next two

decades of chardonnay's future in Australia were revealed to me in a flash of light, but I can't. I remember the wine as a rather softer, oilier version of semillon, but that was my shortcoming, not the wine's. My last bottle of the wine in question, the 1973 Vat 47, showed the wine still in good condition after twenty-five years. It remains Murray's favourite.

That Murray Tyrrell virtually single-handedly established chardonnay as a variety in Australia is accepted without argument. (I am aware that Penfolds had chardonnay in its HVD vineyard for some years before, and that it had been grown in the Kurtz vineyard at Mudgee, too, but these plantings made no contribution to varietal chardonnay as such.) What was extraordinary is that someone with Murray's background would have done so.

At the time when Murray took over the reins at Tyrrell's, he was far more interested in beef cattle and he retains that interest to this day. The previous winemaker was 'Uncle Dan' Tyrrell, who had made wine for the previous seventy-six vintages, an extraordinary record. It was Dan's father Edward Tyrrell who had settled at 'Ashmans' in 1858. Murray inherited a company that sold most of its wine in bulk, to either wine merchants or other wineries like Mount Pleasant. Its cellar door sales were minuscule – no different from the other six Hunter vineyards at the time. His first few vintages were badly hail affected, and his red production in the 1961 vintage was just three casks.

Yet, within a short time of becoming vineyard manager/winemaker/managing director, Murray had started selling all his wine under the Tyrrell's label, had refined his style of semillon to a softer, later picked – and much more palatable – style, and had won a gold medal at the Sydney wine show with the 1962 Vat 5. (An emissary from the show and the local police sergeant were sent to Tyrrell's to check for fraud. They found none.) Then, after barely ten years, and after tasting some French white burgundies because he wondered 'what they were all about', he decided to plant an obscure variety called chardonnay. Cheers, Murray!

That experimentation did not stop with chardonnay, as pinot noir was soon to follow. The 1976 Tyrrell's won international acclaim by topping the pinots noirs at the Wine Olympiad in Paris organised by Gault et Millau magazine, beating several highly regarded French burgundies.

Tyrrell's has now grown to a sizeable empire, with wineries or vineyards in the Upper Hunter and Quirindi, New South Wales, Heathcote in Victoria and McLaren Vale and the Limestone Coast in South Australia. It's now about the fifteenth-largest Australian wine company in terms of sales, with wines that stretch from big commercial lines like Long Flat Red to small parcels of top semillon or shiraz of only 500 cases. Not bad growth from three casks of red in 1961!

In Murray's early years, Tyrrell's' reputation was mostly for reds, but this has completely changed. Throughout the 1970s and 80s, Vat 47's complete domination of chardonnay classes in wine shows did a lot to change this perception, but in recent years I think the semillons have had a greater role. The reds have not shown the same consistency and, while the best have been excellent, there have been some plain wines, too.

The '98 Vat 9 Shiraz shows distinct smoky oak, but it has very rich fruit and good balance, and the flavours will integrate in time. It will be a long-term keeper. The '96 Vat 9 also showed

a lot of charred oak. I had mixed feelings about the 1996 Stevens Shiraz. While is certainly has big flavour, there are some over-ripe fruit characters that I thought detracted from the style of the wine.

1996 Stevens Semillon ($21.70)

If ever a wine reinforced Tyrrell's mastery with semillon, this is it. When I tasted it, four years had added some vanilla and smoky development to the hay-like fruit, yet the palate was still so fresh and fine, combining delicacy with intensity. The Stevens vineyard was the source of some of the great Lindemans semillons of the past and this wine should go the same way. A real pleasure. It'll keep for many years.

1994 Vat 1 Semillon ($40.30)

Well, all right … this wine shows that mastery, too. Vat 1 has, since about 1970, been *the* Tyrrell's semillon and, although another challenger gets thrown up occasionally, this is their really consistent line. The '94's nose is very full and complex, with lemon and toasty characters mingling beautifully. The palate reflects these, with rich, developed flavour, yet in a fine structure and with fresh acidity. The wine is simply delicious and, most importantly, Tyrrell's have done the aging for you. It will age still further if you wish. I still have many older Vat 1s and most are drinking beautifully. Of the recent wines, the 1996 is excellent and the '99 will be great with time.

1996 Vat 47 Chardonnay ($43.60)

Very complex nose with rich fruit that is beautifully assisted by excellent barrel handling, giving some smoky oak and lees maturation characters. The palate is rich and full bodied, with lovely balance and roundness in the mouth. It's a great example of Hunter chardonnay at its peak. The 1997 vintage, although showing some of the leanness of the year, is also a very complex wine and in great shape, while the '93 is quite toasty, yet tight and dry. The '99 Vat 47, tasted in 2000 against some of the best chardonnays in the country, showed me that the quality is there with the young wines, too.

ADDRESS: Yango Creek Road, Wollombi 2325
TELEPHONE: (02) 4998 3322
FAX: (02) 4998 3322
E-MAIL: finewines@undercliff.com.au
WEB: www.undercliff.com.au
ESTABLISHED: 1990
CELLAR DOOR: 11am–3pm Wed–Fri, 10am–4pm weekends & public holidays
OWNERS: Peter and Lesley Chase
VITICULTURIST: Bryan Hubbard
WINEMAKER: Peter and Lesley Chase with David Carrick (consultant)
1999 PRODUCTION: 1500 cases
MAILING LIST: Yes
DISTRIBUTED: Direct from the vineyard
FEATURES: Art gallery and winery building, set in beautifully landscaped grounds in a secluded valley.

Wollombi is one of the most historic spots in the Hunter but, for many years, it was a place that I, like other winos, hurried through on the way to Pokolbin. There's now more to attract our attention than the wonderful old buildings and Dr Jurd's place of refreshment, as there are vineyards springing up in the little green nooks and corners of the Wollombi Valley. One of these is Undercliff, planted by James and Janet Luxton in 1993. Janet Luxton is an artist who has worked and studied in New Zealand, the USA, Israel and Australia.

The property had been operated as a mixed farm from 1846 to the 1960s and was in disrepair when the Luxtons bought it. The quarry, which produced the red clay for the nineteenth century Wollombi brickworks, is next door.

The Luxtons planted 2 hectares of vines – shiraz and semillon – and built a winery, partly from local materials, which also doubled as the gallery in which Janet Luxton displayed her etchings. In 1999 the Luxtons sold to Peter and Lesley Chase.

The winery/gallery building is set against a bush-covered hillside and to reach it you drive across a small creek and through beautifully landscaped gardens. Liquidambars colour the expanses of lawn,

which are punctuated by ponds with bulrushes and lily pads. I'm sure the birds that Janet Luxton used to draw were very much at home.

This was my most exciting discovery for this book – although, checking my notes, I found I had tasted some of the wines before. There are just three wines made: an unwooded semillon, a shiraz and a sparkling shiraz; and they vary from good to simply brilliant.

I had tasted the 1996 Shiraz in 1998, a wine of wonderfully rich flavour and a lush, fleshy balance. It won a silver in the Hunter Wine Show and this was clearly no fluke; the '97 did the same and the '95 won a gold. The great news is that the '98 is even better.

1998 Shiraz ($17.50)

The nose shows very good depth of ripe, berry fruit with a little spice and barely perceptible oak. What's particularly impressive is the palate, which is deliciously soft, lush and round in the mouth. It's one of the most exquisitely supple, balanced young reds I have had for a while. The vineyard must be on a very good patch of dirt to do this so consistently. What's more, the price makes it a great bargain.

This will develop beautifully into a soft Hunter red of great quality and charm.

1998 Semillon ($14)

The nose is quite full, showing some attractive vanilla characters, and is just beginning to develop complexity. The palate is soft and round, with good depth of flavour and acid balance. It's a good each-way bet: soft and balanced enough to drink now but with the capacity to age for many years. The 1999 Semillon ($15) is a leaner, crisper version without the same flavour at present, although it will be a good long-term keeper.

Sparkling Shiraz ($17.50)

This shows the same attractive fruit characters as the table wine, but with a little earthy complexity beginning to develop and some spicy notes. It's drinking beautifully and will develop further.

Van de Scheur Wines

ADDRESS: O'Connors Lane, Pokolbin 2321
TELEPHONE: (02) 4998 7789
FAX: (02) 4998 7847
ESTABLISHED: 1995
CELLAR DOOR: 10am–5pm 7 days
OWNERS: Kees van de Scheur and Helen Palmer
VITICULTURIST: Kees van de Scheur
WINEMAKER: Kees van de Scheur
1999 PRODUCTION: 2300 cases
MAILING LIST: Yes, and City Vignerons Program
DISTRIBUTED: Direct from the vineyard
FEATURES: Annual Teams Winemaking Challenge, including production day
and blending day; annual pre-vintage 'Almost Posh' dinner in winery; annual Planting
Day; annual Wine Challenge Awards presentation lunch.

In the hey-day of The Robson Vineyard at Mount View, the person you were most likely to meet, apart from Murray himself, of course, was Kees van de Scheur. Following Murray's departure, Kees stayed with the winery for a while after it became Briar Ridge and then moved on. He now divides his time between Bimbadgen and the new venture he started with Helen Palmer, the re-establishment of the old Ingleside winery on O'Connors Lane.

Ingleside dates to the 1870s, almost as old as Pokolbin itself, but had not produced wine since about the 1950s. The winery (since renovated – sort of) and the old house (still teetering) are now the home of Van de Scheur Wines, and of an unusual concept, City Vignerons. The idea is, you promise to buy two cases of wine a year of your choice, for which you get your name displayed on a short stretch of vines, join in the pruning, picking, winemaking – oh yes, and the drinking – and have free use of the vineyard and winery grounds. Kees and Helen get some guaranteed sales and a bit of help; you get to have a lot of fun. Sounds like 'Win, Win' to me!

From the tasting I did, those two cases of wine won't prove to be much hardship, either. The seven wines I tasted were of a very consistent quality. A common feature was the low level of new oak. Where it had been used, it was barely apparent, which is as it should be. Some other winemakers would do well to take note. The '99

Chardonnay ($20) is a good example, with quite complex melon fruit, a nice tight palate and good acidity. The oak's there, but almost at the subliminal level, giving complexity but without a flavour of its own. The '99 Cabernet Sauvignon ($22) again shows just a subtle touch of oak, but with nice blackcurrant fruit and a stylish palate. My favourites were these:

1999 Semillon ($20)

Very fine nose, with nice vanilla character typical of the variety. The palate is quite full and round, assisted by a suggestion of sweetness, and finishes with good length. It should develop brilliantly in bottle.

1999 Chambourcin ($22)

A very typical chambourcin, showing ripe, sweet berry fruit on the nose and a lovely, supple palate, with plenty of sweet, black cherry fruit and soft tannins. This really highlights the strengths of this variety. Drink it while it's young and succulent.

1999 Shiraz ($22)

Beautiful, blackberry fruit on the nose. There's considerable depth and character but, again, a relative absence of oak. The palate's quite stylish and medium bodied, with plenty of sweet fruit and fine tannins. Please keep it. You'll be rewarded with a lovely, soft, complex 'Hunter burgundy' in time.

ADDRESS: McDonalds Road, Pokolbin 2320
TELEPHONE: (02) 4998 7668
FAX: (02) 4998 7430
E-MAIL: poolside@hunterlink.net.au
ESTABLISHED: 1972
CELLAR DOOR: 10am–5pm 7 days
OWNERS: Keith Yore, David and Susie Lochhead
WINEMAKER: Monarch Winemaking Services (contract)
1999 PRODUCTION: 4000 cases
MAILING LIST: Yes, and Premier's Club
DISTRIBUTED: Direct from the vineyard.
FEATURES: Four-bedroom house on vineyard, sleeping 8–10 people.
Restaurant – Cafe Max. Harry's lunch bar and sandwich shop.

Verona operates on several levels. The most public face is that of the Small Winemakers Centre on McDonalds Road. This is your best opportunity to taste the wines from several of the smallest companies that have no cellar door of their own, like David Hook's 'The Gorge' and Thomas Wines. You'll also find wines from Reynolds Yarraman, which will save you a trip to the Upper Hunter. The 5 hectare vineyard currently grows shiraz and a small amount of chardonnay.

The Centre is built on a small block, previously part of the Hungerford Hill vineyard, that farmer and irrigation agent Keith Yore bought in about 1980. Yore had previously planted 22 hectares of vineyard on his extensive property at Muswellbrook, in the Upper Hunter, and wine is still produced from these for the Hunter Wine Society and the Verona label. A small amount of wine also appears under the Tullamurra label. Varieties include sauvignon blanc, semillon, chardonnay, shiraz, cabernet sauvignon and verdelho. He grows pecan nuts, too, which are the best you'll ever taste. Both wine and pecans can be bought at the Small Winemakers Centre. (Keith has told me he is very particular about storing the pecans refrigerated to keep their freshness. They can go rancid if stored badly.) When you're sated with pecans, you can satisfy other cravings at either the lunch bar or Cafe Max.

Susie Lochhead is Keith Yore's daughter and, while you won't see her at the Centre, you see her influence everywhere. She's an architect and has designed the Ivanhoe and Gartelmann cellar doors, the Pokolbin Community Hall and the new Lowe Family winery at Mudgee. Her skills are in great demand.

Vinden Estate

ADDRESS: 17 Gillards Road, Pokolbin 2320
TELEPHONE: (02) 4998 7410
FAX: (02) 4998 7421
ESTABLISHED: 1995
CELLAR DOOR: 9am–5pm 7 days
OWNERS: Guy and Sandra Vinden
VITICULTURIST: Tim Lesnik
WINEMAKER: Guy Vinden and John Baruzzi
1999 PRODUCTION: 750 cases
MAILING LIST: Yes, with wine club
DISTRIBUTED: Direct from the vineyard

'We bought four paddocks of weeds with a few trees in 1990.' This was how Sandra Vinden described the beginnings of Vinden Estate. Over the next few years the Vindens cleared the land and planted several cover crops, which were ploughed in to improve the soil. In 1995 they started planting shiraz, merlot, semillon and chardonnay and now have about 3 hectares, which will shortly rise to 4.

Guy Vinden, who has a legal practice in Chatswood, has been studying wine sciences at the Hunter Institute of Technology, Kurri Kurri, and now spends part of each week on the property. The Vindens have built a small winery, where Guy made their first wines in 1998, under the watchful eye of ex-Wyndham and Wilderness Estate winemaker John Baruzzi.

The newly opened cellar door area is at one end of their simply beautiful new house; there are few new buildings in the Hunter with the understated elegance and style of this one.

The wines are made in tiny quantities at present. 'We're starting small so that we can cover the marketing side,' Sandra explained. It's a shame a few other small companies haven't got the same message. The whites are quite forward in style, particularly the semillons, which have good flavours, but without the potential to age much further.

1999 and *1998* Chardonnay ($18.50 and $19.50)

An interesting contrast. The '98 has lovely, lemony French oak, which is of great quality, but overpowers the fruit a little. There's some toasty bottle age appearing, suggesting that it should be kept for only a year or two. The '99 has better oak balance, with fresh melon fruit and good acidity. Drink the '98 and keep the '99 for a bit.

1999 and 1998 Semillon ($18.50 and $19.50)

Another contrast. The '98 is quite full, soft and round in the mouth, with nice honeyed development. It has plenty of flavour and is very good immediate drinking. The '99 is, again, much livelier, although it too is developing fairly quickly. A hint of fruit-salad character suggests there was a touch of botrytis in the fruit. Drink now or keep for a couple of years.

1998 Shiraz ($19.50)

This is one of those soft, elegant young Hunter reds which drinks beautifully young, but often surprises with the capacity to age. The berry fruit has a nice touch of new oak and the palate is soft and well balanced in the 'Hunter burgundy' way, with fine tannins on the finish. It shows the same finesse as the house where you'll taste it.

ADDRESS: Wilderness Road, Lovedale 2320
TELEPHONE: (02) 4930 7317
FAX: (02) 4930 7814
E-MAIL: rwepp@wandinvalley.com.au
WEB: www.wandinvalley.com.au
ESTABLISHED: 1973
CELLAR DOOR: 10am–5pm 7 days
OWNERS: James and Philippa Davern
VITICULTURIST: David Lowe
WINEMAKERS: Karl Stockhausen (2000 vintage), Sarah Kate Wilson
1999 PRODUCTION: 8000 cases
MAILING LIST: Yes
DISTRIBUTED: Direct from the vineyard
FEATURES: Frequent events, such as The Lovedale Long Lunch in May; three jazz dinners (May, June and Aug); two-day Food and Wine Experience with Damien Pignolet and Max Allen in June; 'Words, Wine and Wassail' in Aug; The Lovedale Grand Dinner, Sept; The Macquarie Trio Vineyard Concert, Oct; 'The Feast of the Olive', olive harvest festival Nov. Ruby Pavilion function centre and cricket pitch. Accommodation in 2–4 bedroom villas. Swimming pool and tennis court. Restaurant, Cafe Crocodile. Craft shop, barbecue facilities and children's playground. Space shuttle launch pad (no, just kidding!).

Wandin Valley started life as Millstone, which was established by Peter and Vivienne Dobinson in 1973. Dobinson was a potter and a highly innovative winemaker who produced many individual, if somewhat eccentric, wines. The property was bought by James Davern, a television executive, who, amongst other things, was the producer of the television series *A Country Practice*. Wandin Valley was the town in which the series was set.

The Daverns have gradually developed Wandin Valley into an extraordinary showpiece, with the addition of accommodation, a conference centre, an excellent restaurant in Cafe Crocodile and, in an echo of Gordon Cope-Williams' vineyard at Macedon, a cricket pitch.

Their 2000 calendar shows an amazingly diverse collection of events, some linked with other Lovedale region events and others exclusive to WVE. I've shown the programme above, not suggesting that they'll happen every year, but in the hope that 2001 and beyond will be as good.

The skilled Geoff Broadfield made the wines from 1990 to 1999, so it's no surprise that their quality has been good.

There are now 10 hectares of vineyard planted to a comprehensive mix of varieties – chardonnay, merlot, malbec, shiraz, cabernet sauvignon, verdelho, muscat and, unusually for the Hunter, ruby cabernet.

Of the reds, I preferred the '98 Riley's Reserve Cabernet Sauvignon, which has good minty, blackcurrant fruit and firm but balanced tannin. It should develop beautifully in, say, six years. 1998 Bridie's Shiraz is a soft, round, nicely balanced wine with pleasant fruit and new oak, with a little development adding some earthy complexity. Four or five years should make this a lovely, soft, mellow Hunter.

1999 Verdelho ($17)

This is one of the best Hunter verdelhos I've tried recently. It has really good depth of ripe fruit, with those typically pineapple varietal characters, yet the palate is soft and beautifully balanced. It's a full-bodied white for full-flavoured foods. It should age reasonably well until about 2002 if you're after more complexity.

1998 Reserve Chardonnay ($21)

Quite a striking wine, as it delivers plenty of ripe flavour without a particularly full body or big whack of alcohol. It's very complex, with lovely flavour and balance, and the oak has been so well handled that it's barely apparent. It should develop still more complex, toasty flavours over a couple of years.

ADDRESS: Wilderness Road, Lovedale 2321
TELEPHONE: (02) 4930 7594
FAX: (02) 4930 7199
E-MAIL: warraroongestate@bigpond.com
ESTABLISHED: 1986
CELLAR DOOR: 10am–5pm 7 days
OWNERS: Adam and Jan Rees
VITICULTURIST: Adam Rees with Bryan Hubbard (consultant)
WINEMAKER: Adam Rees with Gary Reed (consultant)
1999 PRODUCTION: 2000 cases
MAILING LIST: Yes, plus membership of the Warraroong Wine Club, which gives discounts for wine and accommodation
DISTRIBUTED: Direct from the vineyard
FEATURES: Lovedale Long Lunch. Self-contained accommodation in Claremont House, a luxurious Georgian style house. Also, a four-bedroom winemaker's cottage.

Daisy Hill was one of the great vineyards of last century, extending for a large distance along the south of Wilderness Road. Part of the property was replanted in 1986 by Peter and Beverley Fraser and named the Fraser Vineyard. I remember their first chardonnay winning a well-deserved trophy at the Hunter Wine Show. Clearly the vineyard hadn't forgotten what it could do. The property was recently bought by Adam and Jan Rees, who offer accommodation for up to eighteen people in Claremont House and The Winemaker's Cottage. The 6 hectare vineyard is planted with chardonnay, semillon, chenin blanc, sauvignon blanc, shiraz and malbec.

The '99 Semillon has delicate, citrus fruit and is quite full on the palate, and with a little tannin that suggests some skin contact before fermentation. It should develop well in the short term.

1998 Shiraz ($25)

I liked this wine for its beautiful, rich fruit. It's a bit on the oaky side at present, but the wine has such obvious depth of flavour, coupled with plenty of soft tannin, that I'm sure it will come into better fruit/oak balance. Give it at least five years, although it will age way past ten. Good value.

ADDRESS: Branxton Road, Pokolbin 2320
TELEPHONE: (02) 4998 7755
FAX: (02) 4998 7750
ESTABLISHED: 1985
CELLAR DOOR: 9am–5pm 7 days
OWNER: Josef Lesnik
VITICULTURIST: Josef Lesnik
WINEMAKER: Josef Lesnik
MAILING list: Yes
DISTRIBUTED: Normans Wines, Wine Works (NSW)
FEATURES: Picnic and barbecue facilities.

In 1982, Joe Lesnik planted vines on a site that had been the Rosedale Racecourse in 1928. His venture started as Lesnik Family Wines, but after a while he decided to perpetuate the name of 'The Wilderness'. This was the name given to a large property to the east of Branxton Road and along what is now Wilderness Road. It was settled and farmed by Joseph Holmes who planted vineyards in about 1862, but they have long since disappeared.

In 1985 Joe added a winery. This is almost directly in line with the northern approach to Cessnock Airport and local scuttlebutt had it that the winery was put up without Department of Civil Aviation planning permission. Whether this is true or not, the winery is still there, and without any re-structuring of its roof.

Joe now has 37 hectares of vineyard, planted to a broad mix of shiraz, pinot noir, merlot, chardonnay, verdelho, semillon, malbec, cabernet sauvignon, sauvignon blanc and chambourcin. The wines appear under several labels: Wilderness Estate, Lesnik Wines, Borradaile Estate and Black Creek Wines. For some years Joe was joined by ex-Wyndham Estate winemaker John Baruzzi, but John departed in 1999 and is now working as a consultant.

I found these wines quite unusual, even problematical. The '98 Black Creek Semillon Chardonnay has plenty of ripe flavour but also carries a little volatility and an odd yeasty character. The bottle of the '99 Black Creek Verdelho ($13.30) I tasted was oxidised. Hopefully neither of these is typical. The '98 Wilderness Reserve Chardonnay ($17.80) has restrained melon fruit and is still quite fresh, even retarded in its development. It should develop complexity over several years.

1998 Wilderness Estate Shiraz ($17.80)

The nose shows some stalkiness, combined with sweet new oak. The flavour is quite complex, with some fruit sweetness and a touch of liquorice, until firm, rather chewy tannins cut in towards the finish. This is an atypical Hunter shiraz that will clearly age for several years, although it will always be on the robust side.

1998 Wilderness Estate Cabernet Merlot ($17.80)

Complex nose, with good depth of berry fruit that's beginning to show some bottle age and some tarry overtones, perhaps from charred oak. The palate has rich flavour and, like the shiraz above, finishes with rather chewy tannins. Another big, strongly constructed red that will take many years in bottle.

ADDRESS: De Beyers Road, Pokolbin 2321
TELEPHONE: (02) 4998 7648
FAX: (02) 4998 7648
E-MAIL: pottersinn@email.com
ESTABLISHED: 1984
CELLAR DOOR: 10am–5pm Tuesday to Sunday and public holidays
OWNERS: Max Andreson and family
VITICULTURIST: Thomas Jung
WINEMAKER: Tom Andreson
1999 PRODUCTION: 25 tonnes
MAILING LIST: Yes
DISTRIBUTED: Direct from the vineyard
FEATURES: Vineyard pottery with a wide range of ceramics, handmade pottery and port crocks (personalised to order). Motel and two-bedroom cottage. German styled Potter's Family restaurant, seating 50, with views over vineyards and Brokenback Range. Oktoberfest and numerous wine and food festivals throughout the year.

Max Andreson is a German ceramics engineer and potter who, in 1984, bought a 26 hectare property on De Beyers Road with a small area of shiraz vines. These had been planted in the late 1960s by Peter Kemp, a Gosford orchardist. Andreson's first priority was to build his pottery, but in 1985 and 1987 he added chardonnay and semillon grapes to the vineyard, which now totals just over 5 hectares. In 1989 he built a winery. A motel and restaurant complete the complex, which is promoted as the German Tourist and Holiday Estate.

The restaurant specialises in German cooking and is decked out with suitably Teutonic decorations. There is a wide range of pottery available in the shop.

I'm afraid I can't recommend any of the wines I tasted but, if you're interested in pottery or German cooking, or want a great view from your motel window, pay Windarra a visit.

ADDRESS: Dalwood Road, Dalwood, via Branxton 2335
TELEPHONE: (02) 4938 3444
FAX: (02) 4938 3422
ESTABLISHED: 1970 (as Wyndham Estate)
CELLAR DOOR: 10am–4.40pm 7 days
OWNERS: Groupe Pernod Ricard
VITICULTURIST: Stephen Gilbaud-Oulton
WINEMAKER: Brett McKinnon
MAILING LIST: Yes
DISTRIBUTED: Orlando Wyndham (Groupe Pernod Ricard)
FEATURES: Wyndham Estate Concert, February; Jazz at Wyndham Estate, April;
Opera in the Vineyards, October.

George Wyndham was one of the first to plant vines in the Hunter Valley when he took up a land grant near the Hunter River in 1830, naming the property 'Dalwood'. He may even have been the first; we just don't know. His first vines died, but he persevered and planted more, making his first wine in 1835. This, by his own admission, was not a success, but he must have been a quick learner as, in time, he became one of the most widely known producers in the Hunter. He also bought land further down the river, which he called 'Fernhill' and much further afield, as far as Inverell. The wine he made there, at his property 'Bukkulla', was dark and strong, and he used this to bolster the lighter wines he made at Dalwood. (Amazingly, Bukkulla ceased production in only 1940 following a severe frost and after fire destroyed the cellars in 1939. With the revival of grape growing around Inverell, maybe Bukkulla will be revived.)

Wyndham died in 1870 but for a while the business continued successfully under his son John, who built the company into one of the most successful in the Hunter. However, it didn't survive the death of John Wyndham and the depression of the 1890s. After a period of receivership, the Wilkinson family

of Coolalta bought the business and then sold it to Penfolds in 1904.

Penfolds' purchase was a particularly significant one. Firstly, I believe it was the first time a wine company had ventured to another state (or, before Federation, another colony). More significantly, Penfolds was to become, with Lindemans, one of the two big players in the Hunter for the next fifty years. It also made Dalwood into a major national brand and, although it disappeared from our shelves in the 1970s, the name is still used in international markets.

At some time or other, Penfolds owned vineyards in many parts of the Hunter. 'Sparkling Vale' was just off Allandale Road, another vineyard lay along the railway line at Allandale, and 'Penfold Vale' and the Hunter Valley Distillery, or 'HVD', were on Hermitage Road. However, in the early 1960s they made a much more radical move, planting a huge vineyard on Wybong Creek in the Upper Hunter and selling the land and cellars to their ex-winemaker and manager Perc McGuigan. For a while Perc's son Brian was the Penfolds winemaker at Wybong and dabbled in a vineyard with David Hordern and Dr Bob Smith, but in 1971 Brian formed a company with other investors, which he called Wyndham Estate. This started in

Wyndham Estate

a fairly small way but was soon growing at a phenomenal rate, acquiring other wineries and vineyards and taking grapes from much further afield. Richmond Grove rapidly became another successful brand for Wyndham, assisted by the marketing genius of ex-Saxonvale winemaker Mark Cashmore, although others, such as Saxonvale itself and Hunter Estate, were less successful.

The secret to this success was simple – if you were Brian McGuigan. Brian had an amazing understanding of what average wine drinkers wanted and he gave it to them. Wyndham Estate grew to be one of the largest brands in Australia and, by the late 1980s, was also making big inroads into international markets. The company had made a widely trumpeted withdrawal from Australian wine shows 'to concentrate on international exhibitions'. It used this departure in a clever way, exhibiting their best 'show' wines to great effect overseas and using that success to promote the standard Wyndham wines in Australia.

Wyndham floated on the Australian Stock Exchange and, not long after, the French liquor group Pernod Ricard acquired the company, changing the name of its Australian operations to Orlando Wyndham.

Those buying and drinking Wyndham wines would not have noticed any of these corporate changes. Apart from a natural evolution of the labels, and the appearance and departure of some lines, little else has changed. Few, also, would have noticed the disappearance of the words 'Hunter Valley' from most of the wines in 1990. Quality has been maintained at previous levels and, if anything, the wines are now better than previously. I was pleasantly surprised by my last taste of Bin 444 Cabernet Sauvignon; it had really attractive berry flavour and pleasing softness. The Hunter Chardonnay remains one of the few mainstream wines to declare its origin and is usually a richly flavoured wine with genuine Hunter character.

The Wyndham label has recently been extended in two directions, the first a group of varietal blends – the 1828 Range – at a price somewhat below the Bin Range. Shouldn't that be the 1830 Range? (Incidentally, I love the marketing hype in the brochure, which describes Wyndham's first vintage in 1835 as getting 'rave reviews'. Were there wine writers around then, too? George Wyndham himself described the wine as 'vinegar'.) However, in a move that gladdens my heart, Wyndham has launched a small group of wines under the Show Reserve label, which are released after bottle age has worked its magic, something that the best Hunters need. It's really good to see that Wyndham is standing by its heritage and releasing classic Hunter wines again. With its vineyard resources, Wyndham is in a better position to do this than most other companies in the Hunter. The two wines below are great examples.

1994 *Show Reserve* Semillon ($21)

Medium–deep yellow. The nose has plenty of ripe, even tropical, fruit, with lovely developed straw characters. The palate is full and developed, with grilled nuts and toasty flavours, and has filled out considerably with bottle age. The fruit isn't hugely intense, but the development has given the wine really beautiful flavours that make it a pleasure to drink. It still has a few years in it, too.

1995 *Show Reserve* Shiraz ($26.30)

Beautiful ripe shiraz fruit on the nose, with lovely, earthy developed complexity. The palate is medium bodied and round, with softness and balance and very attractive flavour. This isn't a big wine, but it has real Hunter balance and style. It's drinking beautifully and will develop further over several years.

Travel*ling*

There are several ways of getting to the Hunter from Sydney, depending on your inclination and, of course, where you're starting. Two main approaches are from Sydney and from the north.

From Sydney

The simplest way for most people is to head north along the Pacific Highway until you pass Wahroonga and then take the F3 freeway towards Newcastle. From the west, you'll arrive at the F3 along the Cumberland Highway. You then have a relaxed hour or so on the freeway until you reach the turn-off to Cessnock, which clearly says 'Vineyards'. This is 100 kilometres from the beginning of the freeway. From there you travel, rather more slowly, through Freeman's Waterholes and over the Wattagan Range to Cessnock, about half an hour away. Don't miss the left turn half way. As you enter Cessnock you'll find the Visitors' Information Centre on the left next to the school playing fields and about 1 kilometre before the town centre. The Pokolbin vineyards lie to the north, between ten and thirty minutes away, the Broke vineyards a little further. For the Upper Hunter, you'll need to take the Branxton Road north from Cessnock and travel about an hour further. After you join the New England Highway at Branxton, either head through Singleton to Muswellbrook or turn left on to the Mitchell Line Road to bypass Singleton and head for Jerrys Plains and Denman.

If you're not pressed for time, there's a much prettier, historic and enjoyable way. I've cursed the Wollombi Road countless times in the past, as you'll know from my introduction, but the road's very good now. Take the M3 as before. After you cross the Hawkesbury River and pass the exit to Mount White, keep your eyes open. Take the turn-off to Peate's Ridge along the old Pacific Highway. At the start, it's wide enough to land a 747, but it soon gets narrower. After Peate's Ridge, take a left fork to Central Mangrove and Kulnura. (Set your odometer.) The road will take you through these two areas, with their market gardens and orchards, where you can stock up on oranges, peaches, macadamias and avocados, if you're there in season. The orange blossom, at times, is simply magnificent. In places, freesias grow wild along the roadside in spring. You'll pass the Central Mangrove Country Club, with its 'Big Bottle'. (Years ago, this was Penfolds Royal Reserve Port but, in deference to changes in the wine market, it's now Tyrrell's Long Flat Red. I was most impressed on my last trip to see that the vintage had changed to 1997.) You'll then pass by several horse studs and through the gum and Angophora forests of the Yengo National Park and the intriguingly named Bucketty (was it often raining on the edge of the escarpment?) before the road from Wisemans Ferry joins you from the left. After this, you're on the old convict-built road that was cut in 1826.

At 34.6 kilometres from the Peate's Ridge fork, park on the right of the road and, if you look carefully, you'll find, chiselled out of the stone cliff, the convicts' drinking trough. More recent travellers have had other things to drink. This was a meeting place for weekend vignerons heading for the Hunter. The compost under the leaf litter is composed of corks from long-past bottles of Bollinger, Krug and, in winter, Ch. Lanessan or Aloxe Corton. You'll hear bellbirds on the breeze. At 40.9 kilometres, you'll pass Murray's Run Culvert, built in 1830, before plunging downhill into the Yarramalong Valley. The road then takes you through Laguna – stop for a beer at the Trading Post – and then to Wollombi. Dr Jurd's hostelry is another natural stop. You may also want to visit Undercliff Vineyard if you need to relax after the hairpin bends below Bucketty.

Most people turn right to Cessnock and the Pokolbin vineyards but, for something different, go straight on and visit the Broke/Fordwich area and then to Pokolbin.

From Sydney's far west, the natural road to take is the first road of all, the one cut from Windsor to Singleton in 1823. This is the famous Putty Road, which brings you out into the Hunter Valley at Bulga, the north end of the Broke/Fordwich area. Don't be in a hurry. The hairpins at the north end deserve respect.

From the north

Travellers from the north of the state, or those from Queensland seeking refuge from their muggy, tropical climate for the fresh breezes of the Hunter, approach the Valley either on the New England Highway or along the coast down the Pacific Highway. The inland route takes you straight through Muswellbrook and the Upper Hunter. You need only turn right at Muswellbrook, where sign-posted, to Sandy Hollow or Denman. Keep going south past Singleton to reach the Lower Hunter and look for the vineyard signs.

On the Pacific Highway, you should turn right after the Hexham Bridge over the mighty Hunter River and follow the signs to either Cessnock, for the Lower Hunter, or Singleton and Muswellbrook, for the Upper Hunter.

Safe travelling!

Eat*ing*

Amanda's on the Edge
Windsors Edge, McDonalds Road, Pokolbin 2320
02 4998 7900

Amicos Restaurant
138 Wollombi Road, Cessnock 2325
02 4991 1995

Black Opal Hotel
220 Vincent Street, Cessnock 2325
02 4990 1070

Blaxlands Restaurant
Broke Road, Pokolbin 2320
02 4998 7550

Blue Bianca and Luke's Unique Eatery
Mount View Road, Cessnock 2325
02 4990 2573

The Branxton Inn
35 Maitland Road, Branxton,
02 4938 1225

Brent's Restaurant
Montagne View Estate
555 Hermitage Road, Pokolbin 2320
02 4998 7822

Buttai Barn
Lings Road, Buttai
02 4930 3153

Cafe Caffe
188 Broke Road, Pokolbin 2320
02 4998 7321

Cafe Enzo
Peppers Creek, Broke Road, Pokolbin 2320
02 4998 7233

Cafe Max
McDonalds Road, Pokolbin 2320
02 4998 7899

Cafe on Cooper
1F Cooper Street, Cessnock 2325
02 4991 2762

Cafe Monteverdi at Catersfield House
96 Mistletoe Lane, Pokolbin 2320
02 4998 7220

Cafe San Martino and Wine Bar
The Hunter Resort, Hermitage Road, Pokolbin 2320
02 4998 7777

Cafe 65
4/65 John Street, Singleton 2330
02 6572 4851

Casuarina Restaurant
Hermitage Road, Pokolbin 2320
02 4998 7888

Cellar Restaurant
Hunter Valley Gardens, Broke Road, Pokolbin 2320
02 4998 7584

Charade's Restaurant at Charbonnier
44 Maitland Road, Singleton 2330
02 6572 2333

Chez Pok
Peppers Guest House
Ekerts Lane, Pokolbin 2320
02 4998 7596

Cliffords Cafe
43 Allandale Road, Cessnock 2325
02 4990 1671

Corky's Restaurant & Function Centre
Wollombi Road, Cessnock 2325
02 4991 6088

The Cottage Restaurant
109 Wollombi Road, Cessnock 2325
02 4990 3062

Courtyard Restaurant
Travellers Rest
35 Colliery Street, Cessnock 2325
02 4991 2355

Elizabeths Cafe
Mount Pleasant
Marrowbone Road, Pokolbin 2320
02 4998 7280

Esca at Bimbadgen
McDonalds Road, Pokolbin 2320
02 4998 7585

George and the Dragon
48 Melbourne Street, East Maitland 2323
02 4933 7272

Golden Grape Estate
Oakey Creek Road, Pokolbin 2320
02 4998 7568

Harry's Sandwich Bar
Small Winemakers Centre, McDonalds Road,
Pokolbin 2320
02 4998 7668

Hermitage Restaurant
Hunter Resort
Hermitage Road, Pokolbin 2320
02 4998 7777

Hope Estate Restaurant
Hope Estate, Cobcroft Road, Broke 2330
02 6579 1161

Hunter Gourmet Pizza
146 Vincent Street, Cessnock 2325
02 4990 8883

Hunter Valley Gardens Restaurant
Cnr Broke & McDonalds roads,
Pokolbin 2320
02 4998 7600

Hunter Valley Cheese Co.
PO Box 722, Cessnock 2325
02 49987744

Il Cacciatore
Cnr Gillards and McDonalds roads,
Pokolbin 2320
02 4998 7639

Isabels at Mid City Motor Inn
180 John Street, Singleton 2330
02 6572 2011

Jack Daniels Tavern and Restaurant
148 John Street, Singleton 2330
02 6571 2712

James Busby Restaurant
Country Comfort, Singleton
02 6572 3288

Kathleens Cottage
228 John Street, Singleton 2330
02 6572 3228

The Kurrajong Restaurant and Cafe
234 Wollombi Road, Cessnock 2325
02 4991 4414

Leith's Restaurant
Kirkton Park
Oakey Creek Road, Pokolbin 2320
02 4998 7680

Magnum Cafe
Peterson House
Cnr Broke & Branxton roads, Pokolbin 2320
02 4998 7881

Mallees Cafe Restaurant
Broke Road, Pokolbin 2320
02 4998 7724

Mulligan's Brasserie
Cyress Lakes Resort
Cnr McDonalds & Thompsons roads,
Pokolbin 2320
02 4993 1555

The Oak Brasserie
The Royal Oak Hotel
221 Vincent Street, Cessnock 2325
02 4990 2366

Palatinos in the Hunter
142 Bridge Street, Muswellbrook 2333
02 6541 2211

Perees at Branxton
72 Maitland Road, Branxton 2335
02 4938 3225

Pipette Restaurant
Cyress Lakes Resort
Cnr McDonalds & Thompsons roads,
Pokolbin 2320
02 4993 1555

Pokolbin Woodfired Bakehouse
McGuigan Wine cellars, McDonalds Road,
Pokolbin 2320
02 4998 7264

Potters Restaurant
German Tourist Centre, De Beyers Road,
Pokolbin 2320
02 4998 7648

Reds Restaurant
Broke Road, Pokolbin 2320
02 4998 7977

Reggio's Restaurant
57–61 Cumberland Street, Cessnock 2325
02 4990 6633

Roberts at Peppertree
Halls Road, Pokolbin 2320
02 4998 7330

Rockgarden Restaurant
82 Wilderness Road, Lovedale 2320
02 4930 7244

The Rothbury Cafe
Broke Road, Pokolbin 2320
02 4998 7363

Shaky Tables
Hunter Country Lodge
Cessnock–Branxton Road,
North Rothbury 2335
02 4938 1744

SJ's Restaurant
Arrowfield winery,
Denman Road,
Jerrys Plains 2330
02 6576 4041

Tallawanta Hotel
Hunter Valley Gardens, Broke Road,
Pokolbin 2320
02 4998 7854

Taylors Cafe
McDonalds Road, Pokolbin 2329
02 4998 7117

*Vineyard Kitchen Coffee Shop
& Produce Store*
Hunter Valley Gardens, Broke Road,
Pokolbin 2320
02 4998 7716

Wyndham Estate Restaurant and Cafe
Dalwood Road, Branxton 2335
02 4938 3444

Stay*ing*

Aberglasslyn House
Aberglasslyn Lane, Aberglasslyn 2320
02 4932 7396

Abermain Hotel
27 Charles Street, Abermain 2326
02 4930 4201

Abernethy Guest House
20 Ferguson Street, Abernethy 2325
02 4990 8303

Alleyn Court B & B
Lot 31 Talga Road, Rothbury 2320
02 4930 7011

Almavale Cottage
Doyles Creek, Via Jerrys Plains 2330
02 6576 4188

Araluen Mistletoe Cottages
108 Mistletoe Lane, Pokolbin 2320
02 4998 7567

Aussie Rest Motel
43 Sheddon Street, Cessnock 2325
02 4991 4197

Avalon House
699 Wollombi Road, Broke 2330
02 6579 1254

Avoca House
Wollombi Road, Wollombi 2325
02 4998 3233

Belford Country Cabins
659 Hermitage Road, Belford 2335
02 6574 7100

Bellbird Bed & Breakfast
275 Wollombi Road,
Bellbird Heights 2325
02 4990 7219

Bellbird Cottages
Mount View Road, Mount Baker 2325
02 4998 1705

Bellbird Hotel
388 Wollombi Road, Bellbird 2325
02 4990 1094

Belltrees Country House
Gundy Road, Scone 2337
02 6545 1668

Benjamin Singleton Motel
24 George Street, New England Hwy,
Singleton 2330
02 6572 2922

Berenbell Vineyard Retreat
60 Mistletoe Lane, Pokolbin 2320
02 4998 7468

Billabong Moon
393 Hermitage Road, Pokolbin 2335
02 6574 7290

Bimbadeen Estate
Lot 256 Bimbadeen Road, Mount View 2325
02 4990 1577

Black Opal Hotel
220 Vincent Street, Cessnock 2325
02 4990 1070

Blackwattle Cottage
16 Talga Road, Rothbury 2320
0417 267 117

Blueberry Hill Vineyard
Coulson Road, Pokolbin 2320
02 4998 7295

Bluebush Estate
Wilderness Road, Lovedale 2320
02 4930 7177

Bonnies
Lot 1 O'Connors Road, Pokolbin 2320
02 4991 4000

Branxton House Motel
69 Maitland Road, Branxton 2335
02 4938 3099

Brockley's Bed & Breakfast
Lot 494 Tuckers Lane, North Rothbury 2335
02 4938 3011

Bronte House B & B
147 Swan Street, Morpeth,
02 4934 6080

Burncroft Guest House
Talga Road, Lovedale 2320
0500 507 246

Caledonia Hotel
110 Aberdare Road, Aberdare 2325
02 4990 1212

Cambridge Retreat
Lot 25 Old North Road, Rothbury 2320
02 6574 7268

Cants Cottage
677 Wollombi Road, Broke 2330
02 6579 1333

Capers Guesthouse & Capers Cottage
6–11Maitland Road, Wollombi 2325
02 4998 3211

Carellen Holiday Cottages
Lot 101 Rosemount Road, Denman 2328
02 6547 2549

Carriages Guest House
Halls Road, Pokolbin 2320
02 4998 7591

Carricks Country House
Lot 172 Wallaby Gully Road, Ellalong 2325
02 4998 1241

Casuarina Country Inn
Hermitage Road, Pokolbin 2320
02 4998 7888

Catersfield House
96 Mistletoe Lane, Pokolbin 2320
02 4998 7220

Cedar Creek Cottages
'Willtun' Wollombi Road, Millfield 2325
02 4998 1576

Cedars Of Mount View
Mount View, Cessnock 2325
02 4959 3072

Cessnock Cabins & Caravan Park
Branxton/Allandale Roads,
Nulkaba 2325
02 4990 5819

Cessnock Heritage Inn
167 Vincent Street, Cessnock 2325
02 4991 2744

Cessnock Hotel
234 Wollombi Road, Cessnock 2325
02 4990 1002

Cessnock Motel
13 Allandale Road, Cessnock 2325
02 4990 2699

Cessnock Vintage Motor Inn
300 Maitland Road, Cessnock 2325
02 4990 4333

Charbonnier Hallmark Inn
44 Maitland Road, Singleton 2330
02 6572 2333

Chardonnay Sky Motel & Skydiving
Lot 210 Allandale Road, Cessnock 2325
02 4991 4812

Chez Vous
138 De Beyers Road, Pokolbin 2321
02 4998 7300

Claremont House
Wilderness Road, Lovedale 2320
02 4930 7594

Cockfighter Creek Vineyard Country House
738 Wollombi Road, Broke 2330
02 6579 1220

Cockfighter's Ghost Cottage
331 Milbrodale Road, Broke 2330
02 9667 1622

Convent at Peppertree
Halls Road, Pokolbin 2320
02 4998 7764

Cottage at Collectables
393 Hermitage Road, Pokolbin 2320
02 6574 7290

Country Acres Caravan Park
Maison Dieu Road, Singleton 2330
02 6572 2328

Country Comfort Motel
Cnr George & Hunter streets, Singleton 2330
02 6572 2388

Cracklewood
21 Lovedale Road, Lovedale 2320
0418 678 161

Cumberland Motor Inn
57–61 Cumberland Street,
Cessnock 2325
02 4990 6633

Cypress Lakes Resort
Cnr McDonalds & Thompsons roads,
Pokolbin 2320
02 4993 1555

Danica House
27 Orient Street, Nulkaba 2325
02 4991 4893

Dingo's Retreat
Lot 11, McDonalds Road, Pokolbin 2320
02 4998 7449

Duck Hollow
103 Deasys Road, Pokolbin 2320
02 9415 6656

Elfin Hill Motel
Marrowbone Road, Pokolbin 2320
02 4998 7543

Ellalong Hotel
80 Helena Street, Ellalong 2325
02 4998 1217

Elysium Vineyard Cottage
Milbrodale Road, Broke 2330
02 9664 2368
0417 282 746

Emma's Cottage & Winery
Wilderness Road, Lovedale 2325
02 4991 4000

Eumalga
13 Talga Road, Rothbury 2320
02 4930 7504

Fordwich Olive Farm
Lot 3 Fordwich Road, Broke 2330
02 6579 1179

Four Horizons
Georges Road, Watagan Forest,
Quarrobolong 2325
02 4998 6257
0407 927 473

Francis Phillip Motor Inn
18 Maitland Road, Singleton 2330
02 6571 1991

Getaway Inn
11 Orient Street, Nulkaba 2325
02 4990 6222

German Tourist Centre
Potter Inn Motel
Lot 181 De Beyers Road, Pokolbin 2320
02 4998 7648

Glen Ayr Cottages
De Beyers Road, Pokolbin 2320
02 4998 7784

Glengarrie Park
Lot 81 Wilderness Road, Rothbury 2320
02 4930 7133

Grapeview Villas
(C/O Hunter Valley Gardens Lodge)
Broke Road, Pokolbin 2321
02 4998 7630

Green Gables Lodge
558 Milbrodale Road, Broke 2330
02 6579 1258

Greta Main Pay Office
RMB Lot 12 Wollombi Road,
Greta Main 2325
02 4998 1703

Guest House
Mulla Villa & Hunter Highland Tours
Great Northern Road, Wollombi 2325
02 4998 3254

Hambledon Hill House
538 Hambledon Hill House,
Singleton 2330
0409 186 599

Heaven & Earth Hideaway
Lot 2 Mt. View Road, Cessnock 2325
02 4990 7823

Hermitage Hideaway
Hermitage Road, Pokolbin 2320
02 4991 4000

Hermitage Lodge
McDonalds Road, Pokolbin 2320
02 4998 7639

Hill Top Country House
81 Talga Road, Rothbury 2320
02 4930 7111

Holman Estate
Gillards Lane, Pokolbin 2320
02 9966 1414

Honeytree Cottage
16 Gillards Road, Pokolbin 2320
02 4998 7693

Hunter Country Lodge
Cessnock–Branxton Road, North Rothbury 2335
02 4938 1744

Hunter Haven
351a Wollombi Road, Bellbird 2325
02 4990 8858

Hunter Hideaway Cottages
Tuckers Lane, North Rothbury 2335
02 4938 2091

Hunter Olive House
322 Harrowby Street, Broke 2330
02 4322 2769

Hunter Resort – Hunter Valley
Hermitage Road, Pokolbin 2320
02 4998 7777

Hunter River Retreat
1090 Maitlandvale Road, Rosebrook 2320
02 4930 111, 0407 256 788

Hunter Valley Country Cabins
C/O Millfield Post Office, Millfield 2325
02 4990 8989

Hunter Valley Gardens Lodge
Broke Road, Pokolbin 2320
02 4998 7600

Hunter Valley Motel
30 Allandale Road, Cessnock 2325
02 4990 1722

Ironstone Cottage
Lot 1092 Londons Road, Lovedale 2325
02 4990 3376

Junburra Hut
Appletree Flat, Via Jerrys Plains 2330
02 6576 4068

Kerrabee Homestead
Bylong Valley Way, Denman 2328
02 6547 5155

Kindred Estate Country Lodge
Cnr McDonalds Rd and Palmers Lane,
Pokolbin 2320
02 4998 7381

Kirkton Park Country House Hotel
Oakey Creek Road, Pokolbin 2320
02 4998 7680

Krinklewood Cottage
Lot 5 Palmers Lane, Pokolbin 2320
02 4998 7619

Kurrajong Vineyard Cottages
614 Hermitage Road, Pokolbin 2335
02 6574 7117

Kurri Conference Centre
Heddon Street, Kurri Kurri 2327
02 4936 0342

Kindred Estate Country Lodge
Cnr McDonalds Road and Palmers Lane,
Pokolbin 2320
02 4998 7381

Kurri Conference Centre
Heddon Street, Kurri Kurri 2327
02 4936 0342

Kurri Motor Inn
313 Lang Street, Kurri Kurri 2327
02 4937 2222

Lancedene
3/115 Vincent Street, Cessnock 2325
02 4991 4000

Leonard Estate Guest House
RMB Lot 1 Palmers Lane, Pokolbin 2320
02 4998 7381

Lochinvar House
New England Hwy, Lochinvar 2321
02 4930 7873

Lothian Grange Luxury Cottage
Cessnock-Branxton Road, Rothbury 2320
02 4938 1530

Lovedale Lodge
Lot 33 Londons Road, Lovedale 2325
02 4991 1628

Madigan Vineyard
Lot 1 Wilderness Road, Rothbury 2321
02 4998 7815

Mid City Motor Inn
180 John Street, Singleton 2330
02 6572 2011

Millbrook Estate
Lot 18/19 Mt View Road, Millfield 2325
02 4998 1155

Mistletoe Guesthouse
771 Hermitage Road, Pokolbin 2320
02 4998 7770

Misty Glen Cottage
Lot 6 Deasys Road, Pokolbin 2320
02 4998 7781
0418 168 788

Molly Morgan
Talga Road, Lovedale 2325
02 4930 7695

Monkey Place Country House
Wollombi Road, Broke 2330
02 6579 1278

Montagne View Estate & Vineyard
555 Hermitage Road, Pokolbin 2320
02 4998 7822

Mt View Cottage
Lot 1 Mt View Road, Mount View 2325
0407 117 874

Mulberry Cottage
65 High Street, Singleton 2330
02 6571 2428

Neath Hotel
Cessnock Road, Neath 2325
02 4930 4270

New Llanfair
165 Hill Street, Broke 2330
02 6579 1056, 6579 1078 A/H

Noonji Homestead
Lot 892 Lomas Lane, Nulkaba 2325
02 4991 4000

North Lodge Cottages
198 Old North Road, Pokolbin 2335
02 6574 7259

Nottage Hill Bed & Breakfast
14 Nottage Hill Close, Branxton 2335
02 4938 3246

Nulkaba House
10 Austral Street, Nulkaba 2325
02 4991 4599

*Oakvale Cottage at
Oakvale Winery*
Broke Road, Pokolbin 2320
02 4998 7520

Parrot Stump Farm
Talga Road, Lovedale 2321
02 9235 3947

Parsons Green Estate
Hermitage Road, Pokolbin 2321
02 6574 7024

Patrick Plains Estate
647 Hermitage Road,
Pokolbin 2320
02 9929 3996

Peacock Hill Vineyard and Lodge
Palmers Lane, Pokolbin 2320
02 4998 7661

Pendarves Cottage
110 Old North Road, Belford 2335
02 4991 4000

Peppers Creek
Cnr Broke Road & Ekerts Lane,
Pokolbin 2320
02 4998 7532

Peppers Hunter Valley
134 Ekerts Lane, Pokolbin 2320
02 4998 7596

Pokolbin Cam-Way Cottages
Campbells Lane, Pokolbin 2320
02 4998 7655

Pokolbin Village Resort
188 Broke Road, Pokolbin 2320
02 4998 7670

Rosedale B & B
Lot 1 Lovedale Road, Lovedale 2321
02 4990 9537

Royal Oak Hotel
221 Vincent Street, Cessnock 2325
02 4990 2366

Shellshock Country House
48 Olney Street, Ellalong 2325
02 4998 1055

Southwood Park Village
101 Carrs Road, Neath 2325
02 4930 4565

Sovereign Hill Country Lodge
Lot 34 Talga Road, Rothbury 2321
02 4930 7755

Splinters Guest House
617 Hermitage Road, Belford 2335
02 6574 7118
0412 479 402

Sussex Ridge Guest House
Lot 4 Deaseys Road, Pokolbin 2320
02 4998 7753

Tallawanta Hunter Valley Gardens
Hunter Valley Gardens,
Broke Road, Pokolbin 2320
02 4998 7854/7819

Tara Cottage
530 Wollombi Road, Broke 2330
02 6579 1063

Thalgara Estate
De Beyers Road, Pokolbin 2320
02 4998 7717

The Hunter Habit & Rothvale Vineyard
Lot 2 Deaseys Road, Pokolbin 2320
02 4998 7290
0418 462 899

The Olives Country House
Campbell's Lane, Pokolbin 2320
02 4998 7838

The Ridge at Yango Creek
Lot 3, Yango Creek Road, Wollombi 2325
02 9969 4901

The Vicars House
36–38 Wollombi Road, Millfield 2325
02 4998 1336

The Woods at Pokolbin
Halls Road, Pokolbin 2320
02 4998 7368

Thistle Hill Guest House
591 Hermitage Road, Pokolbin 2335
02 6574 7217

Top O' the Hill
Lot 16 Mount View Road, Millfield 2325
02 9416 3244

Tranquil Vale
325 Pywells Road, Luskintyre 2321
02 4930 6100

Travellers Rest
35a Colliery Street, Cessnock 2325
02 4991 2355

Trinity Cottage
Lovedale Road, Allandale 2321
02 4930 7948, 0412 787 685

Tuscany Estate & Resort
Mistletoe Lane, Pokolbin 2320
02 4998 7288

Twin Trees Cottages
Lot 108 Halls Road, Pokolbin 2321
02 4998 7311

Valley Breezes Guesthouse
83 Redmanvale Road, Jerrys Plains 2330
02 6576 4134

Valley View Cottage
Old North Road, Pokolbin 2320
02 4998 7619

Valley Vineyard Tourist Park
Mount View Road, Cessnock 2325
02 4990 2573

Verona Cottage
McDonalds Road, Pokolbin 2320
02 4998 7668

Villa Provence
15 Gillards Road,
Pokolbin 2320
02 4998 7404

Villini Estate
Lot 77 Talga Road, Rothbury 2320
02 4930 7384

Vineyard Hill
Lovedale Road, Allandale 2320
02 4990 4166

Wandin Valley Estate
Wilderness Road,
Allandale 2321
02 4930 7317

Wattle Grove B & B
Lot 163 Wallaby Gully Road,
Ellalong 2325
02 4998 1637

Wentworth Hotel
36 Vincent Street, Cessnock 2325
02 4990 1364

Wilderness Cottages
Lot 82 Wilderness Road, Rothbury 2320
02 4930 7689

Windsong Country Accommodation
Deasys Road, Pokolbin 2320
02 4990 4807
0417 448 836

Windsor's Edge Vineyard
McDonalds Road, Pokolbin 2320
02 4998 7737

Winemakers Cottage at Warraroong Estate
Wilderness Road, Lovedale 2321
02 4930 7594

Winters on Wollombi
188 Wollombi Road, Cessnock 2325
02 4991 3688

Wirral Grange Vineyard
Lot 4 Lomas Lane, Nulkaba 2325
02 4990 5877

Wollombi Barnstay
Singleton Road, Wollombi 2325
02 4998 3221

Wollombi Cottage and Antiques
Maitland Road, Wollombi 2325
02 4998 3340

Woodlane Cottages
Lomas Lane, Lovedale 2321
02 4991 3762

Woolshed Hill Estate
106 Deaseys Road, Pokolbin 2320
02 4998 7685

Yango Park House
Lot 1 Yango Creek Road, Wollombi 2325
02 4998 8322

Staying

Festivals and *Events*

The festivals listed below are regular, annual dos, but it would be wise to check on their timing as the years go by. There are also other events on a less regular basis. To find out more, contact:

The Wine Country Visitor Information Centre,

Turner Park, Aberdare Road, Cessnock,
NSW 2325
tel: (02) 4990 4477
fax: (02) 4991 4518
e-mail: info@winecountry.com.au
web: www.winecountry.com.au

Tourism Singleton,

Singleton Shire Council,
Queen Street,
Singleton, NSW 2330
tel: (02) 6578 7267

January

Seems like most people are away.

February

This is the peak month for vintage, so the wineries have little to time to organise regular events. However, it's an exciting month and there's plenty to see.

March

Broke Fordwich harvest festival.

April

Harvest festival. Celebrate the end of vintage with musical acts, brunches, lunches and dinners.

May

Mt View autumn festival (sometimes April). Join the winemakers of Mount View in a weekend of gourmet foods, wine and music.

Lovedale Long Lunch. The Lovedale wineries combine with local chefs, art and music, to bring you a food and wine extravaganza.

June

Arts crawl. Hunter Valley artists and artisans display their creativity and originality in local wineries, restaurants and guesthouses.

July

Singleton art prize.

August

St George Hunter Valley wine show. Exhibitors' tasting and awards dinner.

September

Budburst Festival. Two-week long festival with wine, food, banquets and street parade.

Wollombi Folk Festival. A film festival, street theatre, comedians, music, bush dancing and aboriginal cultural performances.

Broke Village Fair. Broke Fordwich wine and food stalls, pipe and drum bands, craft displays, national parks and wildlife displays.

October

Jazz in the Vines. Tyrrell's Long Flat Paddock provides the stage, where renowned artists perform as you enjoy your food and wine.

Opera in the Vineyards. The Wyndham Estate Amphitheatre, set amongst the vines, is the venue for some of the country's biggest opera talents.

Singleton Festival of Wine and Roses. 'Party in the Park', cultural and heritage events, open garden visits, street parade.

Singleton Show.

November

Brokenback Trail Wine Affair weekend. The wineries, guesthouses and restaurants of the Brokenback area combine to bring you winery activities, gourmet treats, art and entertainment.

December

The year winds down and the silly season approaches.

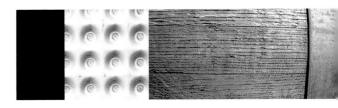

Dis*tributors*

New South Wales

Adderley Hammond Liquor Distributors
28 Montrose Avenue
Adamstown Heights 2289
(02) 4920 6120

Aria Wine Company
Suite 15/44 Bridge Street
Sydney 2000
(02) 9251 4866

Bacchant Wine Merchants,
Suite 23/ 330 Wattle Street
Ultimo 2007
(02) 9212 5658

Benchmark Wines
124 Walker Street
North Sydney 2060
(02) 9460 2944

BHM Liquor Distributors
(07) 3368 0830

BRL Hardy Wine Company
27 Myrtle Street
Pagewood 2035
(02) 9666 5855

Broken Bay Beverages
Shop 1/ 315 Trafalgar Avenue
Umina 2257
(02) 4343 1550

Classical Wines of Australia Pty Ltd
21–32[crosses the road?]
Carlingford Street
Regents Park 2143
(02) 9742 5099

**De Bono Fine Wine & Brew
Merchants Pty Ltd**
86 Vore Street
Silverwater 2128
(02) 9748 8456

Estate Wines
74a Buckingham Street
Surry Hills 2010
(02) 8399 0000

Fesq & Co.,
Fesq & Company Pty Ltd
45–55 Epsom Road
Rosebery 2018
(02) 9662 3111

Fine Wine Specialist
39 Wolseley Road
Point Piper 2027
(02) 9363 4845

Harbridge Fine Wines
10/56 O'Riordan Street
Alexandria 2015
(02) 9667 1622

Haviland Wine Merchants
19 Northcliff Street
Milsons Point 2061
(02) 9929 3722

Inglewood Wines Pty Ltd
18–20 Cleg Street
Artarmon 2064
(02) 9436 3022

Fergus Hurley
18c Lawley Crescent
Pymble 2073
(02) 9449 6464

**Halloran Manton
Pty Ltd**
3 Welder Road
Seven Hills 2147
(02) 9624 7244

Lewis Fine Wines
14 Hosking Street
Balmain 2041
(02) 9810 0177

McGuigan Wine Co.
4a–4c/ 6 Boundary Road
Northmead 2152
(02) 9630 7565

McWilliam's Wines
68 Anzac Street
Chullora 2190
(02) 9722 1200

The Main Domain Pty Ltd
261 Harris Street
Pyrmont 2009
(02) 9552 2466

National Liquor Company
114 Alexander Street
Crows Nest 2065
(02) 9966 4804

Negociants Australia
6–8 Crewe Place
Rosebery 2018
(02) 9313 8177

Normans Wines Ltd
9 Wrights Road
Drummoyne 2047
(02) 9719 2099

Orlando Wyndham Group Pty Ltd
1 Figtree Drive
Homebush Bay 2127
(02) 8762 5666

Premier Estate Wines
191 Reservoir Road
Cardiff Heights 2285
(02) 4954 0328

Red+White
302 B/ 12 Waters Road
Neutral Bay 2089
(02) 9908 5299

Red Rock Beverages
3 Towns Place
Millers Point 2000
(02) 9252 2282

Rosemount Estates Pty Ltd
18 Herbert Street
Artarmon 2064
(02) 9902 2100

*Rutherglen Wine and
Spirit Co. Pty Ltd*
1800 466 666

*Southcorp Wines
Pty Ltd*
2 Marple Avenue
Villawood 2163
(02) 9795 8666

Southern Cross Wine Co.
124 Walker Street
North Sydney 2060
(02) 9460 2633

Southwell and Garrett
PO Box 399
Brighton-Le-Sands 2216
(02) 9567 5443

Tempus Two
PO Box 664
Rozelle 2039
(02) 9818 7222

*Tucker Seabrook (Aust.)
Pty Ltd*
40 Lord Street
Botany 2019
(02) 9666 0000

Tyrrell's Vineyards Pty Ltd
106 Alexander Street
Crows Nest 2065
(02) 9439 6399

The Wine Company Pty Ltd
1800 677 443

Wine Source
Suite 302/ 12 Waters Road
Neutral Bay 2089
(02) 9908 5322

Wine Works
Ground Floor 102 Alexander Street
Crows Nest 2065
(02) 9438 2988

World Wine Estates
Shop 99/460 Jones Street
Ultimo 2007
(02) 9211 2380

Young & Rashleigh Wine Merchants
327 Pacific Highway
Crows Nest 2065
(02) 9929 3544

Victoria/Tasmania
Alepat Taylor
400 Victoria Street
Brunswick 3056
(03) 9380 6199

BRL Hardy Wine Company
61 Nantilla Road
Clayton 3168
1800 335 469

Dilettare Pty Ltd
235 Broadhurst Avenue
Reservoir 3073
(03) 9462 2763

Halloran Mantn Pty Ltd
33 Smith Street,
Springvale 3171
(03) 9546 6644

Flinders Wholesale Wines
and Spirits Pty Ltd
3 Wandarri Court
Cheltenham 3192
(03) 9584 5233

Hill International Wines
Suite 6/19
Norwood Crescent
Moonee Ponds 3039
(03) 9372 0322

McWilliam's Wines Pty Ltd
756 Stud Road
Scoresby 3179
(03) 9764 8511

Maxxium Australia Pty Ltd
Office Level 2/20
Council Street
Hawthorn East 3123
(03) 9813 0523

Negociants Australia
109 Hyde Street
Footscray 3011
(03) 9268 1750

Nelson Wine Company
253 Johnston Street
Abbotsford 3067
(03) 9482 3866

Orlando Wyndham Group Pty Ltd
6 Kingston Town Close
Oakleigh 3166
(03) 9564 2333

Prime Wines
PO Box 392
North Melbourne 3051
(03) 9372 6777

Rosemount Estates Pty Ltd
58 Duerdin Street
Clayton 3168
(03) 9562 5770

Rutherglen Wine & Spirit
241 Normanby Road
Port Melbourne 3207
(03) 9646 6666

Southcorp Wines Pty Ltd
60 Terracotta Drive
Nunawading 3131
(03) 9875 0200

Southern Cross Wines
21 Henderson Road
Knoxfield 3180
(03) 9764 1822

Tucker Seabrook (Vic.) Pty Ltd
Syme Street
Brunswick 3056
(03) 9388 0400

Vintners Pty Ltd
Unit 2/50 Rooks Road
Nunawading 3131
(03) 9872 5775

The Wine Company Pty Ltd
4/ 56 Smith Road
Springvale 3171
(03) 9562 3900

David Johnstone & Assts
201 Collins Street
Hobart 7000
(03) 6234 9999

Wine Source
PO Box 5177
Burnley 3121
(03) 9429 9199

Winter Fine Wines
35 Smith Street
North Hobart Tas. 7000
(03) 6231 4491

Queensland
Aria Wine Company
9/ 8 Petrie Terrace
Brisbane 4000
(07) 3369 1870

BHM Liquor Distributors
Petrie House
Level 3, 80 Petrie Terrace
Brisbane 4000
(07) 3368 0830

BRL Hardy Company
43 Murray Street
Bowen Hills 4006
(07) 3252 7933

Fesq & Company Qld
21 Ledbury Street
Aspley 4034
(07) 3263 5773

Hill International Wines
2 Henley Street
Coopers Plains 4108
(07) 3344 7300

McWilliam's Wines Pty Ltd
Bldg 2/243 Bradman Street
Acacia Ridge 4110
(07) 3272 8299

Maxxium Australia Pty Ltd
Level 1 25 Donkin Street
West End 4101
(07) 3255 2096

Negociants Australia
120 Factory Road
Oxley 4075
(07) 3373 5788

Orlando Wyndham Group Pty Ltd
16 Parkview Drive
Archerfield 4108
(07) 3273 933

Pacific Liquor
PO Box 1103
Cleveland 4163
Phone:
(07) 3286 3233 /0411 139 973

Rosemount Estates Wines Pty Ltd
26 Virginia Street
Virginia 4014
(07) 3265 6999

Southcorp Wines Pty Ltd
129 Kerry Road
Archerfield 4108
(07) 3259 1400

Southern Cross Wine Co.
16 Theodore Street
Eagle Farm 4009
(07) 3868 3411

Trinity Wine Agency
32 Colonsay Street
Middle Park 4074
0418 788 100

Tucker Seabrook (Qld) Pty Ltd
Unit 4/19 Murdoch Crescent
Acacia Ridge 4110
(07) 3272 1711

Wine Source
U 4/ 1106 Ipswich Road
Moorooka 4105
(07) 3892 7788

Wine 2000
Moggill Road
Kenmore 4069
(07) 3878 4586

South Australia
Australian Boutique Premium Wines Pty Ltd
PO Box 10468
Gouger Street
Adelaide B/C 5001
(08) 8351 0377

BRL Hardy Wine Company
Reynell Road
Reynella 5161
(08) 8392 2222

Hill International Wines SA
Suite 30a 283–287 Burbridge Road
Brooklyn Park 5032
(08) 8238 3492

Jonathon Tolley Wine Merchant
8 Opey Avenue
Hyde Park 5061
(08) 8271 5218

McWilliam's Wines Pty Ltd
Unit 4–5, 348 Richmond Road
Netley 5037
(08) 8352 5911

Maxxium Australia
(02) 9418 5000

The National Wine Group
185 Sturt Street
Adelaide 5000
(08) 8231 1066

Negociants Australia
205 Grote Street
Adelaide 5000
(08) 8410 2982

Orlando Wyndham Group Pty Ltd
33 Exeter Terrace
Devon Park 5008
(08) 8208 2444

Porter & Co. Wine & Spirit Merchants Pty Ltd
8 Hampton Street
Hawthorn 5062
(08) 8373 3010

Southcorp Wines Pty Ltd
78 Penfold Road
Magill 5072
(08) 8301 5400

Southern Cross Wine Company
80 Grove Avenue
Marleston 5033
(08) 8297 4544

Rosemount Estates Pty Ltd
23 Rundle Street
Kent Town 5067
(08) 8363 5110

Western Australia
BRL Hardy Wine Company
Houghton Wine Company
Dale Road,
Middle Swan 6056
(08) 9274 5100

Decanter Liquor Merchants
4/ 272 Selby Street
Wembley 6014
(08) 9387 5877

Fine Wine Wholesalers
32 Parkinson Lane
Kardinya 6163
(08) 9314 7133

McWilliam's Wines Pty Ltd
Poynter Drive
Duncraig 6023
(08) 9246 4189

Maxxium Australia
(02) 9418 5000

Moss Stirling Vintners
88 Beaufort Street
Northbridge 6003
(08) 9227 7007

Negociants Australia
114 Radium Street
Welshpool 6106
(08) 9350 5544

Orlando Wyndham Group Pty Ltd
26 Twickenham Road
Victoria Park 6100
(08) 9472 2888

Rosemount Estates Pty Ltd
252 Cambridge Street
Wembley 6014
(08) 9382 2233

Southcorp Wines Pty Ltd
307 Collier Road
Bassendean 6054
(08) 9377 3522

Southern Cross Wine Co.
118 Radium Street
Welshpool 6106
(08) 9451 8455

Tucker Seabrook (WA) Pty Ltd
18 Narloo Street
Malaga 6090
(08) 9248 2150

West Coast Wine Cellars
8 Carbon Court
Osborne Park 6017
(08) 9446 3565

Bibliography and *References*

Cessnock City Tourist Board, Hunter Valley Wine Country, 1999

Department of Mines, Geological Survey of New South Wales, Geological Map of Singleton, Sheet SI5601, 1969

Dunne, Mike and Maguire, Moira The Winelover's Companion to the Hunter, Dunne Thing, 1993

Evans, Len Complete Book of Australian and New Zealand Wine, Paul Hamlyn, 1973

Gladstones, John S, Viticulture and Environment, Winetitles, 1992

Halliday, James and Jarrett, Ray The Wines and History of the Hunter Valley, McGraw-Hill, 1979

Ilbery, Jaki 'The History of Wine in Australia' in Evans, Len Complete Book of Australian and New Zealand Wine, Paul Hamlyn, 1973

Lake, Max Hunter Winemakers, Hill of Content, 1970